D-Day Plus One

D-Day Plus One

Shot Down and on the Run in France

FRANK "DUTCH" HOLLAND

with

ADAM WILKINS

GRUB STREET · LONDON

Published by
Grub Street
4 Rainham Close
London
SW11 6SS

Reprinted 2007, 2008

British Library Cataloguing in Publication Data
Holland, Frank
   D-Day plus one: shot down and on the run in France
   1. Holland, Frank 2. Escapes – France – History – 20th
   century 3. World War, 1939-1945 – Personal narratives,
   British 4. France – History – German occupation, 1940-1945
   I. Title II. Wilkins, Adam
   940.5'48141

ISBN-13: 9781904943938

Cover design by Lizzie B design

Typeset by Pearl Graphics, Hemel Hempstead

Printed and bound by MPG Ltd, Bodmin, Cornwall

Grub Street only uses
FSC (Forest Stewardship Council) paper for its books.

With thanks to Hart McLeod, Cambridge

Contents

Prologue

Today, everyone goes to France. It's one of the chief holiday destinations for Brits. But long before it became so popular, more than 60 years ago, I visited France, not just once but twice. The two trips, however, could not have been more different. The first, when I was 22, was with two friends, in the summer of '39, just before the war. It was a young person's motorbike holiday. We saw a lot of France, its villages and countryside, probably covering over 3000 miles, going in a big clockwise loop out from Calais, and around the north and east, then south through Nice. We had planned the trip well and it was great fun.

The second visit to France took place five years later. Unlike the first, it was not planned and it was not fun. It began on June 7th, 1944, or D+1, the day after D-Day. I was an RAF pilot and my Typhoon had been hit by German anti-aircraft fire during a low flying attack my squadron had made on a marshalling yard in Normandy. I had managed to take the aircraft up to about 1200 feet but the engine had then gone dead and my Typhoon soon began heading toward the Normandy countryside at accelerating speed. I just barely got free of the cockpit and baled out, maybe no more than 4-5 seconds before the crash. My parachute didn't have time to open but I fell into a wood and, crashing through the branches of an oak, suddenly found myself dangling by my 'chute straps about 15 feet over French soil. Breathing hard, I experienced a few seconds of great relief that I had survived. But there was no time to savour the feeling. I'd heard my aeroplane crash. Maybe it was just 500 hundred feet away. German troops would almost certainly be swarming around the crash site and the wood within a few minutes. I had to get out of there, and as quickly as possible. This was how my second visit to France began.

* * *

Today, for part of each year, I live in the south of France, with my French wife. We have a flat within a large building complex, in the small town of Mandelieu, near Cannes. We have owned the flat since they built this development, more than 20 years ago, though we still spend most of the year in our old family house in Cambridge.

Our Mandelieu flat is a quiet, peaceful place. I like that. Our balcony faces toward a large grassy and tree-filled garden, bordered by the curve of the buildings that make up the complex. Even with the windows open, as we have them on summer nights, there is usually little outside noise. But this morning, I awoke to some noise. Somewhere down below in the grounds of our building, a dog was barking. I rolled over in bed, tried to ignore it at first, then opened one eye and could see that it was just beginning to be light. The barking wasn't very loud but it was just enough to keep me awake. I wondered if someone's dog had got out and was chasing a cat.

After a minute or so, I knew I wasn't going to go back to sleep. Olga, my wife of more than 30 years, was still sound asleep. Breathing quietly, lying on her left side, as she does. When I met her, she was in her mid-40s, a beautiful woman, with lovely blond hair, even then cut short, and incredible azure-blue eyes. Olga's hair is no longer blond but white – she doesn't dye it. She is now in her late-70s, after all, but her eyes are just the same. And when she smiles, it's dazzling. She's still a beautiful woman. But, more than that, she's a good woman. Knew it the day I met her. We had been introduced by my good friend Armand. That was early in the year after Suzanne had died. Armand I had met, in fact, through Suzanne – they had been old friends. One of those chains of connections that shape your life.

I put my dressing gown on and walked barefoot down our little hallway, then through the living room and out onto the balcony. The tiles are cool underfoot, quite pleasant on a summer's morning. It was about 7.00am. I stepped out onto our balcony and looked around. We are three storeys up and have a good view of the building and the grounds. Not another soul was visible on any of the balconies or down on the grounds but there's nothing surprising about that. Early on a Saturday morning, there's no reason for anyone to be up and about. Things are quite lovely at this hour in summer, with the early morning light on the tiers of the awning-shaded balconies, which curve around both to the left and the right from where we are, all five floors' worth.

Over to the left, beyond our complex, in the direction of Nice, you can see a view of two tall structures. Unless your eyes are really good, it is hard to see exactly what they are. One of our first days here, more than 20 years ago, I noticed that smoke was coming out of one. And I thought, "Christ, it's a fire! We'd better call the police or the fire department." Armand and Alice were visiting us and I said something to Armand about calling the emergency service. He just smiled broadly, under his big white moustache, the way he does, and told me that there was no need for the emergency service, this was the local crematorium. And the other structure, well that, it turns out, is the flight control tower at the Mandelieu Airport. Later, I had a thought and then it was my turn to smile. You could say that the two tall structures represent Departures and Arrivals.

Down below, the dog, wherever it was, had stopped barking. It had sounded like a big dog but there was no sign of him now. Most of the French, at least the ones here, seem to like small dogs. Lap dogs we call them in England, don't know what the French phrase is. Never did like lap dogs, myself. If you're going to have a dog, make it a proper dog, an Alsatian, a Labrador, a Golden Retriever, not one of those small, yappy kinds. But it takes all kinds to make a world, I suppose, both of men and dogs. Chacun à son goût, as they say here. Down below, on the grass, maybe 30 feet in front of our building, a tabby cat was lying on the grass, licking a paw, the only sign of life. Otherwise, the place was as still as could be. The tops of the big cypress trees in the garden, just in front of us, were beginning to catch the light. When we first moved to Mandelieu, the whole development was new and the trees were small. You could see right over them to the pool in the middle of the grounds. Now they reach as high as the top floor of the buildings. These big cypresses give the whole place a nice park-like feeling.

In the first years here, I thought that the flat was too small. It is, of course, much smaller than our house in England. But Olga liked it. And that was really enough for me. The golf course here is good, Armand and Alice live nearby, the shopping is convenient, and the weather is great, except in the summer, when it gets too hot, and the place fills up with summer visitors. Then we clear off back to our place in Great Shelford, just outside Cambridge. But our flat in Mandelieu now seems like home to me. If you live long enough in a place, you get used to it. If there are things that might have seemed not quite right, at first, you learn to accept them, you even stop noticing them. It's like a long and good marriage. You make your adjustments and then emphasize the positive. After a while, you don't even feel the negatives. Mandelieu has been a good place for us.

And looking out this morning, on what you might call my domain – it feels like my domain though I share it with hundreds of people and we only own a little part of it – I thought once again how odd life can be. The funny paths it can lead you on. They have been good paths for me, I've been a lucky man. I survived the war, built up the family business into something much bigger than it had been and made a success of it. I have two fine daughters, two wonderful grandchildren and now, six great-grandchildren. And, not least, I'm lucky to have Olga as my wife.

But I wouldn't have predicted the way things turned out when I was in my early 20s, especially my connections to France over 60 years. I'm a true Brit and both sides of my family have been English for generations, centuries really. Both sides of the family are from the Cambridge area, as far back as we can trace. The family legend is that, on my father's side, we were Dutchmen who came over in the 1600s to help drain the fens. But maybe if our name wasn't Holland, we wouldn't have that story in the family.

Yet, British to the bone, my links to France have been a big part of my life. Margot, my beloved first wife, after all had a French name though she was English. I liked the sound of it and we then gave our daughters French names, Paulette and Louise. Suzanne, my second wife, whom I married three years after Margot's death, was French and so is Olga. Do I speak French? Of course, and I would say I speak it well. My vocabulary is good and I speak fluently enough. But my younger daughter, Louise – we've always called her Lollie – thinks that my grammar is pretty awful even though my vocabulary is great. For Lollie, it's the other way around: good grammar but her vocabulary isn't as good as mine. We've joked that if we could only combine the way we spoke French, we'd be brilliant. Haven't quite figured out how to do that, however.

How did I make my own personal French connection? Well, it began with that landing in a French oak tree on D+1. It was then, quite by chance, that I ended up conducting my own personal invasion of Normandy. That certainly had not been in anyone's plans, not Eisenhower's, not Montgomery's, not Air Vice-Marshal Broadhurst or, least of all, mine. But that's the way it began. The tree was a Godsend, a real stroke of luck. If I'd left the aircraft maybe even a second later, I might well have fallen into the nearby field and died instantly, a sorry, bloody corpse of a young RAF pilot, dead at 27.

"Dutch", I should mention, is my nickname. Has been ever since I was "baptised" by my fellow choristers at Trinity College, in my initiation into the Trinity choir, aged 10. With the surname of Holland, I suppose it was inevitable. And some of my oldest friends call me Dutchy. But, deep inside, though it's not something you say out loud, I've sometimes thought that "Lucky" might have been even more suitable. Not that it's all been luck and plain sailing. No way. I've had some heartbreak, too. Margot's early death in pregnancy in 1957, later Suzanne's from a stroke, were incredible blows. But who could reach 90 without some tears along the way?

I've always said, "Don't live in the past" and I've been true to that. It's the present and the future that count and that's how I've lived my life. But when you get to your late 80s, you can't help but reflect a bit. It's not living in the past, it's just reflection. And my daughters and their husbands, not to mention some of the other members of the family, have been saying for years that I should write my story, especially the story of what happened to me on June 7th, 1944, and the two months that followed. Is it a special story? Well, there were no heroics about it, and not for a second would I say I was any sort of hero but the experience was something special all right. Besides, it is my story and it did lead on, not right away but later, especially after Margot's death, to this unexpected set of ties to France, which have shaped my life.

Maybe there were hundreds of stories like this one during the war, possibly thousands, but most of them never got written down and are now lost. God knows there aren't that many of us left anymore. Every 10 years, when we celebrate D-Day, the contingent of those of us who were part of the fighting force – Brits, Americans, Aussies, Canadians, the lot – there are fewer and fewer of us. And some of the politicians who lead the commemorations hadn't yet been born while most of the others were just kids at the time. The American President, Bill Clinton, came over for the big 50th year celebrations in 1994, I remember. At the time, he wasn't even 50 himself.

But though most of us who were in the thick of it at the time and lived to celebrate V-E Day are no longer here, there were so many of us who didn't even make it through the war. Keeping alive the memories of those who made it is part of the way one honours those who weren't so lucky. Because the family have been urging me to write this down for years, I'll give it a go and we'll see how the telling of it develops. It can't be a perfectly 100% accurate history – I can tell you that I wasn't taking notes at the time.[1] But I have a pretty good memory and what I can relate is close to the actual way things happened, though many of the details are now gone and there will be some gaps. At least, I'll try to tell it as straight and accurately as I can. And I'll tell it as if I'm speaking it because that is the most natural way for me.

But I won't start the story with D+1. I'll go back a bit and begin with my childhood in Cambridge, then the early war years. Those times and experiences made me, I'm sure of it even if I can't say exactly how, into the young man of 27 who found himself dangling by his 'Chute straps in that tree in German-occupied Normandy the day after D-Day.

---

[1] I would, however, like to acknowledge how helpful a history of 184 Squadron, compiled by one of our members, Mike Williams, has been. Without it, I would never have been able to reconstruct the details of the squadron's various moves and operations.

1

A Cambridge childhood: from yeast-delivery boy to Trinity Chorister

For people who live in big places like London or Birmingham or Reading, it might be hard to imagine what it's like to live in a town that's dominated by one enterprise. Particularly when that enterprise owns most of the property, sets the rents, and generally makes the rules. The Americans have a term for that kind of place; they call them "company towns".

Well, Cambridge is a company town but the "company" is the University. It has dominated the town for centuries. But to say that the University owns most of the property and controls things, however, is not really correct. It's the colleges, thirty-plus of them, the oldest going back 800 years or so who are the real property owners. When it comes to setting rents or deciding what happens and when to particular pieces of land, the Colleges are a law unto themselves. Often, when an old shop closes down it's because the college that owns the property has decided to raise the rents and the owners can't afford it any more. More and more of the locally owned businesses have disappeared in the last 20 years, replaced by shops of the big chains, which can pay the high rates. The other side of the coin, of course, is that the colleges provide, directly or indirectly, a lot of the employment in the town. Some of the older members of my family were "bedders" in the colleges, others were "bulldogs", the uniformed men who patrolled at night and made sure that the male students were back in their lodgings on time. My maternal grandfather was a bulldog.

But the colleges certainly don't own and control everything in Cambridge. Far from it. Most of the people of Cambridge and the local businesses just get on with their daily lives, as they do everywhere. An example would be our family business, which was founded by my paternal grandmother, Catherine Holland, in 1894. C. Holland's business was supplying yeast to the local bakers. This might sound too small a service to support a family but in those days, it wasn't. It was a good business.

Catherine was a strong woman and an independent one. And, in her later years at least, when I knew her, a large one. She lived with us in her old age, after my step-granddad died, and I remember her in her big armchair, often dozing in the afternoon, sometimes snoring. Even asleep, you couldn't ignore her. Just what she did as a young woman, how she earned her living before marrying my grandfather, "Happy" John Holland, is something of a mystery. There certainly wasn't a lot of opportunity for single young women to earn their living as they do today. And maybe it's best not to know how she got her start but, however she did, she saved up enough to start the business that became our family business. But a strong and independent character Catherine Holland certainly was. And whether my father was really the son of Happy John Holland we also don't know but marry him, and take his name, she did. I don't know too much about him but he was an itinerant Methodist preacher and before that a man, whom we might say, had been a bit too fond of the bottle. We think that's where the nickname "Happy" came from. He died, I think in 1909, eight years before I was born and some years later, Catherine remarried.

My grandmother's second husband was a man named Bill Doe, a hide, skin and wool merchant. His business was located on Cherry Hinton Road, which is well away from the University, on the other side of the city, and still mostly a street of small businesses, shops, and modest housing, though there's now rather a smart shopping centre just past where it comes off Hills Road. Tourists visiting Cambridge often "ooh" and "ahh" about how beautiful Cambridge is, but what they are talking about is the fairly small part of the town around the University, particularly, the big lawns and gardens at the "backs" of the Colleges. But a large part of Cambridge is like Cherry Hinton Road. It's not ugly but it's not beautiful either, just ordinary British town-scape.

I liked my step Granddad. He was a great character, too, with his bow tie, bow legs, and small stature (though it has to be said that none of us in the family are giants). When I was a boy, I would often open the car door for him, as he was leaving, after one of his visits, and he would give me six pence and always say "Boy, you'll never want," a kind of a blessing, I suppose.

Grandmother's business was, at first, on Sedgwick Street. Later, when the family moved, it was in the back part of our next house at the corner of Ross Street and Mill Road. Ross Street is just a residential street but Mill Road is one of the big com-mercial thoroughfares in Cambridge. It starts and runs south from the southeast corner of Parker's Piece, the largest green in the town, which, in the spring and summer, is filled with students lolling on the grass in the sun on nice days. The place where our Mill Road house was is now known as Dutch's Corner, from the time in the '50s and '60s when I ran the business. When I was a kid growing up there, there were six of us altogether in the house, Father and Mother, the three of us kids and my mother's younger half-sister, my Aunt Hilda. Aunt Hildy, as we called her, helped Mother with a lot of the domestic chores plus looking after the three of us children. When Hilda one day announced that she was getting married, Father was none too pleased. He had liked having her as a helper around the house.

I was born at home, delivered by a midwife, on January 12, 1917. I was born in a caul, a sign of luck. Sailors, in particular, used to value them because it was thought that if you had a piece of one, you would never die of drowning. And, as a result, there was a black market in them. When the doctor came, he asked to see it but it had disappeared. My mother was certain that the midwife had taken it to sell.

I was the youngest of three children. The eldest was Fred, six years older than me and the middle child was my sister, Doris, nearly four years older. As the youngest child, my Mum's "baby", I was her favourite child, at least I think so. She never said so, of course, but you can just tell. Nanna Holland, as my daughters came to know her, was a wonderful woman, she looked after us all, you couldn't want a better mother. She could be a bit vain about her appearance, about her clothes but that was the only foible I remember. She looked after us all, with love and generosity.

If I was Mother's favourite child, Fred, the oldest and the oldest son, was my Dad's favourite, at least when we were children. Doris, as the middle-child, had the hardest time, I think. Father was particularly strict with her. If she went out with friends, she had to be back by 10.00pm, no exceptions made, all that sort of thing. In one of the pictures we have of the family, there is my father, in his early 30s, dark hair and black moustache, quite serious. You can see he was a strong and strict character just in the set of his face.

But he had two weaknesses. The first was gambling, betting on the horses and at billiards. The second was drink. As for drink, though, I have to say that he only indulged in it when he was having a good time. Certainly not all the time. He wasn't an alcoholic. And he was a good man. But his love of horse racing, betting and a good drink, led to some interesting things.

For anyone who lives in Cambridge, the centre of horse-racing is Newmarket, which is only about 15 miles away, just about due east. The race track looks out over the big grassy expanses of Newmarket Heath. It has been a great place for horse racing for centuries. There are stories about Charles II and his favourite lady, Nell Gwynne, going to the races there back in the late 1600s. And it's where Father always went to watch the horses and gamble.

He often got his tips on which horses to gamble from Teddy Goater, the head lad at one of the stables there. Teddy wrote to my father every week, with the latest news on which horses were running and which were the favourites. Father usually followed these tips. Once he had a big win, winning enough, it was about £600 I believe, to buy a house on Windsor Road, number 68 Windsor Road, in the northern residential part of Cambridge. We moved there from our old house on Mill Road, sometime in the early 1930s. That was my home right up until I joined the RAF.

Father and I would go out to the races in Newmarket, going in the van from the business. Afterwards, we would stop at the Conservative Club in the town. Now, I had learned billiards when I was fourteen or so and I wasn't bad. Father would challenge anybody to play me at snooker for half a crown a time and I used to win more often than I lost. One day there was a big tournament at the Oddfellows Club, which was on the High Street in Newmarket. They auctioned off the players, to raise money for the club, and the prize was something like £250, a lot of money in those days, along with a cup. This was my final year in school, so it would have been 1933. I played against the son of the bookmaker in the final and I can remember playing the black off the middle cushion into the middle pocket to win the game. My father nearly went mad with excitement but so did everybody else in the room. He then went to the bar and bought everyone, and I mean everyone, the stable boys included, a whisky, even though most people at the club usually had just a half pint of beer for their standard drink.

But that win wasn't the end of the story because the

bookmaker came up to my father while the celebration was going on and asked for a return match. To cut a long story short: he accepted, we played again and I won again on the black. It was quite fantastic. This led to more drinks all round.

Whisky then was only 4d or 6d a tot but I still remember exactly what the total bill came to: £27 10s, quite a sum in those days. So, afterwards, I came up to my father and said, "Look, you're buying all these drinks, what's in it for me?" And he said, "Well, you can go to Norman Bradley's" – they were pawnbrokers in Cambridge – "and spend up to 15s". Well, I played cricket at school and I did go to Norman Bradley's a few days later. Their shop was on Bridge Street, just opposite St John's college, and I bought myself a cricket bat for 12s 6d. I also got the cup from the competition, of course, which I still have somewhere in the garage.

On the way back home from the match, however, Father was really quite intoxicated and not feeling at all well. We had to stop the van along the way, at Nine Mile Hill where he got out, rushed up the slope and was sick as a dog on top of the sandhill. The rest of the way home, he hardly said anything – whether it was because he was still feeling ill or out of just plain embarrassment, I don't know – and as soon as we got there, he went upstairs without another word and straight to bed. The following morning, he came down, looked at me, obviously a little embarrassed but trying not to show it, and said, "Frank, I've lost my teeth." It was pretty obvious when he said this that he didn't have them in. I figured out immediately what must have happened. I said, "They must be on the sandhill on top of Nine Mile Hill". We promptly got back in the van, drove back to where we'd stopped the previous evening, retraced our steps, and sure enough, found his dentures there.

But, if my father was pleased with my skills at snooker, he was also proud of my singing ability. I have to say that I had a good voice but I wasn't alone in the family in being musical. Fred had a good voice too and had been in the choir at St John's College, ending up as head chorister there. Doris played the piano. When people would come by to visit, my father would get me to sing, with Doris accompanying on the piano. I remember, in particular, that he loved me to sing "Charmaine". Yes, I can still remember singing "Charmaine, I wonder why you keep me waiting, my Charmaine, my Charmaine." There was no question of not singing, when Father asked me to, but I have to say I enjoyed it.

And it was my ability to sing that led to what was probably the most unusual thing about my childhood, namely being a chorister at Trinity College. There has probably always been a big town-gown divide in Cambridge but this was one way it was bridged, with townie boys singing in the choirs in the older, big colleges. As I mentioned, Fred had gone before me in this way, becoming the head chorister at St John's College, which is situated just next to Trinity.

When I was 10, my father said to me, "Well, you ought to get into the choir at Trinity". I can't remember my exact reaction to this but I think I was pleased. It seemed like a special thing to do, or would be, if I could get in. Maybe I felt a little competitive with Fred, too, who had made his mark at St John's in this way. So I went along to the interview for new choristers at Trinity chapel and the choir-master, Dr Alan Gray, a big man, sat down at the piano and asked me to sing some hymns. The "interview", of course, was really an audition to see if you could sing well. Dr Gray asked me to choose a hymn. I chose "There is a green hill far away without a city wall". I must have sung it well enough because he accepted me as a probationer for the Trinity College choir.

Dr Gray was a fine man and a good teacher, though I think his greatest love was playing the music, not teaching. By the time I came along to Trinity, he must have been in his early seventies but when you are a child, you don't really think about people's ages that way. I think I just thought of him as an old but kind man. What counted was his love of music and his wish to get the best out of us. He had come from a prominent family in York and had gone up to Cambridge, to Trinity, as a young man, to study law, but music was his great love and he had not stayed with the law long. He had become the chief organist at Trinity in 1889, succeeding the great Stanford, who had moved to London. Gray also became the conductor of the Cambridge University Musical Society (CUMS) and stayed in that post until 1912. As organist and choirmaster of Trinity and with CUMS, he introduced the playing of Bach's mass in B minor, a difficult piece, to Cambridge. But he was also a composer. His best remembered piece, still occasionally played today, is his anthem, based on Christina Rosetti's poem, "What are these that glow from afar". He had composed several anthems in 1916, after two of his three sons died on the Western Front in the First World War. He never talked about that to us boys, of course, and I didn't know about it till much later. And we really only knew him as our choirmaster, not as a composer.

But what struck you immediately about Dr Gray was his size. He was a huge man, very tall, with a frame to match. When talking to you, he would always lean down slightly. This was partly out of courtesy and, I suspect, to be less conspicuous but also, probably, just to make sure that he could hear you. In fact, he really had a perpetual stoop, which emphasised his scholarly nature and, somehow, his kindness.

He also always moved with great slowness and dignity. The story that I heard much later was that the doctors had told him that he had only a normal size heart and that for a man of his great frame, it might not be strong enough. Whether that was the reason for his measured, slow pace in everything or not or whether it was just his temperament, no one can really know. But he moved slowly in just about everything he did. It was said of him that he could ride a bicycle slower than anyone else in Cambridge. Certainly, no one ever saw him peddling fast on his bike.

Trinity chapel is just to the right of the Great Court as you enter the college from Trinity Street. The Great Court itself is the biggest and most impressive college quadrangle in Cambridge, with its large lawns, footpaths and the big ornate stone fountain in the centre. It is where Harold Abrams ran his famous race, completing the outer circuit of the quad in less than a minute, something that had never been done before. That was in 1919 or 1920, I believe, just after the Great War. This race was later made famous in the film *Chariots of Fire* but the filming of the race was at Eton, not at Trinity itself. The film-makers wanted to recreate the race and film it in the Great Court itself but the College vetoed this. I heard that the reason was that it was because in one scene, the Master, who was played by John Gielgud, makes a mildly anti-Semitic remark. Apparently, Trinity felt that would put them in a bad light so they didn't allow any filming there. Pretty silly, if you ask me. That scene with Gielgud was in the film anyway.

But my connection with Trinity began in 1928, so about eight or nine years after Abrams' famous race in the Great Court. The chapel itself is impressive. You enter the building through an antechapel, all whitewashed walls and statues of some of the great men of Trinity – Newton, Francis Bacon, Tennyson – with busts of others on plinths. But you enter the chapel proper by walking through a passageway from the ante-chapel under the organ loft and immediately there's a different feeling. The chapel is lined from the back to just before the altar with wooden pews along the walls, the ones in the centre with candle holders for the choir. Behind the pews are tall oak panels just against the walls and, above them, long stained-glass windows. The building itself was erected during the reigns of Mary I and Elizabeth I but the windows were put in during the Victorian era. Each of the latter shows a great church or academic or royal figure. The ceiling is decorated with wooden beams in a rectangular crossed pattern, while the floor of the chapel consists of black and white marble tiles. The whole length of the room must be 120-150 feet. As you approach the altar, you notice that it is framed from behind by two pairs of gold-painted columns that bracket a large dramatic painting of the angel Gabriel pushing Lucifer down into the fires of hell. To the left of the altar as you face it are several panels with the names of the hundreds of young Trinity men who died in WW1. Trinity chapel isn't as grand or beautiful as King's College chapel, or as old, but it has a certain beauty and dignified austerity.

It felt special to become part of the Trinity choir. But becoming a member was not just a matter of simply showing up one day and starting. No, there was an initiation procedure for new choristers. To be accepted by the other choristers, you had to bring your own "footing", which was a present for them. The footing consisted of twelve one penny Sharp's cream toffee bars. So, my first day, just after I arrived, I gave these to the head chorister, who then distributed them to the other members of the choir, who ate them, while I looked on in envy. There were other rituals, as well. Some of the new boys were put down the coal hole but this didn't happen to me. I did go through another initiation rite, however. On Saturday evening, before the practice and service, a new boy had to walk into the chapel, up the main aisle, in the dark, while the other boys stood on the ramparts above looking down and shouting "Melchesidek will get you!" The new chorister would walk up the central aisle, aware of the darkness, the size of the place and the other boys watching and shouting. You can imagine, it was quite an atmosphere. And then he would kneel down before the altar, which was covered with a red surplice, and say, "Thank you Melchesidek". Melchesidek was the name of the ghost that supposedly haunted the chapel but I have to say, I never saw any ghostly goings-on. Just pranks from the boys themselves. Every now and then, for instance, we would place books on the lintel of the door that Dr Gray would come through. Sure enough, the books would come tumbling down on him when he entered. Another sort of man would have been mad as hell but he just smiled, after the initial surprise, and took it in his stride.

But it wasn't all fun and games by any means. It was hard work. I bicycled to the chapel every day, for choir practice between 5.00pm and 6.00pm every weekday afternoon in term time, in preparation for the Saturday and Sunday services. Between the practice sessions and the weekend services, there were almost never any "days off" in term time. We also had special rehearsals for performances on feast days and Saints' days. And, as one of the top college choirs, we gave recitals outside Cambridge, which involved special trips and all the necessary rehearsals before each of these performances. I remember, in particular, that we sang at Canterbury and York Cathedrals several times. There were also choral recitals at the other Cambridge colleges. Every year, for instance, we sang as part of the Three Choirs Festival at King's College, Cambridge. The three choirs were those of King's, Trinity and St. John's. And, virtually every week, we were learning and practising new pieces. Some of the ones I remember in particular are the Magnificat, Nunc Dimitis, Handel's Messiah, and various non-religious but deeply moving songs like Mendelssohn's "O, for the wings of a dove".

One of the special performances we gave was particularly memorable for me. The year after I had become head chorister at Trinity, the head chorister of King's got the mumps and was unable to sing. I was assigned to take his place. Since the Three Choirs Festival was always broadcast on the wireless, it was a special honour to be doing the solo. I don't remember if I was nervous but I don't think so. What I do remember is singing the music that was sung at the crowning of Mary Queen of Scots. I have always remembered the first phrase, "She shall be brought unto the king in raiment of needle-work".

Being a member of the Trinity choir felt a real privilege. On Sundays, going to and from Sunday services, we choristers had to wear our mortar boards and gowns. Our uniforms we called "bum freezers" and in the bitter Cambridge winters – it was a lot colder and windier in the winter than it is now – that was a pretty good description of how much protection the outfit gave you. But trooping across the Great Court in your mortarboard and gown, one of a dozen boys, you knew that everyone would recognise you as a chorister and it did feel special. There was also a little money that came with the privilege. Our school fees were paid each term and the college also gave each chorister 5 shillings a term while the head chorister got 10 shillings a term. These were not princely sums, of course, but you didn't join a college choir to make money, and the small stipend was a little recognition from the college that what you did was actual work and was appreciated.

Being a member of the choir squeezed down the time for everything else, of course. There really wasn't much time for the normal fooling around that boys do. And for me, there were other duties, as well. On Saturday mornings, I had to deliver packages of yeast by carrier bike, for Father's business. My pocket money for this was 6d, which I collected when I had delivered the yeast to the last customer. Doing these rounds ruled out playing rugby on Saturday morning and I missed that as I liked rugby. On the other hand, I got to play football on Saturday afternoon for Trinity against the other colleges when I was older. In school itself, there was cricket, as I mentioned. Of course, another thing that took time was homework. I had started out at Romsey Council School in Mill Road. But, once I began high school, I was at the County High School which charged, I believe, £4 10s a term but Trinity paid the tab for the choristers.

As for school itself, I have to say that it was never something I really enjoyed, either at Romsey School or the County High School, though I was alright at my school work. In other words, I was an average student, overall. Some subjects, of course, had more appeal than others. I hated Latin and the man who taught it but French, as it happened, was one of the subjects I liked most. By the time I left school, I had obtained "distinction" in mathematics, French and English, scraped through with passing grades in history and chemistry and failed in biology and Latin. Not a great record but not a terrible one either.

Dr Gray retired before I left the choir. He was well into his seventies at the time. One day, shortly before he left, he introduced us to the new choirmaster, Dr Hubert Middleton, who would be taking his place. Dr Middleton, at the time, was the organist and choirmaster at Ely Cathedral. I remember Dr Middleton, who was not a giant like Dr Gray but an average sized man, coming in and greeting all of us, "Good evening Doctor, good evening boys". Alan Gray introduced him to us in turn and then Middleton sat down on the music bench and said, "Boys, I want you to learn a song. I'll take you through it in phrases but I want you to sing it all when I've finished". I will never forget that song. It went like this:

"Never let your braces dangle, dingle, dingle, dangle,
One old sport, he got caught, went right through the mangle,
Over the rollers he went by gum, came out as flat as linoleum,
You could wipe your feet on his rum tum tum.
Never let your braces dangle."

Not your average Cambridge choir piece, to be sure. Hubert Middleton had a sense of fun. And he took us on trips to the country. I have a picture somewhere of us on a picnic, with Dr Middleton eating kippers. He looked after us. And he gave us more active instruction in singing than Dr Gray had.

Naturally, we wanted to do a good job and please him. Once I really let the side down, however, and, more than seventy years on, it is still a painful memory. The choir itself consisted of both boys and men. In the men's choir there was an alto professional, Benjamin Bails, I think his name was, and a tenor professional, Josh Reed, and a bass professional named Armitage but the rest of those taking part were all choral scholars. It was a good group to be singing with. One day we had to sing at a communion service. It was the first time we had ever done this, and as the head chorister, I had to sing a solo. The introduction to the piece was made by the organ and we were kneeling. Dr Middleton played the introduction three or four times and, finally, I whispered to the boy next to me, "What's the old man doing?" And he said, "Well, he's waiting for you to sing," and I felt such a fool for not having realised this. Somehow I got through it but I will never forget Hubert Middleton coming down from the organ loft when the service was finished and saying, "Dutch, I never thought you would let me down". But, of course, he forgave me and became a great friend to me later on. When I was sixteen or so, my voice broke but Dr Middleton kept me on in the choir, allowing me to sing alto.

And then in 1931, we heard that Dr Gray had died. He was seventy six. Maybe his heart had been too small for his body, as the doctors had told him, but it had served him well enough to let him make it to his late 70s. There were two big services for him, one at Trinity – all the important Trinity fellows came or most of them, including Nobel laureates, Fellows of the Royal Society, important professors – and one at York Cathedral a few days later, given his prominence as a native son of York. For the remembrance at Trinity, I sang with the choir at the gates of the college, singing "Nunc Dimitis". I remember that the tears streamed from my eyes. Dr Gray had been a good man and it was hard to accept that he was gone. Years later, I learned that he and I had another link. He had been a golfer and in fact, a good one. He had been the captain of the Gog Magog Golf Club, the second in its history, taking the post in 1903. I mention this because golf became part of my life and sixty eight years after Dr Gray, in 1971, I became captain of this club.

But in 1934-35, golf was not one of my concerns. Finding work and making a living was. The question was "*how?*". This was, of course, the time of the Great Depression and there weren't lots of opportunities. Going into the family business, of course, would have been one option but that had absolutely no appeal at the time. My brother was already working with my father in the business and the strictness of my father made him quite unreasonable at times. It was quite enough for me to have to put up with that at home in the family; I had no wish to be with him during the day as well.

One thing that had caught my fancy was the idea of being a pilot. I think that my first interest in flying was born at an air display given at Marshall's, the local airfield, in 1933 or '34. It was the Cobham air show, called the Cobham air circus, I believe. Cobham was the name of the pilot and I can still see his aeroplane, a Tiger Moth, diving in on the crowd and then pulling out at the last minute. That was the first time I really became interested in flying. I thought it would be great to learn to fly. And then, a little later, after I had started in my first job, in '34 or '35, which I will describe in a moment, there was an advert in the paper for apprentice pilots. The training was to be at Marshall's and it was a five year programme. The first year the pay would have been 5s a week, the second and third years this would increase to 7s 6d, and the third, to 10s. I went to my father and I told him about this, hoping he would agree. But all he said was, "That is daylight robbery, you stay where you are." That put an end to that. There was no arguing with Father when he had made up his mind.

But another possibility involved Trinity. When I was sixteen, nearly seventeen, before I left school, Hubert Middleton said to me, "You've been one of the best choristers I've ever had. Would you like a choral scholarship?" I said, "What does that mean?" He said, "Well, you would come here, sing as a choral scholar and study here at Trinity. And the college will pay you £180 a year. But, of course, there will also be extras, for which you will have to pay, so you'll have to ask your father." I said, "How much is it going to cost him?" He said, "I think about another £100 a year." Well, I liked the idea a lot and I went home and told my father. He was completely negative,

however. All he said was, "No way, get to work." I don't think
that I ever forgave him for that. Though £100 was a lot of
money, he could have afforded it. He always used to carry a
large wad of money in his hip pocket, a big load of cash. His
refusal was just meanness on his part.

When I left school at 16+, my mother suggested that I try to
get a job with the local government. As she said to me, those jobs
were secure, jobs for life. Today, of course, there are practically
no jobs for life but when I was growing up, that was often the big
distinction between different kinds of job, whether they were
secure for a lifetime or not. But I wasn't sure how to approach
the local government for getting such a job. It was, again, Hubert
Middleton who offered to help. He said, "Well, why not join the
County Council?" and he told me that he knew Henry Morris,
who was the director of education though his title, at the time,
was Education Secretary. Henry Morris was a big figure in local
government in Cambridge. He had built up all the village colleges, first at Sawston village, then later in Impington, Bottisham,
and Melbourn. Middleton told me that Morris was a friend of his
and he told me that he would write to him on my behalf.

And that's how I got my first job outside the family. I had an
interview with Henry Morris, a distinguished-looking bachelor
gentleman, at Shire Hall and it evidently went well enough. I was
given a job as junior clerk at £51 a year, to rise by annual
increments of £10. Today, these sums sound like nothing at all
but, at the time, they were reasonable, at least for a young man
starting out. It wasn't enough to live independently on, however.
And, as a result, I continued to live at home, right until the start
of the war.

One of my first duties was cleaning out the inkwells at the
office every day, filling them with new ink and supplying new
pen nibs. I was doing this one day when Henry walked in. We
always started at 9.00am sharp but he always arrived a little
later, at 9.15am or 9.30am. He looked around and then said,

"Morning, Holland, what do you think of the plaques on the walls of this room?" I looked up at the plaques and, at first dodged the question, asking him what he had in mind for them. He said, "I'm going to put them in Sawston village college." But he came back to his question: "Well, what do you think of them?" I took another look at the plaques, turned to him, and said, "I doubt that the art education at Sawston is any better than what I had at school, but even if it's as good as mine, I think they'll say they are pretty terrible." He smiled and said, "Holland, you're the only person who's dared tell me the truth," and from that moment onwards, every time there was a possibility of my advancement, he gave it to me.

The first promotion involved becoming School Attendance Officer. In a little Austin 7 convertible, which was supplied by the council, I used to go round to the schools, making sure the children went to school, and filing reports and prosecuting where the families had truant children. I liked the job but one day I was called into the Chief Clerk's office, a man named Reg Ayres. He told me that I was driving too fast, particularly when I cornered. I told him that I'd had no complaints from anybody else but he warned me that one day I would have an accident. Well, he was wrong but his mentality was typical of some of the petty-minded bureaucrats you run into. In fact, I never had an accident with the car but not having the car led to a small accident with a motor-bike.

It happened this way. One evening I wanted to go to a dance with a girl I was friendly with, Mary Tibbetts, and I asked my father for permission to have the car. He said, "No, I want it for myself tonight." Well, I thought, I'm going to be independent, I'm not going to let this stop me. As it happened, I had been given a £50 bonus by Trinity when I left school, and I had put this in a Post Office account. It occurred to me that this might be just enough to buy a motorbike. So on that Saturday morning, I went to Hallens in Union Lane and bought a brand new AJS350. Unfortunately, the price was £52 and, with my Trinity bonus, I had just £51. They wouldn't let me have it for £51 – it had to be their asking price of £52, not a pound less – so I did the only thing I could. I went home to my mother and asked her to lend me £1 out of the money that I paid her each week from my wages for room and board at home. She agreed, got the £1 for me and I went back to Hallens to pick up the motorbike.

The only trouble was that I knew nothing about motorbikes. "How's it work?" I asked. "Well, you turn this grip, the gear change is below and that changes the gear up," the salesman said. He showed me the ignition and a couple of other things. So, I thought, this doesn't sound too hard. I got on and started going down the road. It seemed fine at first. But the road was narrow and I had to make a turn to come back. I made the turn too quickly and hit the retaining wall on the other side. Not very badly, just making a slight dent in the tank but I went over. Everybody from the shop rushed out and asked how I was. I was alright, only had a couple of scratches, and rode it home without any further trouble. Unfortunately, Father was at home. He must have seen me from the front window because he came out of the house and immediately asked, "Where'd you get that?" I said, "I bought it," and he then asked, "What with?" I told him that it had been the bonus money from Trinity. He said, "You can't bring that here, take it away." He was like that. So I had to go and find some other place to leave my motorbike. Luckily, one of my friends, who only lived two or three doors away, was able to let me keep it in his parents' garage.

The motorbike, in fact, gave me a lot of independence. The next year, I used it to go to an interview for another local government job, this one as the School Attendance Officer in the village of Battle, in East Sussex. But something happened the evening before that interview, one of the oddest experiences I ever had. Mary, my girlfriend, and I were out walking round the town that Sunday evening when all of a sudden it started to rain.

As it started to pour, we were walking through Market Passage, just off Market Street, which comes off the main market square. Market Passage was where the old cinema was. That evening there was no film but a sign outside said, "Séance. All people welcome." This sounded interesting and I said to Mary, "Let's go in. At least, we'll stay dry." We bought our tickets, went in and then went upstairs to the balcony and took a seat in the back row.

The medium came on to the stage, an older woman, looked around and then made some introductory remarks, in a normal voice. But then her voice dropped, almost to the timbre of a man's voice, and she started picking people out of the audience and giving them messages. It was interesting but I was only paying it half my attention; I wasn't gripped exactly. But then she suddenly looked up and said, "That young man, second from the end of the top row." I looked around and then at Mary and said, "That's me." The medium said, "Put your hand up." I said to Mary, "No, I'm not going to put my hand up." I had no wish to become part of the show. But the medium continued, as if she heard me, which I don't think she could have, "Well, you needn't do that," and then said that she was going to describe someone that I knew. And blow me down, she did. She described my step-grandfather, with his little nanny goat beard, his bow legs, his funny way of walking. And then she said, "You're thinking of changing your job." This, remember, was just the day before I was set to go for my interview in Battle. "Well," she continued, "he [my step grandfather] says don't change your job." She paused, "He says, 'You'll never want'." Hearing this was pretty incredible, of course. That is what he always had said, when I opened the car door for him and he would give me six pence.

Mary and I talked about it after we left the theatre but neither of us really knew what to make of it. Still, I went to the interview at Battle the next day and I was offered the job after the interview. But the whole experience at the theatre had stayed with me and I turned it down. The next morning, Tuesday, I reported for work as usual. I was just starting some clerical work when my bell rang. There was a bell for each person in the office, I should explain, which Henry Morris could ring when he wanted to speak to one of us about something. It was about 9.30am or so and he must have just arrived. I went in to see him and he immediately asked, "How did you get on yesterday, Holland?" I said, "Fine, Sir, I was offered the job but I turned it down." He looked at me, smiled and said, "Good. I want you to fill in an application form for the Assistant Juvenile Employment Officer." I looked back at him, trying to see if he was joking, and said, "I haven't got a chance, Sir. I've seen the shortlist and you have two MA's and four BA's on it." He just repeated, "I want you to fill in the form for this post." I felt that this would be a pointless exercise but, since he was insisting, there was no choice. However, I said one more thing. "Well, it will have to go to the council." And he said, "Of course. Just fill in the form and submit it."

The following week I was called for the interview. The bigwigs of the council were there, in particular Mrs Melhuish H. Clark and Mr Jackson, who was chairman. I don't remember much about the interview itself but I got the job, despite having nowhere near the qualifications of the other candidates. I had no doubt that Henry Morris had put his oar in and that had made the difference. And, so turning down the job in Battle, thanks to the "advice" of my late step-granddad, relayed by the medium in the theatre, led to this much better job. It was better paid and more interesting than being a school attendance officer. And I held it until the war came along.

My new boss, I should mention, was a lady named Iris Davis. She was not only smart but quite a bit of stuff, really beautiful. One morning, she came in and first thing, called me into her office. She said, "From now on, Holland, you won't know me as Iris Davis but as Mrs Iris McGary." And that's how I found out that at the weekend she had married one of the well known QC's in Cambridge, Mr McGary.

The summer of '38, Mary and I, and another friend, Ken

Dawes, did something special. We took a motorbike trip through France, from Calais in a big loop around the north and west of France, down through the Brenner Pass into Italy, through Turin and then across to Nice on the Mediterranean coast. Young people today do trips like this all the time but, back in 1939, this was pretty unusual. Ken had his own motorbike, a Raleigh 500 and I had mine, the AJS 350 from Hallens. Mary, when she heard about our plans, announced that she wanted to come along. Her brother was keen on motorbikes and so was she. We fixed a sprung saddle on the back of mine for Mary and, a day or two later, we were off. We rode to Dover, took the ferry to Calais and proceeded from there. Of course, there were no motorways in France then, or in England either for that matter, but there were two-lane main roads that ran right through the towns and villages, most of which had cobbled roads. We had fitted panier boxes on each side of our motorbikes with nuts and bolts but after a while, the bolts started coming loose, with all the bouncing over the cobbles. So, we frequently had to stop to tighten them up.

Altogether, we reckon we travelled about 3000 miles on this trip in a fortnight. And it was great, riding through the country-side and villages and towns and eating French and Italian food (even on a budget), which was a novelty for us. Often, people in the villages would stop to chat and I, with my school-boy French, was able to tell them about our trip. By the time we reached Nice, we felt like seasoned travellers. Nice itself looked much as it does today, with the great sweeping curve of the Promenade des Anglais facing the sea. But, of course, it was much less crowded, with much less traffic, in summer than it is today. This was a great trip, it really was, and it would be my first and only experience of France till I came down out of the skies six years later in Normandy.

What, you might be wondering, was going on between Mary and me during this trip? Well, I confess that I was quite keen on Mary but while she liked me as a friend, she didn't want things to develop further. I brought up the idea of getting engaged and she turned me down. Maybe she had another boyfriend, I don't know. But she let me down gently, saying that she had a friend whom she was sure I would like and who would like me. I asked who that was. And she said her friend's name was Margot. Margot, as it happened, also worked in local government, at the Shire Hall, along with her older sister, Peggy. Peggy was in Reg Ayre's department, the same fellow who had warned me about going too fast in the car. From that time, in fact, I had never been able to stand him. He seemed like a meddlesome busybody. But I would be glad to meet Margot. Peggy worked as secretary to the council while Margot was in the agricultural office. A few days later, Mary introduced me to Margot and I have to say that I liked Margot right away. She was a tall, attractive brunette with nice green eyes and a pleasant voice.

Margot, as I found out soon, was a golfer. One day she suggested that I come and play golf with her, her sister Peggy, and her father, Henry Notley. The next Saturday, I took my motorbike and rode over to the golf course at Saffron Walden to meet them at the agreed time. Margot, Peggy and Henry were already there. Henry was a tall, distinguished looking man. That day, I just walked around with the three of them as they proceeded doing 18 holes of the course, and watched them play. I knew nothing about golf but what I saw was a game that looked pretty easy. About the fourth hole, after Henry had hit the ball, I said, "Well, this is a bloody silly game." It really looked almost too easy to be a decent sport. Henry sort of smiled and said, "Well, you try." He put a ball on a tee, gave me a driver, and said, "Go on, hit it." It took me three swings before I even touched it and then only managed to knock it on the top. They all laughed at me. Well, that of course was a challenge. I said, "Give me a month and I'll play you nine holes around the golf course." Henry accepted the challenge.

So I started practising. I cycled to work at Shire Hall every morning, from our house on Mill Road but now I got up even earlier and at 7.00am every morning, practised hitting the ball on Coldham's Common. After a month, I said to Margot's father, "Henry, I'm now ready for that match." So, we went to the golf course at Saffron Walden on Saturday and started playing. We had agreed to play 9 holes and by the 9th hole, where we were all square, I was on the green for two and Henry was on the green for three. And I thought, I'm all square but I shouldn't try to win this game. You don't do this to your girlfriend's father, at least not the first game you play with him. So I deliberately knocked the ball harder than I would have done to hole the putt, and it went three yards past the hole. Henry had a big laugh at this and we then finished off the game, all square. "Ah," he said, "well done".

And that was my start in playing golf. I had no idea that that would be the ticket to becoming an RAF pilot. But, as I'll explain in a moment, it did.

2
The war begins and
I take wing in the RAF

Like most young men, I was mostly interested in my own life
and didn't pay too much attention to politics. But in 1938, you
couldn't help notice there was big trouble brewing in the world.
Hitler was making this demand, that demand, taking over
Austria, threatening Czechoslovakia, building up the German
military the whole time. As everyone knows, our Prime Minister,
Mr Chamberlain, came back from Munich in September that
year, proclaiming that his agreement with Hitler over
Czechoslovakia had brought "peace in our time". But most of us
felt that it had bought peace for only a year or two, at most.
Probably Chamberlain himself knew that was all his agreement
with Hitler had done, it had just bought some time.

The country began speeding up her preparations for the war
we were all sure would come. In particular, we started producing
more Spitfires and other aircraft, in particular the Hawker
Hurricanes. The inventor of the Spitfire, R.J. Mitchell, had seen
the danger coming, years before Munich – he had been to
Germany and met some of the top people in Hitler's government
– and had designed the Spitfire, for fighting the Germans in the
air. Leslie Howard made a film about this in '42, *The First of the
Few*. He directed, produced and starred in it. Must have thought
it was pretty important. As fate would have it, the film came out
a year before he himself was in a plane that was shot down by

German fighters, returning to London from Lisbon. Later it came out that the Germans brought it down because they thought that Churchill was aboard.

Germany invaded Poland on September 1, 1939. Chamberlain gave Hitler an ultimatum, two days to pull back and get out of Poland. But no one believed he would and on September 3rd, when the ultimatum expired, Britain declared war on Germany. I remember listening to Chamberlain's morning broadcast on the wireless. The event we had feared for years might happen had at last come. We were now at war. Later that day, I was at the station in Cambridge, where people were getting ready to receive the children evacuees from London. The country was already getting on to a war footing and the fear was that the Germans might start bombing cities, especially London, right away, so many Londoners were trying to get their children out of harm's way.

The station was filled with people, waiting for the train to arrive. You could feel the tension in the air and then the air raid warning went. Everybody thought "Christ, we're going to be bombed right away" but within a few minutes, the sirens stopped, the all clear was sounded. It had been a false alarm. Or, maybe they had sounded the alarm, just to make people realise that, after months and years of waiting and worrying, the war really was on, that this was serious. For me, it certainly brought it home that my life was about to change in a big way. I was 22 and in a reserve occupation to start with but it was just a matter of time before I would be called up. Nobody had wanted this war but once it had started, you wanted to be part of the action. But if you wanted to be in the RAF or the Navy, not the Army, you didn't wait to be called up, you volunteered, putting your name down for the service you wanted to be in.

And that's what I did. I volunteered, put my name down for the RAF. I'd thought about it and knew, ever since the Cobham air show, that I wanted to fly. And I thought that if I was going to get into this war, this is what I want to do. But things moved much slower than I had imagined. It was three months before I heard about my application. I kept on at work during this time, waiting to be called up, wondering when the letter would come. Finally, in December, I got the letter. I was asked to report for the interview at the RAF office in Cardington, near Bedford.

I knew that I wanted to be a fighter pilot and not anything else. The problem was that every other young man trying to get into the RAF also wanted to be a fighter pilot but what they were short of was tail gunners, for the bombers, not pilots. The Battle of Britain had begun, with lots of bombing raids from Germany on airbases and other military targets – London would not begin to be seriously hit for a year – and the RAF was already beginning to lose tail gunners in action. Lots of them; it was probably the most dangerous position in fighting aircraft. So what they wanted was more air gunners, not pilots. On the application form, you had to put down "air crew", which was one of the listed choices, not "pilot", which was not listed. Whether or not you got to be an RAF pilot depended on the interview and if you were assigned to be something else, you couldn't complain because after all, you had put down air crew.

There were 52 people called up that day to report to the Cardington office. I was told to be there at 9.30am. As it happened, they were way behind in the interviewing and you just waited in this big room, sitting on wooden benches until they called your name. I asked everybody who came out what he had been assigned. "Air gunner", "air gunner", it went. It was pretty discouraging. I had already decided that if they offered me this, I would turn it down and wait to be called up and just go into the Army and take my chances there.

Finally, my turn came. I was right near the end of the crowd, the last but four of the 52 to go in. There were three officers there, an air vice-marshal, a wing commander and a squadron leader. I sat down in front of them and the questions began. One of them, of course, was what position I wanted in the RAF. Like everybody else, I told them pilot. But most of the questions were basic ones, to see if you knew anything, simple ones in trigonometry and judging the height of hills. No problem with those. Then one of them asked if I knew the difference between a two stroke and a four stroke engine and I did. The interview was just about at an end when one of them said, "What sport do you play?" So I said, "I play a bit of cricket, rugby, soccer and, oh, golf." "Golf! What's your handicap." Well, I didn't have one but this didn't seem to be the time to admit that. "18", I said. The wing commander turned to the squadron leader and said, "Ah George, you'd have a hell of a job to give him a shot per hole, wouldn't you?"

That did it. "Pilot", they wrote down. I was in. Of the 52 of us waiting that day, only one other candidate was made a pilot. I came back out into the waiting room, as surprised as I was pleased.

Then, things moved quickly. About a week later, I was told to report to the allocation board in Cambridge for assignment to the first stage of training. There was a flight sergeant and a warrant officer in charge of the assignments. The warrant officer motioned me to a chair and asked me straight away about where I wanted to go. There were only two choices, Cambridge and Hastings, that's where the initial training wings for the RAF were.

I wanted to stay near Cambridge but I knew that they always sent you somewhere you didn't want to go. So, when the warrant officer asked me, "Where do you want to do your initial training?" I said, "Hastings". And he said, "But you come from Cambridge? Why do you want to go to Hastings?" Well, like a fool, I levelled with him, told him that I had been told that they always sent you to the place that you didn't want to go to. He smiled, told me that this wasn't so, that since I had chosen Hastings, that's where I would go. A few days later, I was on the train to my first posting in the RAF, at Hastings.

Our living quarters were a small hotel on the promenade. Every morning we would walk from our hotel, and show up for classes at 9.00am.

I liked the group I was with. They were all intelligent, well educated lads, had all got school certificates or the like. But in the morning, for what we were doing, brains and education were pretty irrelevant. It was all square bashing, that is, drilling – marching: turn left, turn right, about face, at ease. It went on and on that way, every morning. Fortunately, the afternoons were more interesting. We had lessons: lessons on aircraft maintenance, engineering, map reading, morse code, navigation, everything except flying lessons, which would come later. There were regular exams, of course. They kept us on our toes and paying attention. And, all the time, we were being instructed in the basics of following orders, waking up smartly at 5.30am, getting your kit right, polishing your buttons, cleaning your shoes, that sort of thing. We had as our warrant officer a really strict ex-Grenadier Guard, who drilled us in square bashing. It seemed like being bossed around for something that had precious little to do with fighting the Germans. But pretty soon, with something like this, you develop an interest in getting it all right, looking smart and well turned out, being able to follow orders smartly and looking good at it. And I have to say we built ourselves up into a bloody good squad. We were proud of it, proud of ourselves.

This initial training period lasted a little over a month. But, halfway through, there was a bombing raid on Hastings. I remember the sirens going, taking cover but not many of the details. A moment of fear, I think, but the whole thing was over in a few minutes. However, some of the bombs had hit, there had been damage to the town and the result was that it was decided we would be transferred to Bournemouth, to finish the initial training course. Not everybody made it through this first phase, I should say. It was competitive and it was tough. But I was determined to make it and I did.

From Bournemouth, those of us who passed went on to the next stage, actual training in the air, to the airfield at Hatfield, just north of London. This was the number 1 Elementary Flight

Training School, or 1EFTS, in the country. It was also a development centre for the de Havilland company; they were testing one of their first jet engine aeroplanes there. For the student pilots, all training was on the Tiger Moth, a sturdy, pre-war aircraft that was used only for training. There were about 35-40 at Hatfield.

At Bournemouth, I had learned all the theory you needed for flying but it was at 1EFTS that I got my first real experience of being a pilot. The basic learning drill at 1EFTS was that you would do the first 8 hours of flying with an instructor, just one session per day, of 45 minutes or one hour, never more. Then, after your 8 hours of instruction, you would go solo and they would see how you did. If you were judged not ready after those first 8 hours of assisted flying, you would be washed out of the training programme.

The de Havilland Tiger Moth was a single-engined biplane with fabric-covered fuselage and wings. It was open cockpit with two seats, one for the instructor, one for the trainee pilot. The Tiger Moth had been used for training through a good part of the 1930s; the RAF had about 1500 for training purposes at the start of the war. Its top speed was only 110 mph. But they were good machines for training and for learning the basics. They were sensitive to outside conditions, however, and one could never forget that. If there was a hail-storm, you had better not be flying at all, because big hailstones could puncture the fabric-covered wings. Another peculiarity was that there was no electronic communication between the instructor, who sat up front, and the student, in the seat behind. You communicated through a tube-like device called the Gosport tube that connected the two cockpits. There was a sort of vibration-sensitive piece at the end of each tube and the instructor and student were wearing ear-pieces that allowed them to hear each other. It was usually the instructor, of course, telling the student what to do or – more often in the beginning – what not to do. Since you couldn't directly see what the instructor was doing with the controls, you were learning from his verbal instructions, not watching him.

At Hatfield there were no runways, it was an all-grass field. We would taxi to the take-off point, check right or left to make sure that all was clear, then turn the aircraft, using the rudder, to the take-off line. Take-offs were always into the wind. You would push the control column forward and open the throttle. Then as you accelerate and the tail lifts up, you're doing about 50-60 miles per hour, you pull the control column back ever so slightly to the central position. On take-off in a Tiger Moth, when you open up the throttle, the aircraft shudders and, the first time, I wondered if it was strong enough to lift off. But it did, every time, slowly leaving the ground, rising into the air. And, as it does so, you continue to pull the control column back toward your stomach, which points the nose further up and the aircraft rises up, the ground dropping away.

You take the aircraft to about 500 feet, slowly pushing the control column forward to level off. When you see the horizon cutting the windscreen you know you are now level. There was always a left turn at 500 feet and then you would pull the control column back again and go to whatever height was planned for the lesson or the exercise.

In my first lesson, the instructor kept full control of the flying at all times but he started getting me used to the handling of the basic controls once we were airborne. The bit he stressed in particular was the importance of not holding the control column in too tight a grip. If you do that, you are bound to create sharp movements in the aeroplane while the objective was to move the aircraft as smoothly as possible at all times. Moving the control column, either forward or back, makes the aircraft either rise or fall. Keep the control column in the centre and you fly level. After about 10-15 minutes, I had a feeling for how to handle the control column. A second basic feature to get used to was learning how to handle the throttle, to give the acceleration and power you wanted. A third feature was the rudder pedals, which, together with the control column, governed the movement of the aircraft either to the right or left. For each of these controls, the thing you needed to learn was smooth handling for smooth movements of the aircraft. The Gypsy Moth was a good flying machine to learn on but it was very light on the controls. That made it good for aerobatics but it also meant that you had to be careful not to jerk the controls or it would respond too much.

The first lesson was basic familiarisation, with the instructor controlling the plane nearly all the time. In the second, the instructor lets you take over the controls for much of the time. You are really flying the aircraft together at this stage but the instructor is gradually shifting control to the student. That second lesson, and the third, involved primarily instruction in take-offs and landings. And, after about two hours of this practice, I was basically comfortable with it though judging just how close the ground was as we came in for a landing was a problem and remained one for a while. There was a tendency to come in a little too abruptly which caused the aircraft to bump back into the air, maybe 10 feet or so. And when you do this, you have to open up the throttle a little and then ease the plane down again.

The next task was learning how to put the aeroplane into a spin but the real point of the lesson was learning how to come out of a spin, if you find yourself in one. For this, you take the aircraft to 5000 feet, climbing the whole time, nose pointing to the heavens and then, slowly, you ease back on the throttle, cutting the speed, until the plane stalls. As the plane stalls, it starts turning in the direction you have applied the rudder and within a few seconds, you are spinning round and round, heading faster and faster toward the ground. The earth is rushing up toward you and it is terrifying the first few times you do this; it seems impossible that you can come out of the spin quickly enough.

To do so, you need to do three things. First, you slowly push the control column forward. Then you press on the rudder pedal in the direction opposite to the spin, so if you're spinning to the right, you press on the left rudder pedal, to fight the spin. But the correction doesn't happen right away; there might be 3 to 4 spins while you are doing this. But, then, as the spin is easing off, you open the throttle and within a few seconds, as you ease back on the control column, you are flying on the level again. What a relief! The first time, the instructor demonstrated the whole thing; I was just the slightly terrified student in the back. The second time, I took charge. By the third or fourth time, it was beginning to feel almost natural – and not so frightening at the start, when you are just beginning the spin and the earth starts rushing toward you, as it was the first couple of times.

After the student had mastered coming out of a spin, there were the basic acrobatic manoeuvres: the loop-the-loop and slow rolls. And there was basic instruction for each. For the loop-the-loop, the practice was, again, at 5000 feet. To do it, you pulled the column straight back but slowly. Do it too fast and the plane stalls and you suddenly find yourself in a spin, plummeting to earth. (This is why they teach you how to come out of a spin before you learn any of the other manoeuvres.) At the top of the loop, the earth is beneath you, then slowly, things come right again and you level off. It is, of course, important to be strapped in tightly. The first time we did this, the instructor asked me, "Are you strapped in tightly?" I said "Yes sir". I certainly thought I was. But I wasn't; at the top of the loop, I felt myself leaving my seat, as if I was about to fall out – but was caught and held by my harness. Remember, the Tiger Moth was an open cockpit plane; there was no canopy to hold you in. Though the feeling of falling out probably only lasted a second or so, it was a deeply frightening experience. It taught me the importance of being strapped in tightly, I can tell you.

The slow rolls were a challenge. The trick was learning how to keep the nose of the plane up when you are upside down. At the top of the roll, when you are upside down, you want to pull the control column backwards, the normal move for raising the nose. But you have to do the opposite, push it slightly forward and, again, you have to do it smoothly and slowly or you can end up in a dive.

We also had to learn how to do a forced landing. This was essential: at some point, almost every pilot has to make a forced landing, either due to running out of fuel – if you'd gone too far from your base to make it back – or engine stalling while in level flight or some other mechanical defect. If you suddenly had to land, you had to have the reflexes for quick decision-making, to bring your aircraft down quickly but safely. For a practised forced landing, the instructor would pull the throttle all the way back, cutting the power, and say, "No throttle, now land in a field", so you had to choose a field quickly as the plane descended. If there were cows grazing in it, you could judge the way the wind was blowing because cows always graze into the wind, and then manoeuvre the airplane to come in with the wind, if you could.

My last lesson before going solo on the Tiger Moth started at 4.00pm in the afternoon, a nice clear day in late May. I practised a spin and a roll and then did about half a dozen circuits and bumps (landings) because the latter, getting the landings smooth, was still my big problem. I had pulled up in front of the aerodrome, the engine was still running and I started to unstrap but the instructor said, "Sit there", and he got out. At this point, the chief flying instructor, the CFI came over and got into the front seat. "Holland," he said, "I want you to take off, climb to 5000 feet, do a spin and return to the aerodrome." By now, I was confident that I could do this if I could remember all that my instructor had taught me. My only worry was getting the landing right.

I did just as he instructed, taking the Gypsy Moth to 5000 feet, putting it into a spin, pulling it out and then making the approach toward the landing strip. But I could see that I was going too fast, more than the 60 mph that was right for a landing. I throttled back gently but still the ground was coming up too fast. Suddenly, bang, the wheels hit the ground and the aeroplane bounced at least 10 feet into the air. I opened the throttle just a little, then let the aeroplane float to the ground as I gently eased the control column back, just as the instructor had always told me. This time, we made contact without a bounce and I eased up on the throttle and taxied it to a halt at the dispersal area. As I was doing so, I was down-hearted, certain that I had messed it up, failed the test.

"Stay there, Holland," the CFI said as he undid his safety straps and then got out and jumped to the ground. He then said, looking at me, without any hint in his expression as to whether he thought I had done a lousy job or a satisfactory one, "Take her up for one circuit and bring her in gently. Don't kill yourself." He then just walked away.

He hadn't praised anything I had done but I was relieved. "I've passed the first hurdle," I thought. I took off, singing something quietly to myself now, in a good, optimistic mood. But, at the same time, I was concentrating hard. This was, after all, my first solo flight after 8 hours of instruction. I taxied out to the runway, slowly opened up the throttle and took off and soon began the circuit, climbed to 500 feet, left turn to 1000 feet, then another left turn downwind, parallel to the aerodrome. I levelled off, chose the point to turn and lost height, coming down to 500 feet, turning left into the wind. But the acid test, the landing, came soon enough. This time, however, it went fine, a perfect 3-point landing. I taxied to the dispersal area, a happy and confident young man.

My instructor came up to me, as I turned off the engine. "Well, done, Holland," he said. This was a great relief. I had passed, after all, despite the first dodgy landing. I had truly passed the first hurdle at this point and was ready for the next stage of my training, which would be fifty hours of combined instruction and solo flights at Cranwell. Cranwell, it should be said, was the best posting you could hope for, the equivalent of

Sandhurst in the Army. Pupils leaving Cranwell were always passed out as officers, provided they survived the rigorous test in flying and ground training that you got there.

Two friends I'd made at Hatfield at this time – not close friends, I didn't really have any during the war, but fellows I liked – Bill Laidlaw and Tommy Dorwood, were also assigned to Cranwell. Bill Laidlaw was the Assistant Golf Professional to Henry Cotton, a famous golfer of the time while Tommy was a Scotland Rugby International player. I was glad that we would all be going to Cranwell but, tragically, both Bill and Tommy were killed in crashes during operational training. Bill Laidlaw crashed during a training exercise while flying a Whirlwind, I can't remember how Tommy Dorwood died.

When I look back on it, I think that, in general, one did not make close friends while you were in the service. You had mates, of course, but not close friends. Because anyone you liked could just disappear at almost any time, once you were on ops, so you didn't want to get too attached to anyone. It was a much lonelier business than being in the infantry, where you might be fighting side by side with the same fellows for weeks, months or even years.

When on operational squadrons in the RAF, you'd be having dinner at the mess with the group one night, there could be an operation that night or the next day and, the next day, if someone's chair was empty, you knew what it meant, of course. Some did come back the following day, of course, while others were captured and became prisoners of war but many never came back at all. And, for anyone killed or captured or missing in action, someone else would soon come along at dinner time in the mess hall and be sitting at his place. So, you stayed focussed on doing the job and, of course, did not spend any time thinking that it could be your turn to disappear next time. You just didn't. And when someone you liked bought it in action, you felt sad of course, but you just moved on, you didn't dwell on it. You couldn't afford to.

Cranwell is just outside Sleaford, the other side of Stamford, in Lincolnshire. It was the Advanced Flying Training College (AFTC) for the RAF and was a much bigger, and more important, place than the training centres at Hastings or Hatfield. This was the real thing, where the serious training began and where you felt that you were really becoming part of the RAF. For one thing, we were taking the first step toward being part of the officer corps, as leading aircraftsmen or LACs. LACs weren't actual officers but we felt that we were entering the officer corps. We had a special white flash in our hats to show our status as training pilots. Instead of boarding in the nearby town, as we had in Hastings, we lived in the college. Each of us had his own room and a batman who looked after his kit. He would polish the buttons on your uniform and get your gear ready for the afternoon sport. If you needed something cleaned, he took care of it.

Everything was very strict. Pupils weren't allowed to simply walk at any time. Wherever you were going, you marched, as if on parade. Every morning, in fact, there was a parade, marching drills and the raising of the flag before we marched off in groups either for training flights or lectures. Sport was taken seriously, with one major sporting event each week such as a big cross-country race or a serious rugby match. There was also a lot more course work than there had been at Hatfield, with continued training in navigation, Morse code and aircraft recognition. For the first time, also, there was gun training.

But the main work, of course, was training to become a pilot. Altogether I had about 50 hours of flight training in Cranwell. We flew most days but flying depended on good weather and the lack of air raid warnings, which were numerous owing to the fact that we were not that far from London. I started with a couple of training flights on a Master; these were single-engine aeroplanes and were the training aircraft for Hurricanes, which I flew later. I also had one flight in a Hart, a single-engine biplane, a very nice aeroplane to fly though an older model. Doing aerobatics on a

Hart was a pleasure; it handled beautifully. It had been in service before the Spitfires and the Hurricanes but was now used just for training. However, at Cranwell, you were soon assigned one main type of aircraft to train on. My training aircraft was the Oxford, a good, twin-engined monoplane, with two Bristol engines. It had been introduced into the RAF in late '37 specifically as an advanced training aircraft. It was a two seater. It also had two throttles, one for each engine, and you had to keep them synchronised. The main exercises were simple cross-country flights and how to come out of stalls and spins but you didn't do aerobatics in an Oxford.

One of the things I learned early on was that each type of aeroplane was different in its handling, in the way it felt. When you think about it, it's not surprising. The early models, of course, weren't nearly as good as the later ones for fighting but they were fine for teaching purposes. The various kinds of actual fighter plane were very different, too. They all had different top speeds, different kinds of handling, different weaknesses and different strengths, different stalling speeds, and of course different capabilities. The Spits, of course, were purely for aerial combat, for taking out Gerry aircraft in the air, both fighters and bombers, while the fighter bombers were designed to do that too but, just as importantly, to take out targets on the ground. Needless to say, the different kinds of aircraft also felt different when you were in their cockpits. The Spits were snug. Being in the cockpit of a Spitfire, you felt that you had just got into a custom-made suit or put on an elegant glove. Snug but comfortable. In the Typhoons, in contrast, it felt more as if you were getting into the cab of a lorry – there was a lot more room and a lot more power in the machine but it lacked the elegance of the Spits.

Altogether, during the whole course of the war, either during training or teaching or in combat, I must have flown about a dozen different kinds of aeroplane: Tiger Moths, Masters,

Spitfires, Fairey Battles, Harts, Majesters, Hurricanes, Harvards, Oxfords, Ansons, Typhoons, Tempests, these are the ones I remember. Of course, once you knew how to fly one kind of plane, it was easier to pick up the technique for the next. Like learning to drive a car; once you learned on one type, you can apply the skills to the next. But, with each new type of aircraft, you had to learn the particular machine and its specific quirks and strengths. How fast you can get it to fly, what altitude you can take it too, how quickly you can get it to top speed or decelerate, what it felt like at cruising speed, how manoeuvreable it was. You also had to recognise its signature noises, like what the engine should sound like on take-off and during flight. Pick up an odd sound in the engine and you had better know what it meant, whether it was serious and you should turn back, or whether you could probably ignore it. But, most of all, actually feeling how the 'plane was handling was critical. Was it responding to the throttle or the joystick in just the way it should? When you banked or did a dive, did it respond quickly and in the right way? For all aircraft, it was essential to know your stalling speed. Stall the aircraft and you would start spinning to earth. Each aircraft also had its own way of stalling; some would go into a spin gradually, others would tend to flick over when stalling. And, of course, those differences in stalling behaviour dictated how you had to get out of the stall with each kind of aircraft.

You also had to know instinctively whether it was behaving right or wrong, and what your instruments were telling you and what you needed to do, often in a split second. Your life, and your mission, depended on those instincts and that kind of knowledge. And, when flying in a group, your mates' lives are dependent upon them too. Good pilots learn all this, and get to know it, instinctively in terms of their reactions. Pilots that didn't would often pay the price. The actual fighting, of course, involved an extra set of skills. Operating the guns or bombs or rockets, knowing when to fire at enemy aircraft and getting the deflection just right, and targeting the bombs or rockets from the fighter bombers. All of this took special skills but, above all, a good sense of timing. If you weren't good at handling the aircraft, of course, you weren't likely to be much good at hitting your target, but the training period saw to it that all those who flew for the RAF had the requisite flying skills.

I was at Cranwell altogether for 6 months. This period was one of the best of my life. I really loved it. At the end, there was a big farewell dinner in the mess hall, with a major entertainment we put on. During that time, each squadron had to put on an act at the college hall. If you were in charge, you had to find someone to write the script and you had to line up the performers. Our act went well and the whole celebration was terrific fun.

But just before the gala dinner, I got my assignment: I was to be an instructor. Just why I was made an instructor and not sent into combat, I don't know. I suspect that my background in education before the war, though I had not been a teacher, must have played a part in the decision. In my immediate group, I believe I was the only one picked to be an instructor. The other qualified pilots were despatched to various operational training units around England, some to be trained as fighter pilots, others as bomber pilots. But, whatever the individual assignment, we all felt a great deal of pride. We had all been presented with our "wings" and had been judged competent pilots.

In December, 1940, I was told to report to the airbase at Peterborough for my first stint as an instructor. Peterborough is about 30 miles north of Cambridge and this would be the closest I'd been to home since leaving for Hastings. I was pleased to be stationed so near home. But there were two surprises at Peterborough. The first was that it was a flight school for training on single-engine planes and nearly all of my training at this point had been on a twin-engined plane, the Oxford. But the bigger surprise came the next day: finding out that the whole unit had left for Canada.

I was told to report to Group Captain D'Arcy Greig. Greig had been a Schneider trophy pilot. In other words, he was damn good in the air. When I went into his office and saluted, he looked up at me, sort of squinted, and said, "What are you doing here, Holland?" And, I said, "Well, I've been sent here from Cranwell." He looked at me for a second and said, "Well, that's a bloody silly thing to do, the whole unit has gone off to Canada, to an Advanced Training School." I'm sure that I must have shown my surprise and momentary wonderment at what I was supposed to do now because he added, almost immediately, "You'd better join us."

Canada! So much for being near home. This was certainly news to me but, as I found out a little later, the unit's move to Canada was part of something much bigger, namely the British Commonwealth Air Training Plan, the BCATP. The political and military background to the programme was basically simple. After nine months of the "phoney war", France had fallen in June, 1940, and the Germans had then, without missing a beat, turned their serious attention to Britain. The evacuation from Dunkirk had taken place just a few weeks before France surrendered and the Battle of Britain had begun in July, a month after the defeat of France. That meant that our airfields were under regular, frequent attack from the Germans. You never knew when the sirens would go and you'd have to take cover. Apart from casualties, after the raid, you would have to deal with any damage to the airfield and the aircraft, which could be extensive. Training under wartime conditions was difficult, at best, therefore and, in fact, often a nightmare. Basically, if we were going to train tens of thousands of trained pilots and get them into the fight, we needed space and time to do the training. In Britain, that was impossible under the war-time conditions the Germans were providing for us. Furthermore, as the war developed, and night-time ops became part of the picture, there was also need for flight training at night. Again, that would have been impossible in Britain. We needed help from one of the Commonwealth countries far from the front. That's where Canada came in and where the bulk of the training for the RAF, and for the pilots from other Commonwealth countries, would be carried out.

The general problem had been foreseen before the war started. Some preliminary planning for it had begun several years before but it was only in September of '39, after the war had started, that the two governments agreed and started planning in a serious way. The Prime Minister of Canada, MacKenzie King, wanted it for political reasons though it was also politically sensitive and had to be negotiated so that Canadians would not feel they were being recolonised. On the other hand, our Prime Minister, Neville Chamberlain, knew that Britain would absolutely need this kind of help if it came to war. And, with that incentive and MacKenzie King's support, he was able to get the agreement with Canada. Eventually, there would be 107 training schools and 184 auxiliary sites throughout Canada. Over 200,000 airmen from Britain, Australia, New Zealand and, of course, Canada herself, would be trained there before entering operations in Europe. It would prove to be Canada's biggest and most important contribution to the war effort.

I was going to be part of it, as one of the instructors. The paperwork was organised within a few days and I soon had my assignment. As Greig had recommended, I would be joining the Peterborough group. I was going to be stationed at Service Flying Training School number 31, just outside Kingston in Ontario.

But I only found out about the bigger picture of the BCATP a little later. That day, after telling me about the unit's going to Canada, Greig just said to me, "Now, we're not going for another week or so. You'd better go home and we'll call you when we have to go."

So, within 24 hours of arriving at Peterborough, I left, taking the train back to Cambridge. I was glad to have a few days at home before leaving, particularly because it would give me a chance to see Margot and say good-bye. Since we had started going out together, we knew we were serious about each other. The next day when I saw her, as soon as we were alone, I said to her, "We'd better get engaged before I go abroad. If you can get on a boat and come over to Canada, I'll marry you over there." To tell the truth, I didn't really think she would have the chance to get to Canada during the war and thought that we would get married when I got back from Canada, whenever that might be. But, just in case, we decided that if she should come, she should send me a telegram with some short coded message that meant I should expect her. We picked it out of a book. It's odd, what I can remember today is that it was page 9, line 5 of the book but I can't remember the particular book or the sentence or words that we chose. As it happened, I didn't remember it, even when it was actually needed, about a year later.

The important thing for me, at this time, however, was that we were engaged. I would be going west, across the Atlantic, away from the war actually, not at all what I imagined when I first signed up for the RAF. But it was still going to be part of the war effort and I would be going far from home. It was good to know that there would be someone at home who particularly cared about me and who especially wanted me to come back. Of course, I knew my mother and father did but, in this sort of situation, it is even more important to have a sweetheart who does.

3

The spacious open skies
of Canada

In late December, I boarded a troop ship at Greenoch in Scotland, to embark for Canada. She was the *Duchess of York*, a big grey tub of a ship, as all the troop ships were. There were about three to four thousand of us on board. It was crowded and actually quite miserable. The food was standard Navy fare, in other words, it was bloody awful. And sleeping conditions on a troop ship were what you would imagine. The troops slept in bunks in large dormitory type rooms down in the hold. The officers, of course, had better conditions, their own cubicles on upper decks. During the daylight hours, we could move around the ship on the upper decks but mostly we played cards, read, talked, smoked, looked out at the sea and thought about our sweethearts or wives back home and what the future might hold.

The crossing itself was uneventful. The Atlantic in winter can be pretty dull, just long grey, endless swells as far as the eye can see. Some days, the wind got up and the sea was choppy with white caps. But there were no storms on this trip, which I think took four or five days. More importantly, there were no U-boats. A good thing, too, since we were unescorted. The ship just went flat out all the way and we arrived safely. We landed in Halifax, Nova Scotia, in the morning. With our kit bags, we boarded a train that took us to Montreal. And there, we changed trains.

The group I was travelling with pretty much broke up there, depending on where we were each assigned. For me, the last stage was a further train journey to Kingston, Ontario, where I was to be stationed at the new training base.

When I arrived at the Kingston train station, what hit me was the cold. This was early January, the deepest part of winter, and there was snow everywhere. We had seen a lot of snow-covered ground on the train journey, of course, but it only dawned on me once I arrived in Kingston what a different kind of winter this was to any I had experienced in Cambridge. Kingston in winter is all round a rather bleak place, with bitter cold winds coming off Lake Ontario and snow, banks of snow everywhere in the depths of winter. Another thing that struck me, once I got to see the town, was that so many of the houses were built of wood. Clapboard houses, I think they call them. A different style of building from what I was used to. They didn't look solid enough really but they were kept warm inside. They had to be. They were centrally heated, something that was still unheard of in Britain. Also, the cars had heaters. The extra heating in the houses and in the cars felt like a luxury at first but, in the Canadian winter, it was a necessity.

Kingston was then a town of only about 40,000 people. Though smaller than Cambridge, it is also a university town. Queen's University is one of Canada's oldest and best. Kingston itself lies about 130 miles east of Toronto on the shores of Lake Ontario, and it is sited where the great St Lawrence river flows into the lake. At one time, Kingston was probably the most important town in Canada. In the 1840s, it was the capital of what they then called Upper and Lower Canada, and was a major naval base on Lake Ontario. The potential enemy lay directly across the Lake. This was, of course, the United States, which had invaded Canada in 1812. Later, in the 1860s, the Canadian capital was moved to Ottawa because it was felt that the capital should not be so directly exposed, if there were ever hostilities again with the States. Queen Victoria, it is said, joked about the siting of the new capital, saying the special advantage of Ottawa was that the Americans would never be able to find it.

Though Kingston is a small town, it is more important and interesting than you would imagine from its size alone. Besides the university, it has several key Canadian military training institutions and the International Hockey Hall of Fame. It also has one of the biggest prisons in Canada, a big stone long fortress-like building, with corner watch towers. It is situated on a hill that slopes down in long segments to the shores of Lake Ontario.

For me, however, the most important part of Kingston was Flight Training School, number 31 FTS, of the BCATP. It was situated at the Norman Rogers Airfield, named after the late Canadian defence minister. This was where I would be stationed and where I would start my work as an instructor. There was also a small ancillary field in the town of Gananoque a few miles away but I worked out of the main airbase near Kingston. For two thirds of my 20 months in Canada, this was my base, though in the middle of this period, I was transferred to Calgary for 6 months and continued teaching there. Because we were soon doing training at night, the base was essentially operational 24 hours a day. And it was big: once it was up to strength, about 1200 men in total – officers, flight crews and general staff – called it home. Altogether, about 1800 airmen received their wings here during its period of operation, from 1940 to 1945.

31 FTS was situated about four miles due west of town, which meant that every time you went between town and the base, you had to hitch a lift or take a taxi along the still unpaved road that connected the town with the base. Newly arrived airmen, not knowing better, often thought that they could just walk from the train station to the airbase but in the depths of winter, this was a miserable, freezing experience. In early '41, a bus service was put on but this was primarily for the NCOs and the airmen, not the service personnel. The officers almost always used taxis for

getting to and from town. I always suspected that the Kingston taxi drivers must have had a very good war, that is in terms of having lots of business.

The airfield itself juts out into the lake like a big diamond. This made it ideal for training flights, both for take-offs and landings. There is an island offshore, less than a mile away. In good visibility, this was a useful landmark but, in bad weather especially, it also was the site of a fair number of crashes for aircraft returning to the base. The airfield was big, with barracks for housing the 1200 men, the mess halls, and, of course, the hangars for the aircraft. The officers' mess was a big old stone farmhouse on the other side of the highway, Front Road, that led from the town and it sat right on the lake's shore, at Smuggler's Cove. As a flight officer, this was where I had my meals. The special parties for the officers, on occasions like Christmas, were also held there. For those times, the food was lavish, a nice break from our standard fare. A typical party might involve five-tiered tables loaded with buffet food, and topped with a boar's head with an apple in his mouth. These parties were also a special treat for the Canadian girls who had officer beaux since rationing had come to Canada with the start of the war in '39, just as it had in Britain, and the civilians as a rule weren't eating much better than we were. A primitive feature of the place was that it had no proper toilet facilities, just separate ladies and gents rooms with metal buckets. One of the Kingston girls told me that during dances, the ladies learned to time their efforts with the percussion movements of the bands, so as not to attract attention.

As for myself, I was pleased with my progress. In the space of a year, I had gone from being a raw recruit to a pilot and then an instructor of pilots. But to my surprise, I found when I arrived, that I would be training students on the old-fashioned Fairey Battles. It seemed a backward step. These were single-engine monoplanes and like the Oxford had been in use with the RAF since '37. But they were slow, with maximum cruising speeds of only 150, 160 mph. They were sent into battle in May, 1940 after the Wehrmacht started its offensive against the Low Countries but their slow speed, and lack of sufficient armament, meant they were lost in huge numbers. Soon, they were just being used for training.

But they were no joy to use even for training, especially for night flying training exercises. The instructor had to sit in the back and the student up front – this was the reverse of the situation for the Tiger Moth – but this meant that the instructor had to put his head out of the side to see where the aircraft was going. Another problem was the engine. The Fairey Battles had Merlin engines and these were so old that they cut out frequently. I reckon that while I was in Kingston, there were at least 10 or 15 that cut out on take-off and went straight into the lake. And because of the need for pilots, the training programme pushed everyone hard. Some of the trainee pilots crashed and died on their first solo flights, something that might not have happened, had there been less pressure and more time for the training.

My own closest call, however, involved a night training flight that I didn't take. One snowy, cold night, I was just getting ready to take a student up for a training flight. The procedure was that you would run the aeroplane up so that the cockpit was warm, then trundle it to the runway. That night, I was just about to move off the dispersal point when the flight commander came over and tapped the side of the aeroplane. "Dutch, you've got my aeroplane," he told me. I replied, "Look, I've just warmed this up, I'm all ready with a pupil. Can you go and change the form 700 [this was the form we filled out before each flight] and take my aeroplane? I'd like to continue with this." He said, "Okay", and walked off. Well, I taxied around, got to the stop-start light on the runway, took off and we did one circuit. It was a pretty routine flight, nothing eventful. For night training, we did mostly circuits and bumps, saving the more complicated manoeuvres for day-time flights. Just after we had landed, however, getting back to the starting point, about to do one more circuit, we saw an aeroplane coming in on the right hand side, flames coming out both sides and suddenly it crashed. It had been my original plane. The flight commander, F/Lt Tinney, was lucky. He survived with only a broken shoulder and he had some bad cuts. But he survived. The pupil, however, was killed in the burning aircraft as it hit the ground.

Years later, well after the war, I found out why the aircraft had crashed. I was at the Farmer's Club in Cambridge one evening and someone persuaded me to tell them about some of my war experiences. Normally, I didn't like talking about the war – it was all still too close at this point – but I obliged and this was one of the experiences I was recounting when there was a tap on my shoulder. It was a man named Jimmy Truelove. Jimmy was a big man and I remembered him as the fellow who used to run the sports side of things at the airfield in Kingston. He looked at me and said, seriously and slowly, "I was the cause of that plane going in." I said, "What do you mean?" And he told me. "What happened was that we were doing the 60 hour service on the aeroplane and we were just finishing off the service when the telephone went and they called me over, it was something to do with the sports activities. I said to the corporal, 'well, all we've got to do is put in the junction box and the job is finished'. So I left him to do that and took the call. When I came back, I asked him if he had fixed the junction box and he said 'yes', so I signed the 700. After the crash, I was sure I knew what had happened, that he hadn't fixed the junction box. But it had been my responsibility, I had signed off on the job. I went to see Squadron Leader Moore, a very nice chap who was the chief engineer and told him what had happened. He told me that I wasn't to blame, that it was an accident, so it was left at that and I wasn't court-martialled."

Things like this happened. You always try to set up the best procedures to make things as safe as possible for the men who will do the flying, the fighting, and all too often the dying, but mistakes still happen because of human error. I could tell that Jimmy Truelove still felt awful about it, though it really hadn't been his fault, and he was still thinking about it, two years after the war ended. He too had come back to Cambridge after the war, like me was a golfer and also became captain of the Gog Magog Golf Club.

Soon, however, we were able to give up the Fairey Battles and took on the Harvard, a much better plane in every respect, American made. And the work was steady and the hours were long. In the programme as a whole, we were training men from all over, Australia, New Zealand, Canada herself, South Africa, and, of course, Britain. Mostly, we were training members of the Navy to become Fleet Air Arm pilots. Each trainee pilot had to have 50 hours instruction, which included 10 hours of night flying. The night flying was not too bad, actually, because of the lights of the surrounding villages and towns and Kingston itself, which you could always use for landmarks. (This was long before transponders and automatic flying by instruments, of course.) But, even still, a lot of the pupils found it very, very difficult.

Some pupils just couldn't get the hang of flying because of air sickness or because they simply just couldn't do it. I had one pupil, in particular, whom I have never forgotten, a lieutenant in the merchant navy, a cocky little sod he was. He could not fly at all, he just had no idea how to do it – or the ability to develop the necessary skills. How he got through elementary flying training, I never could understand. For instance, I would try to teach him to do a roll. In doing a roll, as I've mentioned, you have to push the stick forward to keep the nose up at the top part of the roll, when you are on your back. But instead of pushing it forward, he would always pull it back, which would send us into a screaming dive. This must have happened three or four times and each time I had to take over the controls and get us out of it. Then I'd say, "Come on, we're going to do this for a last time. Now, you take over." Well, the next thing I know he'd rolled onto his back, pulled the stick back and we were zooming down again. I said, "For Christ's sake, keep your nose up, man," and he said, "Nose up be buggered, Sir, I can't keep my stomach down," and he was sick as hell.

After awhile, I'd had enough. I went to see the CFI and said, "Look, this man's going to kill himself and everybody he flies with." "Well," he said, "he's a lieutenant in the merchant navy, so you should give him another chance." I, therefore, continued to instruct this lieutenant, though without much faith in his ability to improve, until we had to start night flying. This proved to be even more hazardous than flying with this pupil by day. He could not control the aircraft or instruments and each landing would have been fatal if I had not taken over control. Immediately, we landed I went to the Chief Flying Instructor and suggested that he should be failed for the whole course. The CFI did not wish to do this to a lieutenant who had served in the merchant navy and decided to personally give him another circuit. But this time he would have to do the circuit on his own. I thought that this was a big mistake and told the CFI so. But he had made his decision and was going to stick with it. To watch this trainee's progress, the CFI and I went to the control tower. To make a very long story short, the exercise was disastrous and I am still surprised when I think about it that he didn't kill himself. He had been instructed to carry out one circuit and landing but after trying to land four times, each time aborting the landing when on the approach, he finally succeeded but it was a disastrous landing and a miracle he survived. He approached the flare path on this run at an abnormal speed and then hit the ground with his wheels, bouncing two or three times before managing to control and slow his aircraft, bringing his bumpy and dangerous landing to a close.

We went to meet him when he stopped the engine at dispersal. He got out of the aircraft and walked towards us. It was a cold night but under the lights we could see that he was perspiring profusely. I asked him, with a straight face, how he had got on during the hour and a quarter or so he had been in the air. Since take-off to landing on a routine circuit normally took about 15 minutes and he had been in the air about five times that long, I wondered what he was going to say. He was as usual full of bravado, replying, "Oh, great!" But anyone could see he was shaking like a leaf. "And why," I asked him, "did it take you so long for one circuit and landing?" "Oh," he said, "I was just flying around to enjoy myself." Did he really think we would fall for that story? Anyone who had watched his flight would have known that was a lie.

The CFI kept silent throughout this exchange but he knew now that there was no other option for this navy flier than to be failed. He was a disastrously bad pilot. Fortunately, most of the trainee pilots were much better than this, though, inevitably, some had to be washed out of the programme.

Fortunately, it was not all work. There was, as always on a base, some time for sport. One of the Canadian officials looking over the RAF lists realised that a lot of the top British rugger and soccer players were now stationed in Canada. As a result of this discovery, teams for both sports were assembled and taken to Toronto for games. Of course, Canadian teams were assembled to play against our boys. And it made for some interesting contrasts, starting with the outfits. The British players just wore shorts and jerseys, ordinary socks and not particularly special shoes. The Canadians came out all padded up, as if dressed for Arctic weather, wearing helmets and so on. At first, we thought they were pretty weedy, to need all this gear but I have to admit, they played well. Another problem, of course, was that the rules for both games were slightly different in both countries. So these differences had to be sorted out. Still, it was all good fun.

There was also some fooling around in the aeroplanes, the kind that pilots will always get up to when there's the chance.

One thing that was a good trick was flying under the main span of the Ivy Lea suspension bridge in town. Coming in at it in one direction wasn't so difficult but the other way was tougher because of an island on the other side. Coming from that side, you had to come down, just miss the island and go under the bridge. Coming from the easier approach, you just had to start gaining height as soon as you were out from under the bridge, to avoid the island. My Canadian friend John Leishmann liked to do it in both directions, and claimed it was easy, "a piece of cake". Another piece of mischief we got up to occasionally was low flights over the town, buzzing the houses of some of our acquaintances in town, something that we were definitely not supposed to do.

Apart from the occasional parties at the officers' mess, there were often social events at the weekend and, of course, these included Kingstonians. Basically, the people of Kingston made us feel really welcome and the social interactions were fun and, sometimes had their funny side. At first, we tended to think of the Canadians as basically fellow Brits, even if they sounded like Americans, who just happened to be living in Canada. In fact, Canadian citizenship didn't officially exist until McKenzie King instituted it shortly after the war. For all of the country's history right through to the end of the war, the Canadians were officially "British subjects living in Canada."

But then you would use an ordinary expression, at least ordinary to any Brit, and you could see puzzlement and the Canadians would ask what it meant. Phrases like "that was a piece of cake" or "that was wizard", or "I was really browned off" or someone was having a "rough do" were often mysterious to them. So, it wasn't just the Americans who were divided from us Brits by a common language. The Canadians were too.

And it wasn't just language, there were differences of custom, too. For instance, on British airbases, there was a strict separation between the entertainments that were held for the

NCO airmen and crew and those put on for the officers. This seemed perfectly natural to us but the Canadians, with their lesser class-consciousness, found it odd. I heard about one social evening put on for the NCOs and the men, where some of the Canadian girls were part of a chorus line. Two of the officers' wives were part of it. When the men realised that officers' wives were part of the group, they were actually pelted with beer bottles. The entertainment broke up and the women ended up running from the dance floor under cover of their escorts' greatcoats. In recognition of these British class distinctions, when Kingstonians hosted parties for the men serving at 31FTS, or simply had them in their homes, they made a point of never having NCOs or officers at the same time.

My main social contacts off the base were mostly through a Canadian girl, Lucy ("Bunny") Danby and her aunt, Auntie Lou, with whom she lived, and their circle of friends. I was brought into it by one of my mates, Flying Officer Francis Charles de Havilland Bradley, or Brad, as he liked to be called. Brad was quite a character, tall with a neat black mustache. He looked rather like the young John Cleese of "Fawlty Towers". You never knew exactly how much you could believe of what he told you. Was his mother really a de Havilland? In fact, was de Havilland actually part of his name? Had he really gone to Eton, as he claimed? With Brad, you never quite knew what was true and what was invented. But he had the manners and attitude to go with the background he claimed. I remember once going to see "Gone with the Wind" with him and Bunny Danby. Bunny sat between us. I must have found the film pretty moving because, apparently, at one point I had tears in my eyes and sniffed a little. Brad leaned across Bunny and said, "Frank, pull yourself together, man." I looked over at him and did just that but I also noticed that Bunny was smiling.

Brad was a good mate of mine. He wasn't an instructor but a flight engineer; part of his job was inspecting crashes, to sort out where things had gone wrong. He and Flying Squadron Leader

Alderton, "Aldy", had met Bunny one cold day just before Christmas, 1940, at a restaurant, McCalls, on Princess Street in Kingston. She had been sitting in a booth, having a hot drink, getting warm after doing some Christmas shopping, when she heard these two lonely British officers in the booth just the other side of the partition. They were talking about home, the loneliness of being away from it, and how Canada seemed such a strange place. She felt sorry for them, and, on impulse, came around to their side and invited them to meet her aunt at their home on Earl Street and have tea with them. They were delighted, of course, to meet this very attractive, friendly Canadian girl. She assured me later that this sort of thing – picking up strange men in restaurants – certainly wasn't her habit but, on this occasion, she had just felt strongly that these two men should not feel so lost in Kingston.

So, Brad and Aldy accepted the invitation and, each holding a hand of their new acquaintance, stepped outside and got a taxi to Bunny and Auntie Lou's house on Earl Street. Warmed by the tea, the conversation and the general hospitality, they returned the favour, before catching a taxi back to the base, by inviting Bunny to a party at the base that was to take place a few days later. This incident was the beginning of the Earl Street house as a small social centre for a number of us. Auntie Lou's hospitality, not least her delicious Welsh rarebit, was a key aspect of this. Auntie Lou had served as a nurse on the Western Front in World War I and had a soft spot for British men in uniform. Not a romantic soft spot, a patriotic one. The solidarity that Canadians had for Britain was really great. They weren't under direct threat from Hitler but they had made our war their fight too.

One of my best mates in Kingston, however, was John Leishmann. He had been quite sweet on Bunny. I heard about his meeting her from Aldy, not John himself. Aldy had brought him to meet Bunny and Auntie Lou, and when Bunny came into the room, he stood up and shouted "Yippee", delighted to see this gorgeous brunette. He courted her and thought that they would get married. It was a real blow, then, when she upped and married her old beau, a doctor named Charlie. This was in April of '42 and John and I buzzed Bunny's house the day of the wedding in the planes we were then flying, Harvards. John had felt that this was one way to express his feelings about the matter and, as his good friend, I went along and joined in. The noise brought part of the chimney down. But we didn't feel too bad about it. Auntie Lou may have lost a chimney but John had lost a sweetheart whom he had hoped would be his wife.

I had been at Kingston about four months, when orders came through in April, 1941, to report for duty as an instructor to a newly formed Elementary Flight Training School that was being set up in the Canadian west, specifically in Calgary, Alberta. The stint would be for six months. Winter was now giving way to spring and, by this point, I had got used to Kingston and liked it. But this assignment would be an opportunity to see more of Canada. I had about a week or ten days before reporting in Calgary and I decided to buy a car and drive out there. I bought a grey Chevrolet Coupé for 500 dollars and I was off. I drove in a shallow loop south out of Toronto, entering the US and driving through the northern tier of American states. This took me through the Midwestern states of Ohio, Illinois, Minnesota, then through North Dakota and Montana. Finally, I headed north and after about an extra day's driving, arrived in Calgary, the first week of May, I believe. The whole trip had been quite an experience. The huge size of the American Midwest, with its endless fields of maize and wheat; the bleak rocky badlands of North Dakota, the forests and mountains of Montana; and then the vast Canadian plains, devoted to wheat growing and cattle ranching, and beyond them the Rockies, was a real eye-opener for anyone from Britain. It was pretty fantastic, I can tell you, a new world indeed. The size of the areas I had driven through seemed fantastically large. And, of course, by going west, the war in Europe itself started seeming even more distant. The war in the North African desert was going badly for us in the spring of '41 and Crete would fall in a few weeks. But here I was – I had joined the RAF to fight the Germans – and was even further away from the war than I had been in Kingston.

My new training unit, 3 EFTS, had been set up in Calgary shortly before I arrived. The training aircraft were Tiger Moths; the last time I'd been in a Tiger Moth was when I had been a student at Hatfield. Now, I was flying in them as an instructor. The other difference was that these were equipped with canopies for protection against the weather. Each month every instructor had to undertake one hour's training on instruments, which would be carried out under a hood, with another instructor, as we had to teach the pupils to fly using only instruments. But the life in Calgary was great even though the town itself wasn't much. Today, it's a big city, grown rich on oil, with skyscrapers, shopping centres, what have you. But back in 1941, it was a typical western town, with its share of dirt roads and old saloons. Economically, it was mostly a centre for servicing the ranchers and the wheat growers. Our base, 3 EFTS, was near the western border of Alberta with British Columbia with the foothills to the Rockies laying just to the west of Calgary. On a clear day, and during spring and summer, when most days were sunny and clear, the Rockies were a beautiful sight. And the huge blue skies that stretched over the Canadian plains were just spectacular, whether you were on the ground or flying. In Cambridge, we talk about the big skies over the fens but this was a completely different experience. On weekend leaves, we used to go up to the town of Banff, in the mountains. This was a lovely place. On the edge of the town, there was a waterfall and a golf course. It had everything, really. There was also once an Indian jamboree, a most fantastic sight. Here, the war itself seemed even more something that was happening a world away.

I even bought a pony, a polo pony, and used to go riding in

the hills. I bought this pony from one of the ranchers in the hills. As it happened, he had a niece, let's call her Jean S., and she and I became quite friendly. Yes, it's true, I was engaged to Margot and I hadn't forgotten her at all but Jean and I were close. One day, she said to me, "Shall we have a game of tennis?" I said, "Yes, I'd like that," thinking that probably I'd have to be chivalrous and not play too hard. Well, we went to the tennis court and chivalry never had a chance to come into it. Jean gave me a drubbing, I didn't win a single game off her. At the end, as we were coming off the court, I said to her, "You're a bit good, aren't you?" and she said, completely matter-of-factly, "Yes, I used to play at Wimbledon."

Having aircraft at our disposal, in such a beautiful place, was too much for some of us to resist. We would sometimes take friends up for a flight. Several of us got involved in this. On a couple of occasions, I took Jean up. Some of the Indian girls we got to know also got to go with us and see the mountains from the air. We would land at Jean's uncle's ranch, pick up our passenger and then go for a spin. This was strictly against orders, of course. Anyone doing this could have been court-martialled. But it's probably safe to admit it now; I assume that the statute of limitations ran out long ago. It came to an end one day when the CO, who had heard what was going on, came over and said to us, "Boys, you've got to do your instrument flying and not mess about in the hills." Somebody had spilled the beans. One of us took Jean's uncle up once – it was the least we could do – but that was the end of that.

It had been a great summer for me, though. In late September, I got orders to return to 31 FTS in Kingston. I was back in Kingston by early October, 1941. It was good to be back and see friends though soon the weather was nippy and by November, it was bitterly cold. All the training was now on Harvards, a first-class single-engine aircraft purpose-built for teaching. This was a much more powerful and faster plane and a big improvement on the Fairey Battles we had been using. I had been back more than a month when one evening, while I was having dinner in the mess hall, the adjutant came up and said, "Dutch, I have a telegram for you" and he handed it to me. All it said was "Notice 9 received. Love, Margot." And then there was something more that didn't make any sense either. I looked at it but it just didn't mean anything to me. I said to him, "Get the bloody thing decoded to start with and then I shall understand it." And he replied, "But it's in plain language, it's not in code." I looked at it again and it still didn't mean a thing to me, so I said, "Well, I don't know what that's about" and I crumpled it up and threw it in the waste-paper basket.

And I forgot about this completely, until about two weeks later, when I was standing at the bar one evening. It was 10.00pm and snowing like hell outside. The 'phone went and someone went to get it and then shouted over to me, "For you, Dutch, it's Margot." I said, "Margot! She can't ring from England, there's no way." But I went over, curious to know what this was all about, picked up the 'phone and said "Hello?" And the voice that answered was a woman's voice, a voice I knew well. She said, "Dutch, this is Margot, I'm on Kingston Station. I'm freezing here. Can you come and fetch me?" And then it hit me what the telegram had been about. It had been the private code Margot and I had agreed she should use if she were able to get to Canada. The "9" referred to the day of the month when she got onto the ship.

Well, she had managed to get to Canada. She had taken me at my word that if she came across, we would get married. The challenge for her was how to do it. So, she had waited on the dock at Greenoch, enquiring about berths on transport ships going across to Canada and finally she had got one for a ship sailing to Halifax, an unescorted transport ship. At one point in mid-Atlantic, the ship had lost a propeller and had circled for three hours, before it could be repaired; Margot told me about this only much later. About 14 days after the ship left Greenoch, having taken a circuitous route to avoid U-boats, she docked in Halifax.

I was delighted, of course, but surprised. I hadn't really expected Margot to be able to do this. But maybe I shouldn't have been too surprised. A fair number of the married men had been allowed to bring their wives over in '41 and by the spring of '42, there had been a mini-baby boom, although we didn't call it that, amongst the personnel at the base. Still, it had taken guts to do what Margot had done. The first thing I had to do was to find her a place to stay. She couldn't stay with me – this was 1941, remember – and the base didn't have proper visitors' quarters. The only thing to do was to ring Bunny and Auntie Lou and ask for their advice. And they immediately said that Margot could stay at their house until the wedding, they insisted she do so, in fact. The wedding was set for about 10 days later, on Saturday, December 7th.

On that day, in the early afternoon, I don't remember the exact time, a small group of us assembled in St George's Cathedral, one of Canada's oldest Anglican cathedrals, in central Kingston for the wedding. John Leishmann was my best man and Bunny was Margot's attendant. The service was performed by the Chief Chaplain of the RAF in Canada, Wing Commander Gregson from Cambridge. Another guest was Dr Glen Burton, with whom I had become friends. He had been educated at Kingston University and was, in fact, the doctor for the university. His wife, Edna, sang at church functions and for our wedding, sang Schubert's "Ave Maria".

When you get married, all you are thinking about is just that, about your bride and the future – hoping, particularly if you're in the middle of a war, that you'll have one. But the war itself was moving on. That morning, I would guess within an hour or two of the time Margot and I were getting married, the Japanese made their attack on Pearl Harbor. Within a day, the United States would be at war with Japan, and two days later, with Germany, after Hitler had declared war on the US. At last, the

US would be coming in to help Britain actively and openly. As a result, the long-term odds had clearly shifted, at least a little, in our favour.

After the wedding ceremony at St George's, we took several cars and went back to Earl Street, for a reception at Bunny and Auntie Lou's house. Some more of my mates from the base came and some of our local Kingston friends. I think it was there that we heard the CBC announcement of the attack on Pearl Harbor. The announcer had a deep and sonorous voice and was known all over Canada as the "voice of doom", particularly since in the early years of the war, the news was mostly bad. He was the Canadian actor Lorne Greene, later to achieve fame on the American TV series, "Bonanza".

But for Margot and me, it was time off from thinking about the war for a few days honeymoon in Montreal. I remember the snow piled high on the ground and a wonderful ride we had one afternoon in a sleigh, with a blanket over our legs, through the snowy landscape, up Mont Royal, to look out on the city at night. It was a pretty impressive site, with the cathedral behind us on the summit and the city spread out, and lit up, beneath us. We celebrated with an absolutely first-rate meal at the restaurant on top of Mont Royal. If you wanted lobster, you picked one out of the tanks and they then prepared it for you. A few days later, we were back in Kingston, in our own flat on the second floor of the house next door to Bunny's and Auntie Lou's house on Earl Street. It was a very comfortable place, with enough space inside and a big oak and a big maple in the garden outside.

By this point, I had been in the RAF for two years and still had not seen combat. A few of the pilots at 31 FTS had done operational work but perhaps not more than two or three. By April or May of '42, I was given an opportunity. I was told that I could either continue instructing in Canada, or go back to Britain and join operations. There was no question in my mind: I wanted to go on ops. So, I spoke to Darcy Greig at the first opportunity. I came right to the point and said, "Sir, I'd like to get back to England and go on operations," and he replied, without any hesitation, "Well, if that's your choice, Holland, you have the right but maybe you should think about it another day."

I went home and talked about this with Margot. I said, "I want to go back and go on operations. I don't want to finish this war just teaching these people because it becomes a bit of a bore after a time when you're doing the same thing day in and day out. I want a bit more excitement." We discussed it. She wasn't exactly happy about it. She knew, we both knew, that I was much more likely to survive to the end of the war if we stuck it out in Canada than if I joined ops. But she also knew better than to oppose my decision outright and she finally agreed. But, on one condition. That we have a baby. Agreeing to have a baby when you're not sure you'll be around to see him or her grow up is a bit tough, but that was the condition of her acceptance, so I agreed.

I went back the next day and spoke to Darcy Greig. "I've made up my mind," I said, "I want to go back to England and go on operations." "Okay, Holland, right," he said. I then told him, "I'd like to go to Ottawa to arrange my trip back because I want to take my wife with me." He kind of snorted and said, "You haven't got a hope in hell of getting your wife on the boat, I've been waiting here for 6 months to get my wife back. You just can't go back together."

However, the CO agreed that I could go to Ottawa to apply for permission to have Margot return with me. So, we travelled to Ottawa, to RAF headquarters where I was told to report to one Flight Lieutenant Taylor. I knocked on his door, entered and blow me down, I recognised him immediately. It was Peter Taylor from Cambridge. I immediately asked him what he was doing here and he countered by asking me the same question. We had known each other at grammar school. I had been a junior when he was a senior. He had been a great cricketer and rugger player at school and got a blue at Cambridge University and later became a teacher at Newport Grammar School.

He answered my question first. "I'm in control of all the shipping from Canada, all the berths for shipping." I said, coming straight to the point, "You're just the man I want to see. I want to get back on the next boat back to England with my wife." From what Darcy Greig had said, I assumed that this was going to be the start of a long argument with him. Not a bit of it. He agreed immediately. "You're on it. I can't tell you when but I will tell you that you'll both be on the next ship and in the best cabin."

But it took a few weeks more before we were given our instructions to report to Halifax. Finally, in early September, we boarded a liner at Halifax and were on our way. The crossing was 7-10 days and it was risky. The Battle of the Atlantic was at its height during 1942, with more than 1600 allied ships lost that year alone. But you didn't spend much time thinking about that. If you were making the crossing, you just took your chances, crossed your fingers and only thought about how good it was to be going home. At least, on our trip, we had a naval escort. And it proved an uneventful crossing; there were no alerts, let alone attacks. To be frank, at this point, I remember little about the details of the trip. But the cabin Margot and I had been given was first-rate and we had a lot of time together, which was great. Perhaps it's no coincidence that our eldest daughter, Paulette, was born about 9 months later.

We arrived back in England without incident in mid-September and despite all the grim news about the progress of the war, the constant threat of bombing attacks and the uncertainties that lay ahead for me, as I prepared myself to enter ops, it was good to be back home. By this point, I had had at least 800 hours of flying time under my belt. I was as ready for combat operations as I was ever going to be.

4

The run-up to D-Day, the Isle of Sheppey to Operation Crossbow

We arrived back in Cambridge to the joy of both our families. My father said that he would buy a house for us and he set about doing so. But, in the meantime, while the purchase was being arranged, we lived with Margot's parents in Saffron Walden, which is about 15 miles south of Cambridge, set in the very pretty Essex countryside. Two months passed, however, and I became restless with this long leave. In fact, I even began to think that the RAF had forgotten that F/Lt Holland existed. I, therefore, wrote to the Air Ministry. After a week or two I received a letter from them. My guess is that my records had got lost in the system and that my letter had prompted their's but there was no hint in the communication from them that this was the case. The important information was that I was to report to 184 Squadron. This was a new squadron that was being formed, initially based in Colerne, near Chippenham in Wiltshire. Colerne was the first of several airfields I was stationed at during the 21 months between my return to England and D-Day. They were nearly all in south-east England, where the main preparations for the coming invasion of occupied Europe were taking place.

The news from the Air Ministry of my posting lifted my spirits. It would, at last, relieve my feeling of uselessness and allow me to achieve my ambition to be involved in operations. But Margot was not happy about it. By this point, we were expecting a baby and the possibility of losing the father of her as yet unborn baby must have seemed a bit more real with this posting than when we had first discussed my joining ops, back in Kingston.

Colerne was a fairly new airfield, one of the last of the so called "Expansion Scheme" airfields to be built. These had been commissioned in the late '30s, during the run-up to the war that the government hoped would never come but which it knew it had to prepare for. Colerne had officially opened in January, 1940 but during its first two years, it had not been used as a base for combat operations or for training. Instead, it served during this period as an aircraft storage depot, holding Hurricanes, Whirlwinds, Defiants, and Blenheim and Beaufort nightfighters. But in late '42, its role was about to change. It was going to be used as a base for organising new fighter squadrons.

Our commander was Squadron Leader Jack Rose, also known as "Bunny" Rose. He hated his nickname but we all used it, at least when he wasn't around. It came from the fact that his ears moved a little when he talked. He had served with 32 Squadron, stationed at Biggin, one of the key airfields for combat during the Battle of Britain, in '40 and early '41. But from September, '41, he'd been based at Exeter, flying Spitfires with the Czech and Polish wings based there. His next assignment, however, was to set up the 184th.

Jack had arrived at Colerne on December 1st, 1942. In theory, the new squadron consisted of 20 airmen. In fact, when he started, he had no pilots or aircraft or ground-crew, just a folding table and a chair in the corner of a hangar. But soon both the men and the aircraft began to arrive. I was one of the first to show up. Most of the new airmen for our squadron came straight from Officer Training Units, OTUs. Fred Taylor and Johnny Sellors, who had been with an OTU in Annan, Scotland, also arrived in December. In early March, Archie Lamb, from

OTU 56 in Dundee arrived, and he was followed by Sgt. Pilots Frank Carr and Len Thorpe. In this first phase, we were soon up to about 12 airmen plus support crew. Of this first group, I think it was only Jack Rose, Len Thorpe, Archie Lamb and I who made it through the war.

The 184 was being put together for a specific role. We were to be a "tank busting" unit and we would be flying Hawker Hurricanes for the job. We were being prepared for attacks on German armoured units on the Continent. We knew, of course, that this would help in taking the war back to Germany but we did not know that our operations were seen as part of the early stages of the larger plans for D-Day. Churchill and Roosevelt had met in Casablanca in mid-January, '43, and agreed in principle to opening a second front against Germany. The air war against targets in occupied France, Belgium and Holland would be a big part of the preparations for D-Day itself and for the fighting on the ground that would immediately follow the invasion.

Of course, we airmen were not involved in grand strategy. At this point, the main concern of the 184th was the matter of armament refitting for our tank-busting mission. The particular problem to be faced was that the Hurricanes had initially been designed for aerial combat. They had done the lion's share of the aerial combat in the Battle of Britain, knocking out German bombers and fighter aircraft, though the Spits seem to have got all the glory. Tank busting, however, would be a different kind of fighting altogether. So new armaments were needed. Each Hurricane was to be armed with two 40 mm Vickers "S" cannons. These were to be tucked under the wings, one on each side. These were in addition to the four Brownings in the wings, two per wing, that the Hurricanes had originally been equipped with. The Brownings were perfect for aerial combat but didn't have either the power or the accuracy for hitting large targets on the ground from 500 yards or so, hence the addition of the Vickers S guns, which were already known to be effective against armoured equipment. The Hurricanes that used them against tanks came to be known as "Flying Can-Openers". They were also later equipped with rockets, initially 25lb armour-piercing heads. These, however, were found to be insufficient for destroying tanks and were soon replaced with 60lb semi armour-piercing high explosive heads. The first Hurricane IID's were allocated to the squadron in mid-December and more soon started arriving. The refitting began, I think, in January.

That winter was grey, cold, wet and, at times, snowy. There was a big snowfall on January 4th and on January 5th, we were all out shovelling snow off the runways to clear them. For me, it felt like being back in Kingston. We got a further taste of winter when we found ourselves living under canvas, as part of Operation Spartan. We found ourselves quartered with 174 Squadron. The weather was cold and miserable at this time and bunking down at night in tents in the winter was not fun. But Operation Spartan was important. It was the biggest military exercise, up to this point, ever held in the British Isles. More importantly, it was the first big "composite" action, that is joint Army-RAF. The idea was to simulate battle conditions that we would later face, on D-Day and beyond, when RAF missions in support of the ground troops would be essential. The Army and the RAF had developed some of the coordination techniques in the Desert War but more work was needed and, of course, there were lots of new men, who had not been involved in the Desert War, to be trained. Operation Spartan revealed some of the weak links in operations and led to some big improvements in forward air control for complex battle situations. One change in operations would be the assignment of an Army Liaison Officer (ALO) to each squadron in '43, as the time approached for actual combined air-ground operations.

For us, however, we had more immediate problems to sort out. Like the problem of the food. Someone in the Army had been placed in charge of the catering arrangements during Operation Spartan. Whoever he was, he had somehow managed to leave a nought off the estimated number of RAF personnel to be provided for. The consequence for us was starvation rations all round. In addition, there were a fair number of so-called exercise referees who were, in effect, competing for food with us from the available supplies. Because of their status and preference in the pecking order, we were barred from using NAAFI wagons or even the local pubs. We were reduced to helping ourselves with the occasional hare that someone had shot and some untended potato plants to ease our hunger pangs.

On March 12th, we moved again, this time to the sodden airfield of Zeals in Wiltshire. Zeals was known as one of the wettest bases in England. And, again, for our living quarters, we found ourselves living under canvas. But, luckily, from about the time we arrived, the weather improved somewhat. We weren't getting soaked all the time. One of the more memorable events of our stay at Zeals involved Flight Commander Peter Almack. He had been a motorcycle racer before the war and he was older than most of us. He was filled with confidence, the way you'd expect for someone who'd competed in motorcycle races, but his luck and his skill at flying weren't as great as his confidence. On one earlier flight, he had returned from a low-flying exercise with a bird stuck in his radiator. He didn't even know it till he had landed. During the Zeals exercise, he came in for a landing with a power supply cable wrapped around one of his wings. He had picked it up by flying too low over a farm. That wasn't too serious but the fact that his wheels were still up was. We saw him coming in, wheels up, and sent off a number of red flares to warn him. Jack Rose ran out on to the field, waving his arms to warn him but Peter either didn't see or didn't understand. Still, he managed to make a non-disastrous wheels up landing, the aircraft skidding to a halt. Unfortunately, the two Vickers S guns had been left firmly embedded in the ground where his Hurricane had first made ground contact. Always before, Peter had managed to avoid any major disciplinary action with well placed bottles of Scotch whisky on Jack Rose's desk and that of "Monty" Norman, the Engineering Officer, who would rule that, after all, the damage was fairly minor. This time, however, Peter had gone too far. He was transferred out of the 184th but this was not the end of his flying. He became a first-rate air sea rescue pilot, flying the Supermarine Walrus or "Shagbat" as it was affectionately known.

But I don't want to give the impression that this period was all just routine problems, like finding enough food, making silly mistakes or having narrow scrapes, or boredom. The work was hard and it was risky. Exercises, like normal flight training, were serious business and things could go wrong. Sometimes men died, as they did during normal flight training. In our squadron, during Operation Spartan, F/S Simmons was engaged in "beating up" tanks when he crashed in flames.

The result of Operation Spartan was that the whole RAF system was reorganised, along the new Airfield system, in which squadrons were grouped, three at a time, on a Wing basis. We were assigned to Airfield 122, formed in Eastchurch, and we moved there on April 1, 1943. The other squadrons relocated there were 132 and 174 Squadron. In addition, there were three Servicing Echelons and the 1493 Flight Group, with their Miles Martinets that towed air-targets for practice in air-to-air firing practice. Initially, in the new system, the service units for the different squadrons at each airfield were merged. In principle, this made it easier for squadrons to be assigned to different airfields at short notice. In practice, it led to a weakening of responsibility. Soon, when this problem was recognised, a few key personnel were assigned to specific squadrons.

Although Eastchurch was an established RAF station, with well-built pre-war facilities, it was not being used as a base for combat operations at this time. Its main function was serving as an Aircraft Re-selection Centre, for dealing with the cases of airmen who, for one reason or another, couldn't carry on. Each case was dealt with by a special board, who would either reassign the individual to non-operational flying or discharge him from the RAF, which was always followed by compulsory re-enlistment in the Army as a private. Because the main buildings had been commandeered by the board, we found ourselves again sleeping under canvas. Furthermore, we were barred from the mess during meal-times, reserved for members of the board, and had our meals around the campfire, as it were. Later in the evening, following dinner, we were allowed into the mess. Needless to say, the officers of the board, who tended to be older and more staid men, were highly brassed off by the nightly invasion of the mess hall by the younger and more boisterous officers of our group.

It was here, at Eastchurch, that we acquired the rocket-firing capability for our Hurricanes. We were now flying a later model of the Hurricane, the Hurricane IV. Each of the Hurricane IVs was fitted to carry a bank of eight rockets, four under each wing. Each was also fitted with a rocket rail. With the rocket rails, there was no problem of recoil and without the recoil, you would not have to re-sight each time after firing, which was always a problem with the Vickers S guns. The usual tactic was to fire the rockets in a "ripple", that is letting them off two at a time. But you had to be careful about the timing, allowing just enough space between each round because, if you didn't, the slip-stream of the rockets that had just been fired could interfere with the next round just-fired and shift it off-target. The other alternative was getting in close, firing all rockets at the same time in a salvo. Usually, you would want to be within 250 yards, at most 500 yards, of the target for this to work. This might sound like a good distance. When you are coming at 200-300 mph, it calls for instant responses, lining the target up quickly and pressing the firing button at just the right instant.

Our initial practice was at the Leysdown range and soon we were expert at hitting the early targets, old vehicles of various sorts that were used as substitutes for actual armoured vehicles.

In a typical run at a target, you might hit it either with rounds, up to 32, from your S guns or two to three of your 25lb rockets. The rockets and the S guns were never used or fitted together; it was one or the other. By this point, it had been decided by Jack Rose that we needed to do a test with the real thing. Accordingly, an out-of-service Churchill tank and a smaller, old Sherman tank were donated, minus their armaments, from the commanding officer of an armament brigade stationed near Canterbury. These had to be brought by transport to the Island of Sheppey just off the coast, near the Leysdown range. The initial problem was getting them over the bridge that connected the island to the mainland. The tanks themselves couldn't move and on the transport vehicle, the weight would have been too much for the bridge. So they had to be winched over the bridge and then placed back on the transport vehicle, which had been driven across the bridge. Finally, the two old tanks were set up on an old sea wall.

Jack Rose and I carried out the first attack on the tanks. There was a group of officers, both Army and RAF, who had come to observe the exercise. Jack and I came in, flying at 0 feet (that is, as close to ground level as possible), firing the armour piercing rockets two at a time. He went in first firing at the Churchill which he hit with his rockets. I followed right behind, aiming at the Sherman, firing a salvo. The result of this initial attack was that the turret of the Sherman was knocked off into the sea and several holes left in its armour while the Churchill had its stack blown off and the missiles had penetrated the side armour plating. We wanted to do more damage, however, so we returned to base to reload with 60lb explosive rocket heads. Returning to the attack, we both fired salvos at the two tanks. This time they were left in a very dilapidated condition.

This demonstration had been witnessed by the officers of the 51st armoured division who returned from the range to discuss it with the pilots. There was no question that the demonstration of our tank-busting capability had been very successful. But this success had a sting in the tail, as became apparent in the talk around the tables that night in the mess hall. The reaction of the officers of the 51st armoured division was not "how wonderful!" but to consider that the Germans might well have similar fighting capacity against our tanks. In fact, this tank-busting technique was both new and secret and the last thing that Command wanted was for the Germans to find out about this method too soon. It was being saved for the invasion of France. The result of this secrecy, however, was that while we had been outfitted to be a tank-busting operation, we were forbidden to fly over enemy territory at this point. Instead, our initial orders would be to attack enemy shipping off the Dutch, Belgian and French coasts.

In early June, 184 Squadron moved again, this time to Manston in Kent, near the cliffs of Dover. It was from here that we began our first combat operations. Most of these involved groups of four aeroplanes at a time or more. When you had only four, one would be designated to bring up the rear of the group, watching for enemy aircraft. If you weren't the leader, you were always watching him and listening for instructions, whether to speed up, or turn your aircraft left or right or suddenly dive. And the flight group leader would be listening for any news of approaching enemy aircraft from the lookout in the rear plus assessing when to lead the group down toward the attack. Radio contact between members of the group, and to ground control at the start of the mission, was essential. If you lost radio contact, you turned back.

We arrived at Manston on June 12th, 1943, and our first mission took place on June 17th, with four Hurricanes taking off before dawn, at 4.15am. Take-off was under cover of darkness in order to avoid detection by enemy aircraft. This was necessary because the Hurricanes, armed with the rockets and extra armour to protect the pilots from attacks from behind, had a cruising speed of only 185 mph, far slower than when equipped just with the Brownings for aerial combat. The extra armament also made them less manoeuvrable, hence, without an armed escort for cover, it was essential to avoid detection and interception. The four pilots on this first mission were Jack Rose, Flight Lieutenant W.R. Kilpatrick or "Killy", Flight Officer Doug Gross, a Canadian, and Flight Lieutenant A.W. Ruffhead. (Of these four, only Jack Rose would be alive at the end of the war.)

The target, for this first mission, was enemy shipping outside Flushing Harbour on the Dutch coast. The four aircraft reached the target just at first light and they swiftly came into the attack, firing rockets in ripples at the ships anchored inshore. Three hits were observed but it did not appear that any serious damage had been done. Unfortunately, no special photo-reconnaissance had been laid on to record the damage inflicted. Nevertheless, this was the first use of rockets being fired from fighter aircraft in war-time operations.

But it wasn't all sweet and easy. The surprise element had worked but there was a strong response from the enemy's coastal defences. A wall of heavy flak went up as the aircraft came in for the attack. Some light hits were made but no one was brought down and all made it back to base.

A few days later, a similar attack was made. This time, I was one of the four pilots. Again, it was led by Jack Rose. The other two pilots were Warrant Officer Ken Starmer and Flight Sergeant Wallace. On this attack, however, we had a loss. Ken Starmer was shot down and presumed killed. He was our first loss on ops.

On June 29th, an attack was made on shipping in Dunkirk Harbour. I wasn't in on this one but Len Thorpe was. He said the counter-attack was intense, the Germans threw up everything except the quayside! But no one was lost, despite that. On July 1st and on the 6th, there were more roadstead attacks on shipping off the Dutch coast.

The whole time, of course, we were trying to develop more effective tactics. We felt that if we could conduct attacks at night, under cover of complete darkness, that would be great. We would have surprise on our side and be far less visible to either enemy aircraft or ground anti-aircraft batteries. The problem, of course, would be seeing the targets. A possible way to do it was suggested by the discovery at Manston of a Fairey Swordfish. It had been fitted with an air-sea radar set, one of the first of its kind. The idea was that the armed Hurricanes would accompany the Swordfish, which would use its radar to locate enemy shipping in the Channel. The plan was that the Swordfish would first locate the targets, then drop flares between the target ships and the coast, and the Hurricanes would then come in for the kill.

The attack plan, however, was both new and risky. And, of course, we all knew that it might not work. Jack Rose felt that we needed trial runs. These were carried out using land-based searchlights, as substitutes for the flares, on the Leysdown coastal range. But Jack was not happy with the results and eventually the plan was dropped. The result was that we never tried using flares at night for actual ops. Most of the night ops were carried out on clear nights with decent moonlight. When we were going after specific targets, we would usually go in groups of two, four, or more. At other times, there were no designated targets. Instead, we would be going out on "rhubarbs", where you are just looking for suitable targets – "targets of opportunity" we would call them today. So a typical night op would be a low-flying patrol by moonlight, along the French or Dutch coast, maybe about a mile out, looking for enemy shipping. Whatever the mission, you would be flying low, usually not more than 500 feet. Flying fast at low altitudes tended to give an extra advantage of surprise and, if you were flying at 0 feet it was almost impossible for enemy ground fire to hit you. But for spotting targets, you had to be approaching at higher altitudes. Flying at 0 feet was good for sudden approaches and surprise, when you knew exactly where you were going, and for fast escapes.

Moonlight patrols still had their problems, of course. Sometimes you would suddenly lose visibility. On my first night mission, I was flying at 300 or 400 feet and it started to become misty. I flew right over a ship before I knew it. Saw some lights below me on the water and knew it could only be a ship of some kind but just what kind I couldn't make out. I circled back but in the growing mist, it was impossible to find. I had to give it up. Another time, however, I was flying at night just outside Calais when I saw a ship below. I took it for some kind of freighter and I came in low firing my rockets, not knowing that I was attacking a gunboat. Well, all hell came from the gunboat and off the coast and I was suddenly flying through incredible amounts of flak, bangs and flashes all around. In this situation, you just keep rapidly changing your flight course and your angle – to prevent the gunners getting a good bead on you – and you are praying the whole time that you will not be hit. Of course, you're not praying at all, you don't have time for that, you are just manoeuvring your plane and trying to get through it as fast as possible. In one of these situations, it seems that it is going on forever but it might be only 5-10 seconds or so.

Well, I wasn't hit and got back to Manston all right. But it could so easily have turned out differently, as it did so often for my mates in the squadron. "Wizz" was lost on a night patrol on July 23rd, and "Killy", the Australian pilot whom we all liked a lot, was shot down and killed on July 30th.

And I soon had other close calls.aYou're never far from death in this business, but to do the job you had better never begin dwelling on that fact. Returning from one mission in France, we were crossing over the coast quickly, flying at 0 feet, to minimise any chances of the enemy hitting us. But, in fact, the Jerries had seen us coming and were firing rifles at us as we went overhead. Suddenly, there was a sound in the aircraft, a "booff". I knew I'd been hit. That was all, just that sound, there was no sign of smoke or fire, nothing funny in the instrument readings, the plane kept on handling as it should but I knew I'd been hit. Back at Manston, as soon as I got out of the Hurricane, I told one of the mainten-ance crew that there had been a hit to the aircraft. The crew looked it over and said, "No, you haven't been hit, you haven't been touched." I said, "I know I've been hit, there's a bullet somewhere in this aeroplane." So they went over it again and sure enough, they found a little slit in the fabric underneath one of the wings. They investigated further and when they took the petrol tank out, they found a bullet inside it. Just an ordinary bullet, not an explosive one, not an incendiary one. I'd been lucky the Jerries had been using just normal bullets.

Because we were doing both daytime and night-time ops, there wasn't a set routine that we followed day after day. It would vary. And a lot of time was just spent waiting, either in tents or in the dispersal, depending upon the base we were at, in flying suits, just waiting for the telephone to ring. Time was passed playing bridge, smoking, talking. And then the 'phone would ring and we would scramble for the aeroplanes. At other times, when we knew that a particular mission had been scheduled, we would take off and form up over the airfield, then proceed to the target, maintaining radio silence the whole time.

One thing that became obvious from the early operations was that the 25lb rockets might be fine for attacking tanks but against shipping, they just weren't good enough. They would punch holes in the ship's armour but usually that was all, this was not enough to sink them. So sometime in '43 we switched to the 60lb rockets with the explosive heads.

Altogether, once we were up to full strength in late '43, we had about 12 planes at this point and maybe about 30 pilots. But there were often problems with engine maintenance. You'd set out, sometimes in groups of two but more often as four or more, but almost always someone would have to turn around and go back because something was wrong. The maintenance wasn't easy. For the maintenance crew, you had an engineer, a

fitter and a rigger. The engineer was in overall charge, the rigger
was responsible for maintenance of the controls, the fitter for the
engine. There was also an armourer, the fellow who was
responsible for reloading all the ammunition.

One day in June, '43, I was returning from one dicey mission,
I think it was an attack on an aerodrome in France, feeling
completely shattered. On some of the longer missions, you would
come back with only a few gallons of petrol in your fuel tank,
cutting it close. On many missions, there was often the anxiety
about whether you would have enough fuel to make it back. I
think this had been one of those trips. But I'd made it, if only with
just enough fuel. And as I was walking away from the plane, the
rigger came up to me and said, "Congratulations, Dutch, your
daughter has arrived." I looked at him, amazed. What the hell
was he talking about? I didn't have a daughter. And then it
clicked. Margot had been due for some time. The baby must have
been born. It was a baby girl. I was now a father. Fantastic! My
mood went in a flash from exhaustion to excitement.

I immediately arranged to get leave and took an aeroplane up
to Debden, near Saffron Walden, in Essex, where Margot had
been living with her parents and saw her and the baby in
hospital at Wendens Ambo. We named our little girl Paulette. It
was great to be a father but at the back of my mind there was
the doubt as to whether I would live through the war and have
the chance to see her grow up.

The leave was short and soon I was back at the base. At this
time, our main ops comprised attacks against enemy shipping,
mostly off the Dutch and Belgian coast. And then in August, the
whole squadron had two moves. Each time, we were told a
couple of hours in advance and had to get ready quickly. But this
involved simply packing up your kit in a couple of duffel bags.
Because we had so little, moving was easy. From late '42
onwards, there had been a big building programme of new
airfields, Advanced Landing Grounds, ALGs, they were called.

These were being built for the run-up to D-Day, to handle all the Allied aircraft that would be involved in the invasion. Just about all of southern England was being converted to a "giant aircraft carrier". And in the course of '43, many of the squadrons found themselves being moved from one ALG to another.

The first move our squadron made came on August 14th, when we went to the ALG at Kingsnorth, a few miles outside Ashford in Kent. But we were only stationed there four days before being transferred again. This time it was to RAF Newchurch, only a few miles from Kingsnorth. Newchurch was one of four ALGs in the Romney Marshes and was the most northerly of the four. We would be stationed at Newchurch until mid-October. Our companion squadrons here were two Spitfire squadrons, 132 and 602. The latter had acquired glory during the Battle of Britain.

It was at Newchurch that we were given a new assignment and one that would take us on missions to attack targets not at sea but in the occupied countries: lock-busting. The idea was simple, to destroy the lock gates of crucial dams, to create flooding. This was part of a programme that was called Operation Twitch. We were the only squadron at Newchurch to be part of this but there were other squadrons at other ALGs that would be part of Operation Twitch. These were 164 and 137, these being outfits flying Hurricanes, and 198 and 3, both of which were using a new and powerful aircraft, the Typhoon, which I'll come back to in a minute.

There were several target dams in this operation, in particular lock gates for the canals on Walcheren Island in Holland. The first mission was on August 28th and did not go brilliantly. From the photo-reconnaissance, or PR, it looked as if the rockets hit the lock gates and went all the way through them but because of the time-delay in the explosive, finished up in the water beyond them before exploding. This was also a close run thing for me, in terms of getting back to base. The whole op took 1 hour and 50

minutes and I got back to base with only five gallons of fuel. Too
close for comfort. My second mission was on August 30th but
this one was frustrated by weather. We had to turn back after 10
minutes flying because the visibility was so poor. The squadron
made a number of other attacks on the lock gates. But I think
that none of these missions really achieved major success and
Operation Twitch was rated a failure. Maybe with a different
kind of explosive charge we could have done the job.

In a way, this was typical of so much of the fighting we did.
You were always trying new strategies, not sure what would
work. The war involved constant improvisation. Trying new
things, seeing what would work, and what didn't. At one point,
I was sent to Millfield, on a course formed for wing commanders,
squadron leaders and flight commanders, who would meet each
morning to suggest ways of making the best use of our rockets.
Many suggestions were made and tried but the one I remember
which was thought to have the best chance of being effective
against shipping was made by one of the squadron leaders – I
can't remember his name. "I believe," he said, "the only way to
do it is to put a lot of aeroplanes into attack all at the same time,
all approaching from different directions." Well, it was worth a
try, we agreed. It was decided to have a practice run with three
squadrons, against a group of old cars and lorries, set up as the
target, on one of the islands off the coast near Berwick, just
below the England-Scotland border on the east coast. The idea
was that one squadron of 12 aircraft would come in from one
direction, a second from a second direction a little after, then the
third squadron coming in from a different direction. There would
be 36 aeroplanes altogether. A brilliant plan, if it would work. I
was in the middle section, flying a Spit and we came in from five
or six thousand feet into the attack. But just as I'm approaching
the target at zero feet, maybe a few hundred yards away, I hear
all these bullets whizzing around me, coming right, left and
centre from all over the place. I got hit once in the fuselage and

there were several other hits, in the wings, one near the cockpit. Frankly, I was lucky to get out of this dummy attack alive. And a lot of the other pilots said the same thing, that they had been too busy dodging the other planes and ammunition. So much for the bright idea of attacking in three groups of twelve aircraft from different directions.

On October 12th, we moved again. Our new base was RAF Detling, in Kent, just north of Maidstone. Detling had been a fighter station in WWI but had been abandoned during the early 1920s, reverting to farmland. During the late '30s, however, it had been taken back by the RAF as part of the airfield expansion scheme. After considerable rebuilding and enlargement, it re-opened in September, '38, a year before the war started.

We moved to Detling along with the Spitfire squadrons 132 and 602 from Newchurch. With them, we were rechristened 121 Fighter Wing of the newly-formed Second Tactical Air Force (or 2nd TAF). The Spitfires of 132 and 602 were refitted with Mark 9 guns and were used primarily as escorts in bomber patrols. But for 184, in this first period at Detling, while we continued attacks on shipping in the Channel, this was a relatively quiet time. The incident that all of us remember, however, was a tragic accident, the death of Pam Barton, who before the war had been the British Ladies' Open Golf Champion. She was in the WAAF, stationed at Manston, but had been flown to Detling in a Tiger Moth by her fiancé, F/L A.W. Ruffhead, for a party. Leave had been granted on the condition that she return to Manston early the next day. Ruffhead was planning to fly her back there in the Tiger Moth. But the weather was foul that morning. Finally, when the rain began to ease off, they were ready to go. Because time was getting short, however, Ruffhead decided to take off from the football pitch just to the side of the aerodrome. But the ground was soggy and, it has to be said, Pam, who was in the front seat, was a large girl. Whatever the reasons, ground conditions, weight, whatever, the

Tiger Moth was clearly struggling to get airborne. Jack Rose and I and several other members of the squadron watched helplessly as the aircraft, just after its wheels left the ground, crashed into a petrol tanker that was parked just the other side of the football pitches. The driver of the tanker and his mate must have seen the aeroplane coming and knew what was about to happen because they had just managed to get out of the cab and start running before the Tiger Moth hit. Both the aircraft and the tanker burst into flames. Pam must have been killed instantly and was incinerated in the fire. Ruffhead survived, however. Jack Rose and several members of the squadron raced across the pitch and managed to pull him out of the back of the plane in time. He had only superficial injuries but was suffering from shock. He recovered physically but he was a changed man after that. The enquiry that sat cleared him of negligence and returned him to duty. But he was never the same man he had been and he died in a combat mission a few months later, in January, '44. Jack wondered if, from the time of the accident, Ruffhead had been seeking his own death, and always felt that it had been a mistake not to shift him out of the 184th, which he couldn't help but associate with the tragedy, to one of the Empire Training Schools.

During this whole period, of course, preparations were moving toward D-Day, Operation Overlord. It was already being called that by the high command. Of course, we didn't know when it would happen though the betting at this point was that it would be sometime in the spring of '44.

In late December, '43, we moved to West Hampnett. It would be from there that our operations on D-Day and the following days would be carried out. Soon after arriving there, we got a new mission, directly related to the coming invasion. This was a series of attacks on the V1 flying bomb sites that the Germans had assembled on the French coast. The V1s, and later the V2s, would be used by Hitler for attacks against London and other cities, revenge attacks. But in late '43, the high command was worried that they would be used against military targets, specifically against the airfields being built for Operation Overlord. It was decided that they had to be taken out.

One evening in early December, we got a call. Our CO was on holiday, on leave for a week. The 'phone went and someone got it. He listened for a few seconds, then said, "It's the Air Vice-Marshal on the 'phone and he wants to speak to whoever's in charge of the squadron". Well, that was me. Jack Rose was away and I was the acting CO. I therefore took the 'phone.

Air Vice-Marshal Broadhurst wasted no time in getting to his question. "Now, you are one of the few squadrons that have rockets and we've got a very big project coming up that needs rockets. Can you dive-bomb?" I replied, "Well, we've never dive-bombed with the rockets, we've always had the sights set for low ground attack but I'm certain we can dive-bomb if we have to." He said, "Good. Have all your pilots in the briefing room at 10.00am tomorrow morning."

The next morning, we were all assembled in the briefing room at 10.00am sharp. Air Vice-Marshal Broadhurst, along with two group captains, came in. Broadhurst was a clean shaven man, of medium height, probably in his mid-30s and decorated with the DSO and DFC. Again he went straight to the point. "Gentlemen, now what I'm going to tell you is most secret. We've got a big problem, the new flying bombs that the Germans are setting up. Churchill says that these targets have to be destroyed. He says that we could lose the war if they're not taken out." Yes, those were his words. And he continued, "Now, I want to know if you can sort yourselves out for dive-bombing or whether you can do this with low attack procedures." I spoke up. "Well, our easiest way is to go in at 0 feet and attack them at 0 feet. We're more sure to hit them with low attack than by dive-bombing." He looked at me for a second, then said, "Fine, that's good then. Here are the targets." And he then produced a map, laying it out with one of the group captains, of all the flying bomb sites. Photo-reconnaissance (PR) flights had produced the information. We couldn't believe it, the number of the sites and the great detail of the map. Altogether, there were about 40 to 50 sites, each one numbered, up and down the coast from Calais to Cherbourg.

The Air Vice-Marshal continued, "You'll find these targets very difficult to locate. Most of them look like only a little shed in the middle of the wood. Do you think you can find them and destroy them?" It was a challenge but we felt that with the PR pictures and the map, we could do it.

So, this was the beginning of Operation Crossbow, as it was called. The V1 targets were code-named "Noball" targets. Our first Noball attack was on December 14th, near Le Touquet. Len Thorpe led this mission and he recorded in his log book, "Target well-plastered. No flak." But it wasn't always so easy. On the 21st, Harry Bartz did not return, and was presumed killed in action. On the 30th, there was a big attack on target 24. But this time, there was a big response, with lots of flak coming all around us from German soldiers stationed around the site. But the target was blown to smithereens and no one was lost.

And it went on this way, through January and February. One key thing we found was making accurate landfall. If you got this wrong, crossing the coast too far from the target sites, the Jerries were alerted and you were much more likely to be attacked on your approach to the target. And there could be big losses. In his book, *The Big Show*, the great French airman Pierre Clostermann, DFC, who was with 602 Squadron, tells of one Noball attack where six aircraft and their pilots were shot down. The attacks were usually low approach, our standard method, often under cloud cover. But because it was often easier to spot the targets from higher altitude on clear days, we also carried out attacks by dive-bombing, just as the Air Vice-Marshal had proposed.

But it was in early '44 when the 184th made a big switch. It was felt that the Hurricane IVs had had their day. We were to trade in our Hurricanes and start flying Typhoons, or "Tiffys", as they were called. In early March, '44, a large group of us flew our Hurricanes for the last time, taking them to the fighter station at Redhill and there picked up our Tiffys. (The rest of the squadron traded in their Hurricanes for Typhoons at Odiham.) The Hawker Typhoon was special, probably the most powerful air fighting machine that the Allies, certainly that the RAF, had. With a wing span of 41 feet, it was slightly bigger than the Hurricane and it was the first fighter aircraft to be able to fly more than 400 mph. Like the Hurricane, it was a fighter bomber but it had a longer range at 820 km, which could be extended with disposable fuel tanks to 1500 km. It was also more versatile in its armament. It had four 200 mm cannon in the wings and eight 60lb explosive rockets but it could also carry two 500lb bombs on underwing racks. For any particular mission, however, a Tiffy would be fitted with either rockets or bombs, not both. In general, if the target was known in advance and it was big, bombs were the weapon of choice. For "rhubarbs", where you were just looking for suitable targets, rockets were the standard armament. For either dive-bombing or low level attacks, all four cannon could be used at once, while firing rockets or dropping bombs.

The prototype had been tested in early '40 and the first Typhoons had entered service by September, 1941. At first, there were operational problems, with a fair number of accidents, some causing pilot fatalities, because of engine or structural problems. But these were mostly sorted and by the time we got our aircraft, the Typhoon was a superb flying – and fighting – machine. We would have three months of flying them, learning their capabilities and their quirks, then using them in ops in the run up to the invasion of Normandy. They would be a key fighting element in both the preparations for and the subsequent fighting on and after D-Day.

The early part of our familiarisation with the Tiffys was back at Detling, which the squadron moved to on March 11th. We would be there for two months. Some time during our time at Manston, one member of the squadron painted on the ceiling of the mess hall, with a mixture of soot and water, "184 Squadron. First into France with rockets".

Every kind of aircraft had its own special quirks and you had to learn them. With the Tiffy, there was a tendency for the engine to cut out after take-off. The way the engine was designed, the sabre motor used to oil up, and this could cut the engine out. The precaution we took against this was to rev up the engine as far as you could before take-off. But this method didn't always do the trick. On one of my first practice runs in a Tiffy, I had revved up the engine just this way but it still cut out when I was no more than 90 feet off the ground. This was a forced landing situation, which I had familiarity with, but it was still always a little nerve-wracking – until you were sure you had a field you could safely land in. Fortunately, there was a field straight ahead and I landed in it, coming up close to a wall. This was only about 300-400 yards from the aerodrome. There is always the danger of fire in this situation, so I turned the petrol off, which was the best insurance against fire, got out of the cockpit and ran to a safe distance from the aeroplane. The fire tender came up within less than 15 minutes and a flight sergeant got out, waved to me, and went over to the Tiffy. He looked in the cockpit at the instruments, then got down and came over to me. "Well, Sir," he said, "you can't expect to take off with your petrol turned off." I could hardly believe my ears. "Don't be a bloody fool," I said. "I turned that off before I got out of the aeroplane. That engine cut out just after I got off the runway, maybe at about 90, 100 feet. That's not my fault so you can do whatever you like about it." But there was no disciplinary action. This idiosyncrasy of the Tiffy's was well known.

During this whole period, just prior to D-Day, there was continual reorganisation of the 2nd TAF taking place, which required corresponding on-going coordination with other air fighting forces. This sometimes led to peculiar things. In late April, for instance, we found ourselves the only squadron on the 129 airfield unit of 83 Group when we should have been one of three. This happened because a decision had been taken to let the Canadian Air Force take command of, and help man, this wing. But the Canadians didn't have enough squadrons to carry this out. So while the Servicing Echelon was Canadian and the wing was administered by Canadians, the only airmen in the 129 airfield unit at this time was 184 Squadron, namely us. But this, it turned out, wasn't all bad. The food that we had, as a result of being under Canadian management, was the best we'd ever had.

On April 28th, we carried out our first op with the Typhoons. There were eight of us and it was led by Jack Rose. We took off at 10.00am for a raid on a bridge over a canal in the village of Baupte, just south of Cherbourg. We successfully took the bridge out with rockets and landed back at base at 11.05am. A second op was initiated that afternoon, again with Bunny Rose as squadron leader, to dive-bomb a road bridge at another village, Pont-de-la-Rouge, also near Cherbourg. But this op had to be aborted because of bad weather and consequent poor visibility. On the first run, Jack had had a bomb "hang up". That is, he couldn't release one of the bombs and it only fell off when he landed back at the base. Fortunately, it didn't explode.

Throughout May, the squadron was fully active, as the preparations for the invasion were stepped up. We made frequent dive-bombing attacks on Noball targets, bridges, roads, railway lines, and anything and everything that would disrupt the German communication and transport systems. Our targets were both in the Cherbourg area and inland, where the invasion would be, and heavily around Calais, where we wanted the Germans to think the invasion would be coming.

The Germans fought back, of course. On May 7th, Joe Best's aircraft was hit during an attack on Noball target 59 at Moyenville. Joe bailed out at 800 feet over the Channel. He was one of the fortunate ones of those who ended up in the Channel; he was picked up by the air-sea rescue service. On May 13th, Frank Worthington was shot down during a low level attack on targets in Holland, when he was hit by flak over the island of Walcheren. News reached the squadron many weeks later, on June 30th, that he had been captured and was a POW. On May 25th, Jack Rose led a group of seven for a bombing attack on the marshalling yard at Cisors, taking off at 10.15am. The target was well and truly hit during the attack but Warrant Officer Polkey's aircraft was struck by flak. He was seen to go into a spin, half of one wing came off, and he crashed into a nearby wood, going up in flames. Two days later, a group of 10 pilots attacked a German army barracks at Bailly-en-Rue near Dieppe. The attack was effective and this time, we all came back. On May 28th, Jack led a group of 11 others, including me, to plaster a naval W/T station just outside Bruges. There was lots of flak but we had no losses. Like many operations, it lasted only a little more than an hour. We took off at 11.55am and were back by 13.10. Again, a successful mission. On June 2nd, we attacked a ship reporting station at Barfleur-le-Vicelle. The whole effort during this time was not only to destroy as much of the infrastructure and armament of the enemy but to keep him off balance.

During the month prior to the invasion, the squadron also made two moves. On May 13th, we left Detling and flew our Tiffys to Homesley South. Nine days later, we moved again, taking the aircraft with us, back to Westhampnett in Wiltshire.

At this point, we all knew that the actual invasion was coming soon but we still didn't know when it would be. The history books say that in January, '44, the Allied high command had initially set the date as May 1st but kept on having to move the date back. It was all a matter of finding the ideal conditions of low moonlight and high tides. The Germans were in the dark too, of course, and on two counts: both the date of the planned attack and where it would take place – whether the invasion would be at the Pas de Calais, where they expected it, or the beaches of Normandy. Rommel, it seems, thought it would be Normandy though many on the German General Staff thought Calais, being closer to England, was much more likely. But Rommel got the timing wrong. On June 4th, judging from the poor weather and assuming that the landings would only be attempted under the best weather conditions, he guessed that the invasion would not take place until mid-June and he set off for Germany to wish his wife a happy birthday. For the Allies, that was a gift. And for Rommel, alerted by 'phone the morning of the 6th, it was a huge shock. But, by then, the Allied troops were already swarming ashore and establishing the beach-heads.

On our side, however, we all knew in the first days of June that D-Day was coming very soon. It was more than a guess. We had it from the horse's mouth.

Sometime in this period, maybe on the 2nd or 3rd of June, we were told that the Air Vice-Marshal wanted to see all of us in the middle of the aerodome on the base at midday. All three squadrons were to report. We assembled on the aerodrome and Air Vice-Marshal Broadhurst arrived. He was standing on some kind of platform and addressed us.

"Gentlemen, we are coming to the most important battle of the war. I can't tell you when it is going to begin but you will all be confined to barracks from now until D-Day." So, we knew it was not just soon but imminent. He went on:

"When the battle begins, you will shoot all German pilots who have bailed out, whether they're in parachutes, dinghies or wherever you find them because if they are not shot, they will come back and be in action against you."?That was his order. There was to be no mercy to enemy pilots, whatever their situation.

We were then dismissed. We knew now that it would be a case of waiting until the invasion began. But, despite Broadhurst's words that we would all be confined to barracks, there was provision for a few airmen to be allowed out on leave. The reason was simple: if there was any "unfriendly" observation of our base, it wouldn't have been sensible for all leaves to be cancelled. That would have been a dead give-away that the invasion was about to start. So a few leaves were granted right up until the start of the invasion. But most of the pilots were now confined to base.

After the meeting on the aerodrome, however, we discussed Broadhurst's order to kill all German pilots whose planes had been shot down, whether coming down in parachutes or escaping in dinghies if they were on the water or if seen running on the ground. We thought that this order was all wrong. It had always been reckoned that you would not shoot any pilot who had left his aircraft. That, at least, was the RAF code for British airmen. But the Poles and the Czechs were known to operate differently. They really hated the Germans and were known to shoot pilots in dinghies or coming down in parachutes. We felt that if we started doing that, the Jerries would only retaliate and do the same. Back in the mess, we were talking and talking about it. Broadhurst's order just didn't seem right. So a small group of us went to see the Wing Commander and we said, "Look, we feel that this order should be rescinded." We discussed it a bit with him and he could see our point. Finally, he said, "All right, I'll send a message to Broadhurst telling him your objections and asking him to rescind the order." Apparently, the Air Vice-Marshal was convinced because word came back that the order to shoot all escaping German airmen had been rescinded.

Throughout this period, however, while we were waiting for the invasion to begin, our daily work of destroying military targets, in particular German supply depots and ammunition dumps, communication facilities, and transportation networks in France continued. On June 4th, we'd attacked a convoy and on June 5th, we'd flown a mission bombing a bridge near Rouen. But if the rescinding of Broadhurst's order about escaping German airmen was the first surprise of this period, it wasn't the only one in the run-up to D-Day. One or two days after Broadhurst's speech to us in the aerodrome, Jock Orr and I were summoned to see him. This was June 5th, I believe. His headquarters were in Portsmouth, not far from the base at Westhampnett, and we showed up at his office, a really beautiful caravan, at the requested time. Jock went in first and I waited. Jock came out maybe 5, 10 minutes later. "What's it all about?" I asked him. "It's about permanent commissions," he said. I couldn't tell whether he thought this was odd or not. But I did. "Christ," I said, "we filled those forms in about six months ago." The whole squadron, in fact, had filled them out. I remembered it well because I had been in charge of making sure that the forms were completed and turned in. I still couldn't believe that this was coming up now, just before D-Day. "That's six months ago since we did this." He said, "Well, that's what it's all about." At that point, the Air Vice-Marshal's adjutant came to the door and said, "Right, Holland, in." I went in.

I saluted, Broadhurst asked me to stand at ease but then, as he always did, came straight to the point. "Holland, why do you want a permanent commission?" I said, "Sir, I'm not so sure that I do but on the other hand, I feel from your speech the other day, we are coming very near to the great battle of the war. I doubt whether I shall survive it because the war will not be over quickly. To be talking about permanent commissions when I'm not certain I'll be coming back, I just don't feel that this is the right time to discuss it."

"Well," he said, "why did you put your application in?" I told him that at the time – I'd been flying missions for six months by that point – it seemed a reasonable thing to do. At the present moment, however, it didn't seem appropriate but that perhaps later on – if I survived the coming months – we could discuss it. He looked at me, smiled a slightly crooked smile and said, "Get out boy and I hope you survive." But I didn't want the interview to end on that note and I said, "Well, I hope that if I survive, Sir, you'll interview me again." I saluted, turned and left, thinking that the ways of the military could be pretty strange. And that was my interview with Air Vice-Marshal Broadhurst, the day before D-Day.

I returned to the base but that evening, two members of our squadron, Jock Orr and Ian Handyside, left for London on what was supposed to be a 48-hour leave. This was part of the "camouflage" of the invasion plans, to create uncertainty in anyone who might be watching movements in and out of the base as to when the invasion was likely to take place. In the city, Jock and Ian stayed at the Mapleton Hotel, one of the hotels used by many of the RAF airmen for short leaves to London. But they did not get to enjoy their full leave. The morning of the 6th, when they turned on the wireless first thing, they heard that the invasion was on. They immediately packed all their gear and headed for Waterloo station to get the first train back to Westhampnett. D-Day had begun and we were going to be in the thick of the fighting, to make sure that the landings were successful and took hold.

5
June 7th, 1944, D+1: My longest day

June 6th, 1944, D-Day, the day we had been waiting for, for months. When one says "D-Day" today, certain images automatically come to mind. The endless fleet of barges and landing craft crossing the Channel under grey and cloudy sky..The famous picture by Robert Capa, the American war photographer, of the helmeted GI swimming ashore in the early morning light with his rifle. The soldiers piling on to the beaches from the landing craft or wading through the water. Men being shot and dying in the water or as they stepped ashore. The German pill boxes spewing fire. The American soldiers clambering up the cliffs at Pointe du Hoc. The German fighter planes zooming down over the beaches, spraying machine-gun fire on the landing troops. All told, twelve thousand Allied ships were involved and 150,000 men took part in the landings. It was the biggest armada the world had ever seen and, probably, ever will.

But there's one thing missing from this general picture. All these are images of the sea and the fighting that took place at the sea's edge and on the beaches. What most people forget is the other big battle that was part of D-Day: the air battle. This battle had, in fact, been going on for months before the day of the landings itself. And it was crucial to ensure a chance of success for the invasion, that once the troops landed on Sword, Juno, Gold,

Omaha and Utah beaches, they could move inland as quickly as possible. All the missions flown by the RAF and the American Air Force to cripple the German military machine, to ensure the invasion could first take hold on the beaches and then move inland, had been the essential preliminaries for D-Day itself.

We, the 184th, had been part of this effort for months. Our work, which I've tried to give a picture of, had been to knock out radar stations, supply depots, Noball units, marshalling yards, German army barracks, and not least, any and all targets presented by the French railway system. The latter was a vital part of the German supply machine, hence of German military operations in France. Along with other units of the RAF and various groups from the United States Strategic Air Force, we had been preparing the way for the invasion since January and the pace was about to step up. Ten thousand aircraft were on call for D-Day and the days immediately following, nearly as many aircraft as there were ships for the invasion. And 8000 of these flew missions on D-Day itself. Given the number of aircraft that would be in the air and the need to distinguish friend from foe in the air, at a second's notice, all the aircraft had been painted with a pattern of black and white stripes on the wings and the fuselage. In principle, this distinctive design had been put on to help everyone with instant recognition. But it was particularly important for us of the RAF because the Americans, it seemed, were less good at aircraft recognition than we were. We suspected that their pilots weren't given the training in it that we had been. The last thing any of us wanted was to be shot down by "friendly fire", as it's called today.

Altogether, the 2nd TAF, one of the main British air combat arms of the Allied Expeditionary Force, had over 1300 aircraft ready to fly on D-Day, in direct support of operations on the ground (this was out of about 5000 RAF aircraft involved in total). These 1300 aircraft were split up amongst eighty squadrons and, of these, 18 squadrons were flying Typhoons only. These would constitute one of the major air attack forces of the Allied Expeditionary Force and the 184th was one of these squadrons. Our job on D-Day and the following days was attack operations in support of the troops, in whatever ways and whatever places to help the invasion get a foothold and move into occupied Normandy as quickly as possible.

I was in the group that flew the first mission of the day. The weather was foul, though not as bad as the previous day – cold, wet, grey but with fair visibility. But I will never forget the sight of the Channel as we zoomed over it at about 1000 feet. Flying over the Channel from Westhampnett was normally a 10-15 minute affair, longer if you were heading for the Belgian or Dutch coasts, and whether seen from 1000 feet or 10,000 feet, the sea was normally fairly empty of any kind of shipping. This morning, it could not have been more different. The surface of the sea was just packed with ships as far as the eye could see, mostly landing craft and destroyers. From above, it looked as if you could probably walk across the whole Channel by stepping from one landing craft to the next. Of course, we knew that D-Day was going to be a huge operation but nothing had prepared me for the sight below of so many ships.

And when we crossed the French coastline, immediately below us, there was already a tremendous battle going on. Looking out of the cockpit window, I could see about 20 destroyers and a couple of battleships, which were pumping lead into the coastline, at the German emplacements behind the beaches, at a furious rate. It was incredible.

There were eight in our group and we took off at 6.00am, just after dawn and essentially at the time the landings were beginning. My aircraft was a Typhoon Mark IB, a newer model than the ones we had started with. We crossed the coast near Le Havre and headed south. The mission was to bomb a bridge south of Caen. And for this we were using 250 pound bombs, not the rockets, which were our more usual attack weapon. At

10,000 feet, you are just about flak height but there was no flak coming at us on this mission. We sighted the bridge, just south of Caen, zeroed in, dropping from 10,000 feet to 2000 feet, flying fast, going in one at a time, lining up the bridge in our sights and loosing the bombs. At least some of them hit the target as photo-reconnaissance showed.

Then something happened. Normally, when I did any bombing I would turn the trim of the aircraft so that you could climb up rapidly if one had been hit. Coming at the target in a steep dive, with the trim up, I had to force the control column forward to keep the nose on the target. I let go of the bombs and eased up on the control column but the trim was set so far back that the aircraft immediately went into a steep climb. The change was so swift that I must have blacked out. It might have been for only 5-10 seconds, maybe half a minute at the most, but long enough to be disoriented when I came to. I was on my back but realising that I had blacked out, immediately took control of the Typhoon and levelled out. Not one of the other seven aircraft in our group was visible. I was at about 5,000 feet again but this time, isolated, the sky was empty. I thought, "Right, OK, you're on your own, you've got to get back, there'll be German fighters about."

In this sort of situation, the most important thing is to avoid becoming a target. I immediately took the plane down, as quickly as I could, to 0 feet and started zooming over the countryside, just over tree-top level, setting my compass to return north, towards the Channel and back to the base. There was only one thing that seemed wrong. I was going like a bat out of hell but there was no sign of the sea. I had set my compass to go north, I thought, but if I had been, I would have been over water within minutes. I must have been confused by the short blackout because when I checked my compass, I saw that I had set it on 180° instead of 0°. I was going south, flying deeper and deeper into occupied Normandy. So I gained a little altitude, turned the plane around, increased the speed to 400 mph and headed straight back in the opposite direction, crossing the coast just west of Le Havre and was back at Westhampnett probably about 20 minutes later. The whole trip, from leaving to return, including the 10 minutes of wasted time going south, had been about an hour and a quarter. That was my only op on D-Day.

But other members of the squadron were involved in two further sorties before nightfall. The first was an attack on a German troop concentration to the west of Cabourg-Les-Bains. The group took off at 15.25pm. Initially Jack Rose led it but he had to turn back because his undercarriage had failed to retract. Someone else in the group then took over and led the attack, which was a success and there were no casualties. The group had returned by 16.35. The second mission left Westhampnett at 19.00. This was an attack on some tanks near Caen. At first, we reported three had been knocked out but the air reconnaissance photos showed five had been destroyed.

The squadron had no casualties on D-Day and it had seemed that we had done a good day's work. In the military, however, there's no attempt to keep the men informed of the big picture. For that, we relied on the BBC, like everyone else, and the news was that the beachheads had been established. The mood was quietly celebratory. After all the waiting, D-Day had at last arrived and the landings had succeeded. A foothold on the Continent had been made. But the mood was also tense. We knew that the hard and dangerous part of the campaign was just starting. The Germans would fight back with everything they had.

D+1, June 7th, began for us at 3.30am, when we were rousted out, to be ready at 4.30am for a dawn reconnaissance of the Caen-Mezidon-Falaise-St Georges area. We were to reconnoitre it and attack any obvious targets. The eight pilots – I wasn't part of this group – struggled into the cockpits of their aeroplanes in the dark but were then instructed by radio to come on out and wait by their aircraft until further orders. The delay was because of poor weather. The wait was only 20 minutes and then they were told to go. But the visibility was still poor when they crossed the French coastline and the group ended up being split into three separate units. The results were mixed but everyone returned safely, at least. A second show was planned for 10.00am but, in the meantime, the entire squadron had piled into the mess hall for a breakfast of bacon and eggs. The weather continued to deteriorate so Jack Rose decided that the next sortie would also be three independent groups. I wasn't involved in this op either. All returned in a little over an hour, reporting some successful hits on more motor transport.

We were now operating on a 24-hour basis, with two shifts of 12 hours each, starting at noon and midnight respectively. I was in the second shift that came on at noon. There was some kerfuffle about plans, with an initial decision to fit the long-range fuel tanks for longer and deeper operations in Normandy, which would have meant only four rockets, but there wasn't time to make the change-over. Each aircraft was fitted instead with the usual 8 rockets. For this afternoon mission, I was the leader of the squadron. We took off at 15.50pm to do an armed patrol in the Falaise area. The first hiccup came a few minutes into the flight when Sam Jessee, who had been in both the previous sorties, reported some mechanical difficulty and had to turn back. But the immediate problem was the weather, the lack of good visibility. When you have a known target, you have the compass bearings from base, the approximate distance, and your flight speed but there's always some uncertainty in precisely when you will reach the target zone. As you make the approach, you have to keep your eyes sharp to spot the target itself. On a clear day, this is not a problem. But on this particular day, the cloud cover was low and the visibility was poor, probably not more than 2 miles at best. We flew over the Channel at 1000 feet, round Le Havre, then south toward Mezidon. Like the other missions that day, this was a rhubarb – we were just looking for any and all German military targets that we might hit. About 20-25 minutes into the flight, we passed over some marshalling yards, in the town of Mezidon. We were going at 350-380 miles an hour and I missed the sight at first but suddenly there was radio contact from one of the pilots, who shouted out, "Did you see that below?" The marshalling yards were just below, a huge concentration of rolling stock, tanks on flat cars, troop carriers, jeeps, you name it, plus lots of German troops. Seen from 500 feet, the yard comprised a huge bulge, of maybe a dozen or more lines of track, tapering down to single lines of track running north and south. A couple of road bridges ran over the yards at its two ends.

It was too late to come in for a direct attack, however, as we were already passing over it. I radioed to the group, "We'll continue on the same course and do a reciprocal." In other words, we would continue flying south, to convince the Germans below, who would have seen us, that we hadn't seen the marshalling yards or had other priorities, then swoop back and take them by surprise. That was the idea, at least.

We continued flying south another 10 minutes at most, then did a sharp turn, reversed course and rapidly descended to 300 feet, coming in at 350 mph or so just above the tracks toward the marshalling yards. I was in the lead and as we approached, I was close enough to see the eyes of the soldiers manning the anti-aircraft guns. They were waiting for us. They had known we would be back and had been expecting us. The firing started as we were making our approach.

My aircraft was hit even before firing off my first rockets. I heard the bump, it was considerable, and knew immediately what it meant. But I fired my rockets and could see the explosions down amongst the trucks and rolling stock. Altogether, we had let go with a total of 55 rockets and had done a lot of damage.

But my immediate concern as we quickly flew north and away from the marshalling yards was my situation. I could see that there wasn't a hope in hell of getting the aircraft back to the base. My cooling system was hit and the temperature of the engine had started rising steeply. Also there was a stream of glycol, the cooling fluid, coming out underneath the aeroplane. The hit must have been in the glycol tank, right underneath the aeroplane. In this situation, you know you don't have long to do something. An engine that has lost its coolant and is getting hotter and hotter is either going to explode or just shut down. I would have to bail out. No question about it. But my altimeter showed 200 feet and you don't bail out from 200 feet. I radioed the group to say that I had been hit and would have to take the aircraft up and bail out. I told them to carry on and get back to base. Flying Officer Lamb was to take over. What I didn't know then was that two others in our group had also been hit during our attack. Flight Sergeant Rowland and Flying Officer Tidbury were also brought down by the anti-aircraft guns. Rowland's aeroplane crashed and burned; he must have died either when hit or, more likely, in the crash. Tidbury had managed to bail out but was captured and became a prisoner of war.

As far as I knew, however, the attack had been a major success and my task now was to survive. I quickly took the aircraft up to 1200 feet, just about the level of the cloud ceiling and undid my harness and pulled out the R/T plug. I had never bailed out before but I was not afraid of doing this. The fear I had, at this point, was of being engulfed in flames in the cockpit. This is a fighter pilot's worst nightmare, being burned alive in the cockpit from an engine fire, not the thought of crashing and dying, as you might think. And, in the minute or so that had elapsed since being hit, the danger of fire was real. The temperature gauge had gone to its maximum.

In principle, bailing out of your aircraft is easy. You are already strapped to your parachute, which is folded up and part of your seat. All that you have to do is push open the cockpit hood and let it fall away, then climb out, pulling the ripcord on your 'chute a few seconds into your free fall once you've cleared the aircraft and its slipstream. The 'chute then opens and you glide down.

That's the theory of it. It should have been simple. The reality was proving to be something else, however. The hood was absolutely stuck. I was pushing and pushing with the palms of my hands, with all the strength I could put into it, yet it still wouldn't budge. I had by this point turned the plane upside down so that my full weight was pressing on the hood as I pushed with my full strength, my palms against the cockpit shield, but it just wouldn't go. So I rolled the aircraft back to normal and was flying straight. But by this point, I wasn't really flying, I was beginning to descend – at a steep angle and with increasing speed. The engine had given out. There had been no explosion, no fire, but now there was no power either and I was heading earthwards. There was a different fear beginning to grip me now, not of fire but of the crash that would be coming up in probably 10 seconds or less. I could see the glycol flowing down the body of the plane, the oil was streaming along the fuselage, and the aeroplane was heading for the ground rapidly. The altimeter now said 500 feet. I had to get out. Fast. It might be no more than 7 or 8 seconds until impact. I was already probably too low for bailing out with enough time for the 'chute to fill and get me to the ground safely. "For Christ's sake, get me out of here," I remember yelling.

Things were desperate. I leaned back in the seat, put one foot on one side of the cockpit, the other foot on the other side and pushed with all my might. And, wham!, suddenly I was out.

It all happened very quickly. I whooshed backwards in a somersault, my parachute hitting the tail of the plane. Suddenly I was falling, sky and earth all topsy-turvy. I have no memory of pulling the rip cord but I must have done so or, possibly, it got pulled when I hit the tailpiece because the 'chute had opened. There must have been only a few seconds with it open, however, and it certainly hadn't filled out. I heard the loud bang of the plane hitting the ground not far away and the next thing I knew

I was rapidly dropping through leaves and branches. And then my fall stopped, with a sudden jerk. I was hanging by the shrouds of my parachute from a tree, an oak tree, about 12 to 15 feet off the ground, near the trunk. It might have been only 4 or 5 seconds, maybe less, since I'd left the Typhoon. Clearly, I hadn't had a chance to float to earth in my 'chute. Instead, I'd been grabbed by the shrouds before the 'chute had fully opened and had been caught, and in effect saved, by this big oak near the edge of a wood. Just beyond, I could see a large, gently sloping field with tall grass and beyond that, some sort of hedge in front of another wood.

Suspended there, in my harness, I experienced a couple of seconds of unbelievable pure relief. I had survived, after all. Not only that, as far as I could tell, I wasn't the least bit injured, apart from some minor scratches and bruises. I knew, however, that there was really no time to linger, reflecting on what a lucky bloke I was. The imperative was to get out of my 'chute and away from that tree as fast as I could. It was a dead cert that one or more Germans would have seen the plane coming out of the sky and either seen or heard the crash. If so, they would come looking for the pilot. The parachute itself would be like a great big white sign saying, "Hey chaps, here he is". If they found me there, I would either be shot and killed then and there or taken prisoner. Being made a POW was more likely than being shot but I had no wish to spend the rest of the war behind barbed wire in a German POW camp. My only thought was to get out of the tree and away from there as quickly as I could.

I swung over to the trunk, grabbed it, and with my other hand, managed to release my parachute harness. I then slid part way down the trunk and then jumped to the ground. It was now just a few minutes after 4.30pm in the afternoon. With double summer-time, even on a grey overcast day like this, it would not get fully dark until about 10.30pm or 11.00pm. If the Germans wanted to make a thorough search for me, they would have plenty of daylight – and time – to do so. It had only been a little more than half an hour since I had confidently set out with my group from Westhampnett. But my situation had changed totally: instead of being the hunter, looking for German targets, I would soon be the hunted.

Which way to go? I looked around and decided the best bet would be across the field and into the next wood and then just keep going, as fast as I could, away from the crash site, away from my 'chute. There were only three or four trees between me and the long grass but before I could make a move, I heard a gate creak. My heart skipped a beat. It seemed as if the sound were coming from off to the left, probably at the top of the field. Someone was coming. My first thought was to get away from the parachute as swiftly as possible. I quickly moved to a nearby tree and crouched behind it, waiting to see who was coming. Of course, if the 'chute had been spotted immediately, my being one or two trees over would not have made any difference. But in this sort of situation, one doesn't always think clearly – one is operating on instincts, reflexes and fuzzy half-thoughts.

Maybe 10 seconds later, I saw who was approaching. It was a German soldier, dressed in the standard German army field grey, wearing the standard deep bucket helmet and with a rifle slung over his shoulder. This was the first German soldier I had seen up close. He was only, perhaps, 20 yards away at this point and walking quickly through the grass of the field, which I could now see sloped downwards; I was on a hillside somewhere. Fortunately, he did not see my parachute. This was June, after all, and the trees were in full summer foliage. Besides he seemed to be looking straight ahead and walking purposefully down the hill. What I couldn't see was the smoldering wreckage of my Typhoon but he almost certainly could. It had crashed into the hillside perhaps 100 yards further down.

He kept on walking. Within minutes of landing in the tree, this felt like a narrow escape. I moved forward to a tree just at the edge of the woods to get a better idea of the place. Uphill, toward the left, maybe 50-75 yards, was a wire fence and a wooden gate. This obviously was where he had come through. At the bottom of the hill was a flat area – what wasn't apparent was that there was a small river, really just a stream – down there and behind it, a well-built two-storey French yellow stone farmhouse. With the soldier walking steadily away from my position, down the field, and with his back turned, this was my chance, I thought. I would crawl through the grass, as quickly as possible, and hit the deck if he should turn around. The idea was to get into the wood opposite and then get away as fast and as quietly as I could. It was a distance of 50 yards at the most. Not too bad.

On hands and knees, I started scuttling through the high grass, as quickly as I could, keeping an eye on the soldier the whole time. And then when I was nearly three quarters of the way across, I saw him stop, turn around and begin to walk back up the slope. I immediately flopped down flat and lay there, trying to see through the grass what he was doing. This is it, I thought. I pulled out my service revolver, ready, if it were necessary, to shoot him before he could shoot me. But I knew that if I did that, my chances of escape would be zero. Half the German army would be out looking for me. The sound of the shot itself would bring them running and they would show no mercy to an enemy airman who had just killed one of their own.

Fortunately, after just a few seconds, it seemed, he changed his mind again, turned around and started walking back down the hill again, I assume toward the wreckage of my aeroplane. What a relief! I quickly stuffed my revolver back inside my tunic and completed my rapid crawl to the other side. There was a big brambly hedge bordering the wood here but the top end of it was close to the point I'd reached. I quickly scurried towards it, to get around the hedge and into the woods, but now saw that it seemed to be covering up a big ditch. A drainage ditch of some kind, for drawing off rainwater during storms. And there was a natural opening at this end. I could squeeze into it and under the hedge without creating a visible hole or damage to the hedge itself. I crawled in and was immediately hidden though my hands and face were lacerated and the brambles had made some tears in my uniform, which I only noticed later. The ditch, however, was about 2 feet deep and, covered by the brambles, it was the perfect hiding place. It was also completely dry. This was enough to keep me well hidden but hardly spacious or comfortable. I crawled along it further to get away from the end. It wasn't a hot day but by now, the perspiration was running off me.

Time passes slowly when you are hiding from someone but still it seemed that it was not long before the first soldier was joined by others, with probably somewhere between 10 and 15 of them eventually walking about, searching for me. It probably became obvious quickly to them that there was no pilot's body in the crashed aeroplane. I heard them talking and shouting to one another. I can't say when they found my 'chute but it couldn't have been more than an hour since I had come down. With a pilot-less wreck and an empty parachute, they would have known that the pilot had survived and could not be too far away. Though I know little German, I caught the German word for "river". There must be a river at the bottom of the hill, I decided, and they were assuming that I'd made my way toward it. They had spread out, however, rifles at the ready and were making what looked like a fairly thorough search all around, occasionally shouting to one another. Peeking through the crack between the hedge and the edge of the ditch, I could see snatches of the action but only that. And most of the time, I simply kept my head down, waiting for the sounds of their voices to stop. At one point, a Frenchman appeared and two of the soldiers questioned him. This was only about 100 yards from where I was lying but, thank God, no one spotted me.

This went on for more than an hour but it seemed a lot longer. The whole time, I had been lying there, trying to keep still but taking peeks through the bush to see what was going on. Finally, they were ready to throw in the towel. But before leaving, they did one last thing: they sprayed the hedge and the nearby woods with automatic rifle fire. The bullets were wizzing over my head, some maybe no more than a foot away, making a terrible racket and creating a small shower of leaves and twigs over me. I just hugged the earth. What they didn't do was look at the hedge closely. Had they done so, they would have found the ditch – and me.

And then, it was over. I heard their voices diminishing and then gone altogether. There was just silence now except for the occasional rustle of leaves, a dog's bark somewhere, bird song. Whatever was happening in the fighting on or, by now, behind the Normandy beaches, there were no sounds of the battle here. It was still quite light, around 6.00pm or 6.30pm on a June evening but the best thing, it seemed, would be just to wait, lying in this ditch, protected from view by the hedge, until it got dark.

Where precisely was I? I had no idea, of course, but much later found out that it was a farm on the outskirts of the village of Croissanville in Normandy, about 15 kilometres north of Mezidon. By taking my Typhoon up to 1200 feet after being hit, I had managed to gain this distance from the marshalling yards. All that I knew for sure at this moment was that I was still a free man, lying under a hedge, uninjured but with a scratched face and hands, somewhere in the Normandy countryside.

Around 10.30pm, when I reckoned that it was sufficiently dark, I crawled out of the ditch and from under the hedge, through the opening of which I'd come, stood up and looked around. There was just barely enough light from the night sky to see by. I was wearing my RAF uniform, which included the flying boots that RAF pilots used. On a parade ground, these look great but they are not practical for walking and it was clear that I had a lot of walking ahead of me. With my knife, I cut off the tops, to make them look and feel more like walking shoes, and put the pieces back under the hedge. I also checked my escape kit, which every flier carries with him in case he finds himself in just this kind of situation. But it wasn't much: a small water bottle, a compass button stitched into my tunic, the revolver (which I'd been ready to use six hours earlier), several hundred francs (maybe enough to buy a couple of cheap meals), a Ronson lighter, and a packet of Horlicks tablets, for emergency nourishment.

As for what to do, well, that would be up to me. There had never been any instruction or advice given to any of us on what to do if you found yourself in enemy territory, except to evade capture and make your way back to your own lines. Just how to do all that was left to the pilot's individual ingenuity.

I decided to take a look around first and walked down the field towards the stream. The skies had partially cleared and the moon and some stars were visible, just enough light to see by. The field levelled out at the bottom and there was a little river, as I'd expected from what I'd heard, and a simple wooden footbridge. On the other side of the river, fully visible under the moonlight, was an elegant looking two-storey light-coloured stone country house. There were no lights on that I could see but the blinds or curtains were probably drawn. Even if there had been visible light inside, however, I wouldn't have been tempted to go up, knock and ask for help. Far too risky.

What to do? If I were to get back to British forces on the beachheads, I would have to go north. Of course, there was a large part of the German army in France between me and the Allied forces on the beachheads but I would worry about that complication later. The important thing was to head north and try to get back to Allied lines. I took a bearing from my button compass, which was difficult because the compass was so small and the light from the moon and stars was dim. I looked for the north star but couldn't see it. An idea dawned. The moon, I figured, should be approximately north at this point and it might, therefore, be a good marker for making my way northwards. I would just head in the direction of the moon and thus, I hoped, in the right direction. This, of course, was another instance of fuzzy thinking that day, since the moon, of course, describes a semi-circle in the night-sky as the earth revolves. Doing as I planned to do would guarantee walking in a semi-circle toward the east – which is exactly what happened. But I only realised that later. It seemed to me that the best course would be to stay away from roads as much as possible and just move northwards through the fields and woods.

I began making my way through the fields when, maybe after only 15 minutes or so, I came to a farmhouse. It was now about 11.30pm British time. There was a light on in one of the windows but I carefully made my way around the house to what I assumed was the back door. There was no light visible from within and, luckily, the backdoor was on the latch. I made my way in quietly and could just barely make out in the near total darkness that this was, in fact, a big storage area of some sort. The shelves were mostly quite bare but there were some potatoes and various other items, which I could see by the combination of the dim moonlight coming from the window in the door and some light coming from a crack under the inner door. This big storage area was next to a room in which there were several people, from the sounds of it, in a lively discussion, talking about something in French. I put my ear to the inner door and could make out more clearly the voices within. And with the aid of my elementary French, I could make out some of the phrases and, therefore, the drift of the conversation. Within less than half a minute of starting to listen, I had quite a surprise.

They were talking about me. The discussion was all about the "pilote anglais", and where had he gone and what had he done? They didn't know but they were sure the pilot was alive and probably not too far away. They didn't know how right they were.

Christ, I thought, I'm too close to the area where I was shot down to ask anyone here for help. The Germans were probably still looking in this part and must have stopped at the various houses around and told the people to report the pilot if he was seen. They would have put the wind up the locals. Any Frenchman found helping an escaped Allied pilot would, almost certainly, be shot. The people discussing this on the other side of the door certainly sounded agitated enough. If I asked for help here, I might just as likely find myself being turned over to the Huns. I quickly but quietly stuffed my pockets with potatoes and a bit of bread that was lying on one of the shelves and let myself out as quietly as possible.

I continued my walk across the fields, still using the moon as my guide. There was quite a heavy dew in the long grass and my trouser legs were soon soaked to the knees. I cursed myself for having cut off the top of the boots. Maybe that hadn't been such a bright idea after all. But it was too late for such regrets.

But while my trouser legs were now dripping wet, my throat was awfully dry. I was beginning to be very thirsty. Soon, however, I found myself in a field with some dairy cows, some standing, some lying down, visible in the moonlight. The immediate thought was: milk! If I could just get some milk into my rubber water bottle, that would help. Well, I tried approaching the nearest standing cow but the one I chose wasn't in the mood to cooperate and kept moving off. Finally, she stood still, and with my water bottle ready, I managed to position it beneath a teat and, with difficulty, tried to squeeze a little milk out as I steadied the cow with my other hand. The opening of the bottle was too narrow – the manufacturers surely hadn't thought about this particular use of the water bottle. And the cow continued to be uncooperative, moving off a few feet again. I moved over to her and tried again but after another minute or so of this fumbling, I decided it was not going to work. I let the cow go and moved on.

I felt, by this point, that I had been walking all night. Soon after the incident with the cow, I came to some railway tracks. Thinking that the tracks were patrolled at night by the Germans, I lay down on the grass by the side of them, for perhaps 5-10 minutes, keeping a lookout for soldiers. There was no sign of patrols by this point, so I got up and quickly crossed to the other side. I then walked across a few more fields through the wet grass and came out on to another road. I cautiously looked both ways. Nothing was coming. Just across the road was another farmhouse. This house had dogs, however, as I soon found out because within a minute of my approaching it, the dogs started barking. I thought that they would surely wake all the Huns in Normandy and get them out looking for me. I had to get away quickly. I walked down the road for a short distance, as fast as I could, and then lay down in a dry ditch by its side. If someone had come out of the house, because of the dogs' barking, they wouldn't see me. But there was no sound of an opening door and I was just deciding that the coast was clear when, all of a sudden, I heard the sound of some kind of motorised transport. It was getting louder and louder, and soon it was thunderously loud. It felt as if it, whatever it was, was coming right toward me. I lay in the ditch and looked out over the edge, my gut clenched tight with fear.

It was tanks, German Tiger tanks, the killer tanks that both the British infantry and armoured units so feared. The Germans themselves, we found out later, called them "Tommie cookers" for their effects on the crews of British tanks hit by their fire. I counted 20 in all. There were no escort vehicles, it was just a small convoy of tanks, a full armoured unit. They were probably part of the German 51st division and, if so, had come down from Calais. I reckoned that they must be heading in the direction of Caen from Le Havre. And I thought, if the Germans can muster this kind of force at this point, how the hell is the invasion going to survive? What I didn't know, of course, was that there had been a major cock-up on the German side with respect to deployment of the armoured units as a whole. But what I had seen was frightening enough.

I waited until the noise had died down, then got out of the ditch. It was now, by my watch, which I could just barely make out, just past 4.00am. And I was exhausted. Not from the walking, though that had been tiring and miserable enough, with my legs soaked through, but from the stress of it all. I desperately wanted to lie down somewhere and get some sleep. By chance, I had arrived at a small village and there was a farm on the other side of the road with a large barn next to it. And near the barn there was a granary annexe. I carefully crossed the road, looking both ways to make sure no one was coming, then walked through the gate of the property, closing it as quietly as possible behind me and entered the granary. Inside, there was a ladder on the floor, which I could barely make out and up above it, what I assumed to be a hayloft. I took a further quick look around, using my Ronson lighter to get an idea where the hatch was, put the ladder up to the loft and quickly climbed it. I was right. It was a loft, filled with straw. I pushed the ladder away, trying to make it fall in the position I'd found it. Of course, it made an awful clatter on the stone floor of the barn and I had a minute or so of anxiety, wondering if it would bring anyone running. But no one came and I was almost too exhausted to care, at this point. In the dark, I pulled some hay around me, making a bed and a place to rest my head, and before I knew it, had fallen into a deep, dreamless sleep.

6
On the run and hiding out in occupied Normandy

It was bright morning when I woke up. There were a few seconds of disorientation as I came to, trying to make sense of where I was. Then, it all came back. I got up quickly and crouched over, trying to be quiet, which was easy because of the cushioning provided by the hay. I made my way to the loading door at the front of the loft, which was open a crack. Through it and some peepholes, I could make out the house and had a glimpse of the road. There were already signs of life, with a few French civilians coming and going. I stationed myself there and watched for hours. Though it was another grey day, it was far too bright to think about leaving now, particularly with various people of the farm out and about, and besides this seemed a safe enough place. I decided to wait at least another day here. If the invasion were proceeding well, I figured there might be British or American troops coming through soon. At this moment, that idea did not seem unduly optimistic. Surely, I felt, our troops couldn't have been that far from this place.

There were several people coming and going about the business of the farm. Occasionally, someone would come into the barn but no one tried to come up into the loft or noticed whether the ladder was lying where it shouldn't have been. The hay must have been emergency rations for the cows and not used that often. On the road, there was the occasional German military vehicle but there wasn't much traffic and no more tanks passed by.

Watching and waiting. That was all I could do for the moment. I was beginning to feel pretty filthy, of course, but the bigger problem was hunger. I'd had no real food since the previous day's lunch at Westhampnett. Every now and then I would have a bite of one of the potatoes but raw potatoes are hard to chew and taste awful. Disgusting, really. Then there were the Horlicks tablets and these were better than nothing but hardly what you would call satisfying. And they had to be rationed, there was only a small supply. I decided to have no more than two per day. As for something to drink, that was an even bigger problem. That night, when it was dark again, and there was a light rain going on, I was able to use my water bottle to collect some rainwater from the gutter on the outside of the barn, which ended just outside the hatch of the hayloft. It wasn't much but there was sufficient water coming out, because of the rain, to collect enough for a drink and it was certainly more successful than trying to milk a reluctant cow at night in a dark field. After this manoeuvre and quenching my thirst, if only just, I moved back to my makeshift bed of hay, lay down and eventually fell asleep again.

The next day, the situation was much the same. It would have been too risky to try to leave in daylight and because no one would have dreamt that a "pilote anglais" was hiding in the loft, I felt safe for the time being. I felt this way particularly because I thought I was much further from where I had been shot down than I actually was. That day, there was more watching at the chinks and peepholes and waiting for some sign of helpful developments or a good idea on how to escape. I kept on trying to formulate different plans but ended up discarding each one, almost as soon as it formed itself. From my watching at the peepholes, however, I was beginning to notice something of a pattern. Next to the granary there was a cottage, with a low wall in between. Both the first and second nights, about 10.00pm or so, a middle-aged man, maybe he was in his late forties or early fifties, it was hard to tell, came out of his cottage and went to a lean-to in the back of his property. By daylight, I could see this better and it was some kind of structure that I figured must be an air-raid shelter. He didn't stay long and I had no idea what he was doing but this seemed to be his pattern and, in the late evening, he seemed to be the only person around who was out and about at this time. He had done this both nights. That second night, it rained again and I was able to collect some rainwater to drink, as I had the first.

I woke earlier the next morning and spent the day in the same fashion. But the situation was beginning to feel desperate. I was nearly out of Horlicks tablets, which were hardly much anyway, and was beginning to feel desperately hungry and weak. Something had to be done. I had to get some food. It seemed to me that approaching the Frenchman who visited his air-raid shelter in the evening would be the best bet. It would be a risk, of course, but it would have to be taken.

That evening, as it was getting dark, I lowered myself through the hatch and dropped to the floor. I peeked out through the door. No one was about. I had to find a hiding place from where I could attract this man's attention but without being out in the open. I scrambled over the low wall between the two properties. Fortunately, there was a grass-filled ditch running not far from the path between his cottage and the air-raid shelter. I quickly walked toward it, crouching over, trying to be as inconspicuous as I could and then crawled into it. And waited.

Before too long, I heard the sound of a door open and, just as I'd hoped, it was this Frenchman walking along the path to the air-raid shelter. It was dark, and raining lightly but there was enough light from the surrounding houses just to make things out. Raising myself just enough to be heard but I hoped not seen, I made psst-ing sounds, the kind you use when trying to get someone's attention. It worked. He came over to the ditch. I had drawn my gun to make sure he would listen and not run away at the first sight of me. And when he saw me lying there, looking at him, gun pointing straight at him, his eyes opened wide. He looked like the most startled man on earth. And I must have looked quite a sight by this point, with a filthy uniform and several days growth of stubble on my face. Quickly, I explained rapidly in my poor French that I was an escaped British pilot and asked him if he could help. I told him that I was starving. I also warned him that I would shoot him if he tried to give me away. He must have recognised the uniform as British and evidently decided that I was telling the truth. He looked carefully around, then motioned me to put the gun away and to get up. He actually looked pleased at this point and said to me, "I'm all for the British. Come with me. I will get you something to eat." And he led me into his house.

He showed me into the kitchen, where his wife and daughter, a girl of maybe fifteen or sixteen, were sitting. The wife's eyes were wide with surprise when she saw her husband bringing this stranger into her house but he explained quickly to them who I was and that I desperately needed some food. With that, the woman made me feel welcome immediately, indicating that I should sit down at the plain wooden table. "What would you like?" she asked. "Have you got bacon and eggs?" I asked, almost thinking at this point that it was too good to be true that I would, at last, after several days with almost no food, soon be having a real meal. She didn't have English-style bacon but did have ham and within ten minutes, I was tucking into ham and eggs. I was ravenous and the food seemed absolutely delicious. She also gave me a glass of water but her husband asked if I would also like some cider. I really didn't want to have anything alcoholic and declined but asked for a glass of milk instead, which I drank down in a couple of long draughts. Only an hour before, I was feeling tired, filthy and just about at the end of my tether. One decent meal under my belt and I was feeling restored. Also, to have been welcomed in this way by this family gave me some hope that I would get help from the locals to escape the Germans.

It had been years since I had spoken any French, not since the motorbike trip in '39 but as I sat there in their kitchen and talked with them, it began to come back. And they told me their story. Their name was Laloy and they were from Paris. Some time after the Germans had occupied the capital, in 1940, they had decided to get out and had come to Normandy, buying this house. There were food shortages in Paris and, in general, they felt it would be safer. Exactly how they had managed to get out of Paris and settle here wasn't clear to me. The village they now lived in was called Lion d'Or and it was on the main road between Caen and Le Havre to the east. The neighbouring village and its domaine was called Mery Corbon.

We discussed, of course, what was to be done with me. Even though they were feeding me, I still felt that I needed to be sure that I was safe with them and asked in my halting French, "Est-ce que vous êtes avec moi or non?" M. Laloy assured me that they were with me, not against me, and told me that, from the news of the Allied advance, he expected the English to be arriving soon. But, of course, something had to be done with me in the meantime and he explained that it would be far too risky for them, and for me, to stay with them at their house or in the granary where I'd been hiding. The odds of someone in the village getting sight of me and reporting it to the Germans were too high. He suggested that I hide in another granary, which was about two fields distant, just north of the road that ran through the village. The idea was that he would bring me some food every day when it was safe and I could stay there until the British forces arrived or the coast was clear for making an escape. This all sounded good to me and I agreed immediately. It was now dark and he said that he would lead me there. We made our way through the fields at the rear of the house and arrived at a granary at the edge of one of the fields.

I've called it a granary but it was really more of a cow shed. Like the other building I had hidden in, it had a loft but its most striking feature was that it was absolutely the filthiest place I have ever seen, let alone stayed in. I could see that by the light of the electric torch Laloy held, the moment we arrived and went in. The torch beam also lit up a rat, scurrying away. As it happened, there were quite a few rats that called this place home. But it wasn't the look of the place, or even the rats, that got me. It was the stench from the cow dung that covered the ground inside. My heart sank at the prospect of staying here. But beggars can't be choosers. And it looked as if this, at least, would be a fairly safe haven, at least for a while.

M. Laloy indicated that I should hide in the loft and told me that he would be back the next evening with more food. He said goodbye and I climbed into the loft. Its floor consisted of rough planking covered with hay. There were gaps in the planking and so I had to make my way carefully. The last thing I wanted to do was fall through the flooring into the cow dung below. But the stench was just as strong in the loft as it was below. If this was going to be "home" for a few days, it would take some getting used to. The old air force phrase of being in the shit took on new meaning for me. Still, I told myself, the situation had improved. I had just had a decent meal and wasn't feeling weak from hunger. And, now, at least, I had an ally and the promise of some food every day to keep body and soul together. I lay down on the hay but sleep didn't come immediately. There was the stink of the place and the occasional scurrying sound of the rats. But after awhile, I drifted off again into a deep, dreamless sleep.

I awoke to a grey, cool dawn. It took a couple of seconds to remember what had happened and to take my bearings, to remember where I was, no longer in the barn near the road but in a fairly isolated cow shed several fields away from the village. There was daylight coming in through the open wooden doors down below but there were good peepholes in the walls of the loft from which I was able to get a better idea of my bearings. I was lying there, wondering if I should go down the ladder to take a look at the surrounding field, when I saw a very old man approaching the barn and then entering. I couldn't see him the whole time but a glimpse that I took through the hatch indicated that he was, indeed an elderly fellow, considerably older than Laloy. From the sounds and glimpses through the floor slats, it was clear that he was milking the cows. I could hear the stream of milk hitting the bottom of the first pail, as he began. Then, maybe 20 minutes or so after he had come in, he was done. The milk sloshing in two pails, he left. The whole time, I just lay there quietly on the thin bed of straw, praying that he wouldn't sense that anything was odd or come up the ladder, but luckily he was completely oblivious of me. I just lay there quietly, breathing as silently as I could, until he left.

And that was more or less what I did all day, lying on the thin straw that covered the hard wood planks, just shifting my position from time to time to try to get more comfortable. The day passed boringly and incredibly slowly. The planking had too many gaps to make walking on it much of an option and I was now wary about descending the ladder to take a look around, in case someone should suddenly show up. Laloy hadn't mentioned to me the night before that anyone else would be coming into the granary or, if he had warned me, I hadn't understood the words. At one point, I had to relieve myself in a corner of the loft but the smell of that was lost in the general stink.

At dusk, M. Laloy returned. I heard him coming and cautiously looking down from the hatch I saw immediately that it was him, not the other Frenchman or anyone else. He came up the ladder with a basket with some food – an omelette, bread, cheese, some milk – and cutlery. The fare was simple but delicious and I tucked in immediately. As I ate, we talked. He had some news. The wireless was reporting that the Allied troops were making progress, getting deeper into Normandy, though the fighting was

From left to right, Fred, Catherine land, Frank and Doris.

Bottom left: Frank with his parents on Yarmouth beach.

Bottom right: Frank as a chorister.

Top: Final choristers' outing –
Frank aged 16 (top right).

Middle left: Frank and Margot's
wedding, Canada, December
7th, 1941.

Middle right: Frank on first trip
to France with Mary Tibbetts.

Bottom: Frank, Margot and baby
Paulette, 1943.

Top: Frank (front row second left) with training squadron in Canada.

Middle: Members of 184 Squadron at Westgate, (from left to right) Frank, Len Thorpe, Archie Lamb, Mike Jones, and Dick Houghton.

Bottom: Frank with his fellow 184 Squadron colleagues.

Top: The Typhoon.

Middle: The granary at Lion d'Or where Frank spent almost two weeks.

Bottom: The annexe to Henri Lair's farmhouse where Frank stayed in Norrey-en-Auges.

Top: Frank's identity card as Roger Gasnier.

Bottom left: Frank's first return to Norrey-en-Auges, late May 1945, just after the end of the war.

Bottom right: From left to right: Frank, André Delattre, Henri Lair and Roger Hervieux.

Top left: Outside the Lair's farmhouse on a later visit. Marie Lair, Ginette Lair (their daughter), Frank and Henri Lair.

Top right: Frank with Henri and Marie Lair at the Memorial de Bayeux in 1994, during the 50th anniversary commemoration of D-Day.

Bottom: At the Typhoon Memorial at Noyer-Bocage, May 2004.

Top left: Receiving his medal to commemorate the 60th anniversary of D-Day.

Top right: Frank receiving part of the wing of his plane in a ceremony at Croissanville in May 2004. On the right is Yves Delaunay, the son of the man who owned the field in which Frank came down.

Bottom: Typhoon pilots pay their tribute at the 60th anniversary of D-Day at Noyer-Bocage. Third from the right is Kit North-Lewis.

Top: With wife Olga and daughters Polly (right) and Louise (left), May 2004, Noyer-Bocage.

Bottom left: With Alice Lair (sister of Henri) in May 2004.

Bottom right: Frank's spontaneous rendition of "O, for the wings of a dove" in the church at Norrey-en-Auges in May 2004.

fierce. The British and American lines were now about 10 miles away to the west. Based on this, he felt and told me that the troops would probably be coming through Lion d'Or soon.

Yet, the thought of spending several more days in this filthy place, just lying there, waiting, waiting for a break of some kind or, at least, for something to happen, while enduring the stench the whole time, just didn't appeal to me. I told him that I was going to try to make a break for it that night, to try to get back to our lines. He shook his head slightly; he clearly didn't think this would be a good move. But he wished me luck. We shook hands, said farewell to each other, and a few minutes after he left, I descended the ladder too.

It was quite dark by now and mostly overcast, so there was precious little light to see where I was going. The memories of that night are now pretty hazy to me but what still is vivid was the sense of danger I had the whole time. I made my way through several fields, sticking to the edge of the woods whenever possible. At several points, I heard German troops nearby and altered course accordingly, staying low, walking quickly. I was still wearing my uniform and if they had caught sight of me, they would probably have shot first and asked questions later.

Then I came across something which really did frighten me, a barbed wire fence with little metal tabs on it. By the little star and moonlight that came through the overcast skies, I could just make out tiny skulls and crossbones on these tabs. The markings of a minefield. In the dark, I had managed to make my way toward the edge of a minefield. I took a deep breath, and experienced a few seconds of real fear. Clearly, I would have to skirt around it but just as I started walking along it to find the end, I saw two German sentries ahead. I quickly crouched down, turned around and retreated back through the open fields, away from the minefield, as quickly and quietly as I could.

The whole situation was just too uncertain and dangerous. I didn't really know where I was or where I was going. It seemed to me that I had better get back to the awful cow shed. Waiting there might be the best option after all. But retracing my route seemed almost impossible. Just how I managed to do it, in the dark, without landmarks, doing it from memory, I do not know but, somehow, just as dawn was beginning to break, I found the old barn again. What a relief! When I had left it the previous evening, I would never have imagined that I would be glad to see it again. I climbed back up the ladder and lay down on a thin bed of hay on the planks, to catch up on some sleep.

But it was probably only a few minutes, probably no more than half an hour before I was awakened by some noise from down below. It was the old man, back again, milking his cows. Through a gap in the floor of the loft, I could see this Frenchman attending to his cows. He was only 10 yards, at most, away from me and had no idea I was there and watching him. He finished up, after maybe no more than a half an hour and left with his full milk pails.

So, there I was again, back in this loft, waiting for something to happen, and sleeping in snatches but not very restfully. I could only hope that M. Laloy might come back and check. Which, luckily he did, late that afternoon. He did not seem surprised that I was back and told me that he was glad I had not got myself killed. He hadn't rated my chances of getting through the German lines very highly. Instead of bringing food to me, however, he told me that I should come to his house for supper. He went off to tell his wife, then came back for me, maybe two hours later, as it was getting dark. I followed him at a distance of about 30 yards. And, when he reached his house, he looked around to make sure no one else was about and then signalled silently that I should come forward, which I did.

As before, his wife and daughter welcomed me with a few words and smiles, and again the meal was simple but good: an omelette, bread and butter and cheese. This continued for three nights but after each meal, M. Laloy guided me back to the granary. I was deeply grateful to them and felt that, with my poor French, I could not really properly express my gratitude. Yet, at no time did he offer the chance for me to wash and, by this time, I was utterly filthy and probably, beginning to stink of the smell of the cow barn. Despite Laloy's hospitality and generosity, I was sure that he and his wife were still afraid that I would be discovered while in his house and, quite reasonably, he didn't want to risk his family's safety. Doing what he was doing for me, sheltering me in his cow barn, was dangerous enough. By now, a week had gone by since I had been shot down. The news about the Allied advance, however, as related to me by M. Laloy, was not good. Though it was hard to tell exactly what was going on, the reports seemed to indicate stalemate in the battle going on in Normandy. Or, at most, very slow progress of the British and American forces. I was beginning to give up on the hope that I was going to be liberated by British or American forces any day now.

The days passed as the first one, in complete boredom and inactivity. Laloy had taken to removing the ladder after each visit, so as not to arouse suspicion. This effectively trapped me in the loft, unless I was willing to drop into the cow shit below, which I definitely was not. And then, one morning, my situation took an unexpected turn. It was about 5.30am or 6.00am when I woke to hear someone putting the ladder up to get into the loft. I saw the top of the ladder extending into the hatch, coming to rest against the side, and then the sound of someone stepping on the rungs, coming up slowly. There was just time to shift quietly to face the hatch and pull out my service revolver. It was the old man who had been doing the milking, a timid old Frenchman of maybe about 70. His expression, when he saw the revolver pointing in his face, just two feet away, was one of complete wordless surprise. With the barrel, I signalled to him to come on up all the way, which he did. He stepped off the ladder, looking like a frightened old rabbit, and I told him that I was an escaped British pilot and that if he had any idea of giving me away to the

Huns, I would blow his brains out. I'm sure that my accent was terrible and my vocabulary pretty meagre, but he clearly got the gist. Now, however, knowing that I was British, he relaxed a little and assured me that he was on our side, that his son was in the Resistance and that he would get his son to help me. He told me that he would ask him to come that evening and see what could be done to help me escape. I didn't mention the Laloy family and the fact that they were already helping me. I didn't want to implicate them.

By now, I had put the revolver away and thanked him for the offer of help. He descended the ladder, repeating the assurance about his son and getting some help. But I still wasn't sure I could trust him. He had left the ladder in place and after allowing 15 minutes or so, I went down myself. I peered cautiously around the door but could see no one, just the empty field and the surrounding woods. That day, I hid in the woods, just in case his "son" happened to be a few Germans. Yet, in the late afternoon, four young Frenchmen, about my age, showed up. One was the old farmer's son, the other three, as I soon found out, friends of his in the Resistance. As soon as I saw them, I knew that the old farmer had kept his word. I came out of the woods quickly and went to meet them in the small barn. They had brought food, wine, Calvados and, as the five of us partook of this in the loft, it felt like a real party. They told me that many American paratroops had been dropped in the area, not far away, and that they would get me through the German lines. They told me that they would be back the next day, with more information and a more detailed plan to get me away.

This sounded great and I was beginning to feel new hope. But when I told M. Laloy, who showed up about an hour later, he shook his head and told me that they were a drunken crowd and not to be trusted. "Bavardes", he called them – gossips. It made me think that they couldn't be very effective as members of the Resistance if they were chatterboxes. Maybe being in the

Resistance for them meant being sympathetic and trying to help fight the Germans but only if it involved minimal risk. M. Laloy told me that, in fact, he already knew that they had paid me a visit because there was talk in the village. With news spreading like that, it would be just a short time before the Germans would get wind of it and some would show up to haul me off as a prisoner or just shoot me on the spot.

He said, "We've got to get you away from here." He was quite insistent that I was not safe here and he told me that he had a plan. "I've got a friend who's a farmer near here. He'll put you in his barn tonight." This barn, he told me, was a few fields further west of the village. The idea was that the people in the village would think that the "pilote anglais" had just upped and left suddenly in the night. Laloy felt that if I could be hidden in a new place, things should be safe.

But first he needed to check with his friend. He had brought me some more food – that day, I did quite well in terms of eating – and went away to see his friend and make sure. About 10.30 at night, he and his friend showed up. I heard them coming and went down the ladder, with my pack. By electric torchlight, I could see that the friend was about the same age as Laloy, they were both probably in their early 40s, and he told me, a butcher. Unlike Laloy, who was somewhat nervous, a fidgeter, the friend seemed calmer and stronger. They told me that they would take me to the new place immediately. Now in the dark, the torchlight extinguished for safety's sake, they led me through another three or four fields to a new hay barn, probably about half a mile from where I had found my first hiding place in Lion D'Or.

They put a ladder up to the loft and we went up, one at a time. There was a good supply of hay to lie upon and though there was a smell of cows throughout, the place didn't have that awful stench. In fact, the main smell was that of hay, which is quite pleasant. The building itself was made of red brick, not wood, and altogether, the place was clean and dry and warm. Not least, there was no sound of scurrying rats and, in fact, the whole time I was there, not a single rat showed up. The two Frenchmen told me to stay in the loft until they came back the next day. "Look, we shall come to you tomorrow about this time," M. Laloy said. "If we whistle twice, everything is clear. If you hear only one whistle, stay in the loft." They bid me good night, climbed down the ladder, and, in the dark, I made myself comfortable on a bed of hay. It wasn't long before I was asleep.

That morning, though remembering the caution they had given me, I nevertheless wanted to have a look around. I came down the ladder slowly and then surreptitiously looked outside through the open door. It looked as if this hay barn, which was solidly built of crude red brick, with a roof of red earthenware tiles, was all on its own in the centre of a large field, which itself was situated in a larger group of fields. There were no windows in the loft but a wooden door through which hay could be loaded. Because the front of the ground floor was open, there was a reasonable amount of light in the loft during the day, between that which came up through the hatch and through the loading door in the loft, if it was left open a crack.

Though I couldn't see it at first, there was a small country road maybe 75 to a 100 yards away just beyond a wire fence. But in the hayloft, I would be perfectly hidden from anyone passing by. Here, I was really much more isolated than I had been before. Nor, in the two weeks I was here, was there ever any milking done. M. Laloy had told me that only he and his friend would know I was here. No one else in the village would know and they would simply tell people, including the son of the older man who had discovered me, that the "pilote anglais" had just left, to try to get back to British lines.

The routine that I settled into was comfortable. M. Laloy or his farmer friend, the owner of the barn, would bring me food in the late evening. And the food that the two men brought me was really good. Grateful as I had been to the Laloy family for the omelettes, bread and milk, the food I was getting in the evening now was definitely a step up: thick steaks, strawberries, cherries. This was war-time all right, and I was in the middle of a war zone, but these French farming families, it seemed, were not starving. And, in the evening, the two men would come, always announcing themselves first with the all clear whistle. I was also given a chance to shave myself every evening, using a cut-throat razor. And "cut throat" is a good description of that razor on a leather strap. You handled it with care. Also, talking with M. Laloy and his family became easier with time. Though I certainly didn't become fluent in French, I was tuning into the local accent and speaking with more confidence, and probably a better vocabulary, as time went on.

Yet, to the extent that there was a plan now, it was essentially the same as the one before: to wait for the Allied breakthrough into the area, which, we all felt, would surely be coming any day. In the meantime, however, I just had to do something to pass the time during the day or I felt I would go mad with boredom and inactivity. The loft itself wasn't large, maybe only about 12 feet by 12 feet but it was adequate. Fortunately, it had a decent floor, unlike the cow shed I'd been in before, so I could at least walk around it. And that's what I did, walk, back and forth, back and forth, measuring my steps, in this 12 x 12 space. Counting the steps taken and knowing the rough distance, I was able to do rough estimates each day of how much I had walked. The maximum distance that I did in one day, I reckon, was about 15 miles. If it sounds tedious, believe me, it was. In fact, I can never remember being so bored in my whole life. But it was far better than doing nothing, staring at the ceiling, and was something to do, keeping me, at least, reasonably fit. Besides, and maybe I didn't fully appreciate this at the time, the whole situation felt safe, or at least safer, than that in the previous barn I had hidden in. After all, it is only when you feel comparatively safe that you can have the luxury of being bored.

After awhile, I began to take the mild risk of not only going down the ladder and peeking out but actually going outside in the day. The barn was, as I mentioned, a good distance from the road and the road was not heavily travelled, unlike the main road through the village. Sometimes I would stretch my legs by walking through the field toward the road and along the fence but taking care to lie down in the long grass if I heard the least sound of anyone approaching down the road, in either direction. But this was risky and, mostly, I stayed near the barn.

Behind the barn, however, and quite well hidden from the road was a small, shallow pond partially surrounded by a semi-circle of ash and birch trees. During the day, I would often sit on my haunches by the pond. Just watching and looking and wondering what would happen next and when I would be able to get away, and thinking about home too, in particular wondering how Margot was doing, especially how she was handling the news about me. She would have been told by now that I had gone missing in action, and was presumed dead or captured. Adding to my anxiety was the fact that she was pregnant again, with our new baby expected in September.

But my chief and immediate concern was how and when I was going to get out of occupied Normandy, back to British lines. Of course, I knew that my situation was better than it had been a few short days ago and I certainly felt much safer than I had in the previous hiding places. But it still felt like being in a prison, trapped.

Sitting by the pond, I spent my time just watching and waiting, not even particularly thinking in any clear way about escape or home or the war. I'm an active person and there has probably never been a period in my life when I just sat and looked at something, doing nothing, for such long periods. I remember, in particular, the green and blue dragon-flies hovering and then zipping over the surface of the pond. And the frogs. It was evidently the frog mating season, with male frogs mounting female frogs to get them to release their eggs into the water to fertilise them. And, of course, there were the birds: blackbirds, starlings, magpies, pigeons, mourning doves, crows and goldfinches. One bird I remember, in particular, was a mourning dove on a branch of one of the trees next to the pond. I noticed him when he began to sing. His song was just a few beautiful but sad notes, and then, suddenly, as if he had just remembered an appointment he was late for, he flew off. I remember thinking: oh, if only I were a bird, I could just fly out of here and fly back home. It's a common thought, I suppose, wanting to be able to fly like a bird. But I don't believe I personally had ever felt or thought anything like that before.

But if this description gives the impression that I had settled in to a comfortable rural existence, hidden away from the war in a pocket of peace, that would be incorrect. In fact, you couldn't escape the reality of the war going on all around you. There were frequent overflights by our fighters and bombers. And if I'd been envious of the birds being able to just fly away, I couldn't help but think that these pilots would be back home in 30 minutes to an hour while I was trapped here in this place. But there was more than just the sight of aircraft passing through. Occasionally, there was combat essentially right overhead. One day, I saw a Focke-Wulf 190 chasing a Spitfire. They were all flying low, probably only 1000 feet. The Fw 190 looked as if it was about to fire on the Spitfire. I stood up and shouted – I couldn't help it but I was lucky there was no one around – "For Christ's sake, break!" Well, it was like ESP because a fraction of a second later, the Spit turned, evading the German chasing him and getting away, while the enemy aircraft gave up and headed south.

Every day, the on-going air war was taking place over these fields. Although there were German fighter planes, mostly the Fw 190s, most of the aircraft I saw were our aircraft, of one type or another. That was encouraging; it indicated that the Allies were the dominant power in the air and the attacks I saw indicated that too. In particular, there seemed to be numerous attacks by our fighters against targets on the ground not far from my hiding place, probably lorries or armoured units. My barn and pond seemed like a tiny and vulnerable oasis in the middle of what was clearly an active war zone, with undoubtedly enemy troops and equipment stationed nearby. Nor did the action die down at night. After dark, the sounds of battle were frequent. At times, there was a fairly steady German heavy gun barrage from artillery emplacements close by. Presumably they were firing at Allied emplacements further north. But it wasn't just the artillery I heard. In the quieter periods, lying in my loft, I would sometimes hear Germans shouting to one another, presumably along the road but I couldn't really tell where the voices were coming from. Evidently the enemy was near and, in fact, probably all over this area.

And every day, my two French farmer friends would bring me the news, whenever they had any new developments to impart. But, as the days went by, it was anything but encouraging. The Allies had not broken through to Caen. They had been brought to a halt outside the city, even though the reports indicated that the British and American bombers were reducing it to smithereens. From what I was being told, it sounded as though Montgomery was deliberately holding back, maybe waiting for the Americans to make the break-out through the German lines first. The sources of news were the BBC wireless broadcasts to France and snatches of gossip that were passed around, so it was hard to know or be sure of much of anything in any detail. But the general picture I was putting together was beginning to seem fairly grim. Certainly, from the news and from what little I could see with my own eyes and hear with my own ears, the fighting seemed to be raging throughout a large part of Normandy. While D-Day itself had been a great success, the Germans were fighting back, and hard. Today, when we know the outcome of the fighting that followed the landings, it seems inevitable that the

Allies would sweep the Germans from Normandy. But, at the time, to me, holed up in a barn, getting snatches of news and knowing that there were German units all around, it seemed anything but a sure thing. There was no telling who would win and how long this would go on. My French friends told me that it would be madness to try to go west, to try to get back to Allied lines and I believed them. Occasionally, one or the other would take a different line, and begin talking about helping me to get back to the British lines but it was always in terms of "maybe tomorrow". Yet, the situation each new day looked just as bad as the previous day and, after a while, we stopped talking about this.

Toward the end of two weeks, I felt that I had to do something. Staying in this place indefinitely was out of the question. And it would be unfair to my French protectors. The longer I stayed, the greater the chance that they would be discovered to have been helping me. M. Laloy, in particular, I could tell, was getting increasingly nervous. Finally, he came out and told me so. Yet, who could blame him, considering the risks he was running both for himself and his family?

No, just staying on in this place, day after day, waiting for British or American troops to show up and rescue me, was not really an option. I would have to try to escape. If going west, into the heart of the battle, seemed far too dangerous, with German troops swarming all around, and the prospects of survival not much better if I were to head east or north, then there was really only one choice. I would have to make my way south, away from the battle. My thought was that I would head towards the Pyrenees. The Pyrenees, mind you, were several hundred miles away, so it would be a long and testing trip on foot. If I got there, however, I would be able to escape across the border to Spain, which was officially neutral. And from there, with time and luck, I should be able to make my way back to England. This plan, if one can call it that, may sound so roundabout a way of escape as to be mad. But, at the time, it seemed like the most sensible option, in fact, the only one, given the way the battle for Normandy was progressing, or rather, not progressing. M. Laloy thought it was almost as certain to fail as going west but his friend was more positive about the idea. Anyway, within a day or two of thinking about this possibility, I had made up my mind to try it.

Sometime during this period, M. Laloy brought me some civilian clothes to wear. A rough blue cotton shirt, some striped trousers, a brown jacket, a clean set of underwear, and the kind of cloth cap with a slight peak that most of the men around wore. For footgear, I was still wearing my cut off flight boots but with the slightly ragged tops covered by the trousers, they looked like ordinary shoes. With relief, I took off my by now filthy air force jacket and shirt and trousers and folded them up, stowing the uniform with my pistol in a coarse sack with a drawer string, which he had also given me. In preparation for my journey, I also spent some time tracing maps the two Frenchmen had left me on some tracing paper, noting the approximate distances. These crude map drawings would have to be my principal guide once I left the shelter of the barn. By this point, it had been more than two and a half weeks since I had been shot down and about twelve days since I had taken up residence in this little barn. I knew that I would have to make a break for it some time soon but I was still hesitating. After all, this had been a refuge of sorts for me and, by no means, the worst. But when M. Laloy and his friend came to me the morning of June 26th, they left me in no doubt that it was time to go. "It's too dangerous for you here, there are now some Germans in the village and they are coming along the roads in great numbers. You'll have to get out. It's too dangerous."

"Right," I said. "I'll leave at 12 noon and will get myself ready for leaving." But this was really just a case of getting myself ready mentally. There was nothing actually to do. Having a wash and a brush up before going wasn't an option and as for my "luggage", well my cloth sack was already packed with my possessions, namely my uniform and pistol.

M. Laloy said, and I could see the relief in his face, "All right, we will bring you some food at 10.00am and then you should just head south." He and his friend then left and I began to wait. There was, however, one thing I wanted to do: to try to get word to Margot that I was still alive and would get back to her. I wrote a brief letter to her and when M. Laloy returned, I would give it to him and ask him to give this to the first British Army member he met after the Allied troops began passing through Mery Corbon, and ask him to send it through the Army Postal Service.

M. Laloy and his friend reappeared at 10 as they promised. They handed over my last omelette and piece of bread, and some simple rations for my trek, and I gave M. Laloy the letter, with my request. They bid me adieu and wished me luck on my journey.

Though I had initially set my departure for mid-day, there was really no point in waiting for noon. I decided, soon after they had left that I might as well get going immediately. I took a deep breath, flung my sack with my few possessions over my right shoulder and walked out of the barn toward the road, opening the gate for the first time, and then closing it behind me. I turned right and began my trek south. With my rough country clothes, I would look like an itinerant worker of some sort. I had shaved the evening before so, while I might look dressed like a tramp, I wouldn't seem totally disreputable. The trick would be to stay calm, no matter whom I might meet along the way, to act as if there was nothing more natural than strolling with a sack on my back through a war zone, and to say as little as possible. A "Bonjour" or a grunt or two would be fine but anything more and my accent or words might be a dead give-away that I wasn't a local and probably not even a Frenchman.

My sang-froid was soon put to the test. Walking south, I

crossed the main road in the village, probably no more than 10 or 15 minutes after I'd set out from the barn. The road I had been walking along intersected the main road, which was the principal inland route between Le Havre and Caen and there happened to be several villagers near the crossroads, as I walked up to it. They just looked at me and didn't say a thing, just stared. I'm sure they knew or, at least suspected, that I must be the English pilot who presumably had left the village two weeks before. They certainly knew I wasn't a local and, given the situation all around the village, it was hardly likely that I was just someone out for a stroll down a country lane. As I crossed the main road, I tried to look relaxed, walking at a steady, and not too fast pace and not looking back at the villagers. Yet, a minute or so later, when I went over a slight rise and knew that I had left their staring eyes behind me, it was a great relief.

Ten minutes later, however, there was a much stronger test of my nerves. A camouflaged military motorcycle with a sidecar was coming down the road toward me. It had to be Germans because none of the French civilians used motorcycles and sidecars and it couldn't be anybody from our side, since this was German-occupied territory and no Allied officer would be travelling through like this. Sure enough, it was a German soldier on the motorcycle and with a German officer as his passenger – I couldn't tell what rank he held from my quick glance. As they approached, I lifted my free hand in a casual greeting and said "Bonjour", which they probably couldn't hear. They didn't acknowledge the wave or slow down. I could feel my whole body, which had been tense with fear, relax. They had taken me for a French peasant. So far, so good.

But I felt a spike of fear in my gut every time that I passed German soldiers or was passed by them. About an hour after starting, I was passed by a lorry full of German troops heading north. It was all I could do to just appear to stay calm, my expression impassive, and keep walking at a steady pace. At another point sometime during this day, two German soldiers on motorbikes, whom I assumed were doing some kind of patrol of the road, passed me three or four times. I avoided eye contact with them but each time I feared that they were going to stop and question me or ask for my papers, of which I had none. But, luckily for me, they didn't and I just kept going. Over the next hour or so, there were more lorries with German troops that passed. My confidence that I would probably not be stopped was beginning to grow.

The Normandy countryside is really very pretty, much of it gently rolling countryside, with fields and woods, with hedgerows bordering many of the fields, and plenty of grazing cows and sheep and horses. It was lovely countryside then and it remains that way today. But in the circumstances, I was in no mood to appreciate it. The sky was grey, with only occasional bursts of sunshine coming through, and my mood was edgy. At least, I told myself by way of consolation, it wasn't raining. And so on I went, just walking and walking. Today, Normandy has dual carriageways and other main roads, with the occasional roundabout but in 1944, all the roads were either two lane affairs, of greater or lesser width, while some of the back lanes were basically single lane roads, with occasional passing places. There were a few main thoroughfares, like the one that went through Lion d'Or but most of the roads were fairly narrow, tarmacked country lanes. It was an entirely rural setting, except when one came to a village or town. Yet, this sleepy countryside was simultaneously a war zone and death could appear at any moment.

I had set myself the ambitious goal of 50 kilometres for the day, or about 30 miles, but given the relatively late start, I was unlikely to make that distance. Furthermore, given the way I was sticking to the back roads, I would certainly not make 50 kilometres due south.

The early afternoon progressed in this way without further

incident. Around 3.30pm, I came to the small town of St Pierre, which is nearly due south of Lion d'Or about 12 kilometres but I had walked more than that, by keeping to the smaller back roads, which involved a certain amount of zig-zagging on my course. I walked through St. Pierre – I don't remember any incidents or anything special about it – and kept on heading south. Somewhere not too far past the town, about 4.00pm, I turned onto a new lane and there, straight ahead of me, were two SS guards, stationed on either side of the road. They had on the usual steel square bucket helmets, and were shouldering rifles. Beyond the two soldiers, maybe only another 10 yards further along, was a crossroads where an SS officer had stationed himself, looking up and down the four roads that met there. A man of medium height but a strong, stern expression. I felt my stomach sink with fear but I was only 30 yards away or so from the two guards and there was really nothing to do but proceed as if going by them meant nothing to me. To have turned aside or retreated would have had them on my tail in no time. So I just kept walking and passed the two soldiers, who seemed to pay me no attention. It was the officer whom I feared might make trouble and, inwardly, I was bracing myself for the worst. He was eyeing me up and down. As I passed him, I nodded and said, "Bonjour, Monsieur, Bonjour." He said nothing, only looked contemptuously at me. But before I could even begin to relax, I realised that the road was lined on both sides by troops of the SS, in their black uniforms, with the double white lightning flash insignia. They were sitting on the grassy verge, relaxing, with their rifles beside them, having some kind of rest period.

Again, there was no choice about what to do, there was no possibility of turning back. I had to keep on going but it felt like walking the gauntlet. All of them saw me and some pointed at me and laughed at my appearance – at least that's what I assumed they were laughing about – but I pretended to take no notice. I just kept on walking with as calm an appearance, and as little expression, as I could muster. This walk between the two lines of German soldiers lasted about 3 minutes, I estimate, but it felt like an hour. The real danger of discovery at any point was probably slight – why would they bother with this French tramp? – but my feelings during those 3 minutes, I can hardly describe. And towards the end, as I could see the empty road ahead, I began to think, "Well, if I get through this, the laugh will be on them. They're letting a British officer walk right through their midst." And that's what happened. I came to the end of the gauntlet and soon left them behind. The tightness in my gut soon unwound. It was a tremendous relief to have come through. And I was even luckier than I thought. The whole time, of course, I was carrying what would have been my death sentence in my sack had it been discovered, my RAF uniform and my pistol. An enemy soldier in civilian clothes is treated as a spy and the penalty for that is execution on the spot. Needless to say, RAF pilots weren't given any advice on this point either during the long period of training or at any time during the whole long period of operations.

Having passed the gauntlet of German soldiers, I now had open road ahead of me. But I was feeling stressed and exhausted and very, very thirsty by this point. I decided that I must ask for water at the next house I came to along the road. Only about 15 yards further along, after making this decision, I saw a chateau off to the left, at the end of a 100-metre drive lined with plane trees on both sides. I could see the front entrance to the building from where I stood on the road. This was it, I would ask for a drink, and possibly some food, from whoever lived in this imposing house. Surely, they wouldn't say no. I walked the 100 metres down the gravelly entrance drive and came to the front of the house. It then occurred to me, however, that it might not be wise for someone who looked like a tramp and spoke dodgy French to just knock on the front door. I decided instead to go around to the back entrance and ask for help from the butler or the maid or whomever it might be who answered a knock on the back door. I walked around to the rear and knocked twice on what might be the kitchen door and waited. Barely a few seconds later, a middle-aged, dark-haired Frenchwoman opened the door. She asked me what I wanted and I told her that I desperately needed a drink and could she spare some bread or something to eat? She looked doubtful or disapproving. She sensed that something was odd; it must have been the accent or perhaps just the rarity of people wandering the roads solo in wartime. So I came out with the truth: I told her I was a British pilot trying to make his escape. She looked flabbergasted. "This is the dining hall for the SS. You are not safe here, get out," she said quickly and quietly, evidently trying to control her voice, and closed the door before I could say anything.

Panic! I suddenly felt my heart beat faster with fear. I had walked right into the lion's den. This must be the mess hall for the officers of the SS troops I had just passed. My only thought was to get away from there as fast as possible but without running. I had to restrain myself: walk fast but not run. I retraced my steps as quickly as possible to the front of the chateau and made my way, walking fast, back down the drive toward the road. Somehow I managed to control myself and not look back, not once. The whole time I was striding back up the drive, I was wondering if there would be the sound of an opening door and boots on the drive, following me. Though I was walking faster, getting back down the drive seemed to take much longer than going up it. The thought of being captured by the Germans was intolerable and yet the possibility seemed strong. The woman had not been friendly at all. She could easily have told one of the Germans inside.

But fate was on my side. She had not betrayed me, after all. I reached the road and no one had followed. The thought that I was free to continue my march to freedom boosted my spirits. I was still thirsty but it no longer seemed so important after my narrow escape.

I was back on the road, heading south, always south. And I walked and walked. Wearily, the thirst coming back, wondering where I would be able to stop and when I could get a drink. Around 5.30pm, I found myself walking on the outskirts of an airfield with an aerodrome. Through the tall metal fencing, I could see that some Focke-Wulfs were being warmed up. I thought, "Christ, if only I can get over the fence and get into one of those, I could fly back to England, no problem at all." But a few seconds further reflection, of calculating the odds of getting away with this, and I gave up the idea. My chances of success, even if I could get into the aerodrome itself, would be slight. Someone looking like a French peasant running toward a parked aircraft would be apprehended long before he got into the cockpit. I reminded myself that I had got this far without being captured, and that it would be idiotic to try a stunt like that. So, I kept on going and soon came to what I realised must be the dispersal area for this aerodrome. Somewhere on the other side must be the mess hall for this aerodrome. Again, I started thinking of the need to get something to drink and, if possible, to eat.

There was nothing to do but keep going. Another hour of walking went by and my feet were really beginning to feel the distance they had travelled. My legs were aching with weariness and my feet were blistered inside my by now battered boots. It was very late afternoon by this time but I reckoned that there would probably still be three to four hours of daylight before it got completely dark – this was only five days past the longest day of the year. I, therefore, still had several hours to find shelter for the night. Nevertheless, weariness and discouragement were beginning to dominate my mood. And then I came to a small, and fairly isolated, house by the side of the road. This place, I figured, could not possibly be occupied by German soldiers. It was obviously a simple French residence in the countryside. I decided it would be worth taking the chance to knock on the door and ask for help. The worst that would happen, I figured, would be that I would be turned away and would be no worse off than before. I looked up and down the road. No one was coming. Good. I walked up the short path to the door and knocked.

A few seconds of waiting and then I heard steps, the sound of someone coming to open the door. The door opened and, to my surprise, I saw not one person but two, two little old ladies, in fact, looking at me in a curious but certainly not unfriendly, fashion. This time I did not say that I was a British pilot but only that I had been walking a long way and could they possibly help me a little by giving me a glass of milk or water. "Come in," they said and motioned me in. In my heart, I blessed them. This was the first friendly human contact I had had since saying good bye to M. Laloy and his friend that morning.

The place was fussy in a very comfortable, old fashioned French rural sort of way. It was filled with antique grandfather clocks and china and other knick-knacks on the sideboards and in the cupboards. It seemed like a wonderful, if temporary, little haven from the dangers outside.

The clocks all started chiming just after I entered the room so maybe it was 6.00pm exactly. I assumed that these ladies were elderly maiden sisters. In any event, they asked me to the table in the little dining room and brought me some bread and cheese and milk. It wasn't much in terms of quantity, and they probably had very little food to spare, but it felt wonderful. Only a few minutes before I had actually been thinking that the whole idea of escape was probably hopeless and that it might be best to turn myself in as a prisoner of war. Now, I felt my spirits restored, at least a little, and that I could go on. They asked me no questions – they were discretion itself – but I am sure they must have sensed I was an escaped Allied pilot, who happened to have a smattering of French.

Perhaps the whole respite lasted only 15 or 20 minutes but that was enough. I thanked them as warmly as I could with a few words of inadequate French and then said that I must not stay any longer but be on my way. They showed me to the door, wished me well with friendly smiles, and a minute later, I was walking south again.

Another hour and a half or so of up hill, down dale, past fields with grazing farm animals, the occasional farmhouse and barn, a few French farmers going about their business, all under grey and, by now, darkening skies. It was now about 8.00pm and I felt absolutely shattered with tiredness by this point. I had been walking about 10 hours, with barely a pause, and by now, the good effects of the short rest and meal with the elderly ladies had begun to wear off. I decided that the next village I came to, I would ask for help and try to find a place for the night. It had begun to rain lightly, adding to my misery.

A short time later, I found myself walking down a gentle hill into such a village, that of Grandmesnil. Coming slowly uphill towards me on a bike was an old man, a French postman, judging from his outfit. There was a bit of wobble in the bike, which, at first, I thought must just be due to his efforts in getting up the hill. But as soon as I stopped him and he looked at me, a little red and bleary-eyed, I knew where the bike's wobble was coming from. I could smell his breath. He was pissed as a newt. But I was feeling near the end of my resources at this point and just came straight to the point. "Je suis un pilote anglais echappé," I began, "Je…" but before I could get any further, he raised his right arm in a kind of drunken salute and shouted, nearly falling off his bike, "Ah, vivent les Anglais, vivent les Anglais," then, quieter and more soberly, "Voilà, suivez-moi, monsieur, je peux vous aider, suivez-moi." He dismounted from his bike, a bit unsteadily, turned it around and we walked into the village together, then up a side road to a farmhouse. The old postman was keeping up a friendly chatter the whole time but I really couldn't follow it. As we reached the kitchen door, he knocked on the outside, the lady of the house opened the door, and my guide explained the situation. She indicated immediately that she was willing to help, asked us both in and offered me cider, at first. But Normandy cider was too much for my gut to take so I asked for milk instead. The children of the house had, by now, come into the kitchen and gathered around me.

Their mother told me that the best thing to do would be to try to get the mayor's help and sent one of the older children to tell the mayor. In the meantime, the old postman was evidently still quite excited about the situation and every now and then would burst out with "Vive la France, vivent les Anglais". This was making me jumpy, to say the least. Finally, I told him in no uncertain terms that if he didn't shut up, I would shoot him. He quietened down after that.

The boy who had been sent to the Mairie soon came back and reported that the mayor himself was not around but that his wife had agreed to help me. I thanked the farmer's wife for the milk and her courtesy and was led by her son to the mayor's house in the village, perhaps 10 minutes walk from the farmhouse.

The mayor's wife was very elegant and seemed both concerned and a little appalled at my appearance. In fact, I must have looked pretty dirty and ragged by that point. And it suddenly occurred to me that nothing would feel so good as a soak in hot water. I asked her if I could have a bath. "Bien sûr," she agreed immediately.

Behind the farmhouse was a small pond of some kind, which, she told me, they used for water for washing their clothes. Next to the pond was a wooden shed with an open side and a big tub. Her help soon had the tub filled with hot water and they left me alone to undress and take my bath. A pile of clean towels lay nearby.

It felt like bliss! Hot water, soap to clean myself. I hadn't had a bath since falling into the trees that first day and had almost forgotten how good it felt to be clean. Even apart from beginning to feel clean, just sitting in the bath, feeling my muscles relax after the long march of the day, was pure pleasure and relief.

But it didn't last long. Suddenly, I became aware of the sounds of some disturbance coming from the front of the house. I tensed up, waiting to see what was going on. I couldn't make it out but it sounded like someone shouting or speaking in a very angry, agitated voice. A minute later, the mayor's wife came back to the shed and told me that her husband had returned and had told her that I had to leave, immediately. Apparently, the postman had being going around the village, drunkenly spreading the news about the English pilot. "It is too dangerous for you here," she said. This was the second time that day I had heard that. The unspoken message was that it was also too dangerous for them. She asked me to hurry and then left me, to go assure her husband that I would soon be on my way. I dried myself off quickly, got dressed, slung the sack over my shoulder and walked through the back yard and around to the front of the house. This was on the main street of the village, in a row of houses. The mayor himself was standing at the door of his house, looking both stern and I thought a little guilty, and other villagers were watching from their windows or from in front of their houses. I looked at them quickly, taking in the whole atmosphere, and I swear I never felt so friendless in my whole life. Friendless and truly dejected. As far as I could tell, there were no German soldiers nearby but it looked as if these villagers were not going to take any chances, any risks, in sheltering a British airman. It was the second time that day that I had left a French village with the people looking at me, slightly curious, maybe, but partly hostile, not wanting to get involved in any trouble I might bring them.

I walked down this street, away from the group staring at me, turned right at the first road, and was soon heading south again, up another shallow hill. The bath had helped but I felt so weary. And no wonder. I had in fact walked about 30 miles that day though, because of the many turns in my route, the distance was less than that, as the crow flies, from Lion d'Or. All that marching back and forth in the loft of my brick barn, just in order to do something and keep from going spare with inactivity, had helped keep me somewhat fit. But the march I had carried out that day had still been a big physical effort and my legs and feet were feeling it. It was worse than just physical tiredness, however. Things were beginning to feel hopeless and the thought that maybe it would just be best to give myself up crossed my mind again. But fortunately, there were no Germans around, hence no chance to do anything so foolish.

In fact, with the light beginning to fade, I wanted to find shelter soon. I didn't fancy sleeping rough, without even a thin blanket, in some field. And then, a few minutes after leaving the village, plodding up this hill, I heard footsteps behind me. As calmly as I could, I moved the sack around so that I could reach in and pull out my service revolver, holding it in front of me, and then returning the sack to my shoulder. I had never shot any one but I was prepared to do so, if it was necessary.

When the steps seemed really close, I wheeled around and pointed the revolver at the person who had just come up behind me. I was facing a middle-aged, dark-haired Frenchman, one of the villagers. He was startled to see the gun, and said, "No, no," he was now motioning me to put the gun down. "Just follow me. You want some help, okay?" I lowered the gun and put it back in the sack. "Yes, I do," I said. And he replied, "Right, follow me." We turned around and walked back, maybe only 50 yards to a small house that I had passed, which was evidently his home.

We entered the house and I saw two women and five children. One of the women was quite old – I presumed she was the man's mother – and was sitting at the table. The other woman was a very attractive brunette, perhaps in her mid-30s, standing by the table. She must have been my host's wife and the mother of the children. The children themselves seemed quite curious to see this unkempt stranger suddenly in their midst but they were quiet and well-behaved.

It seemed to me that within a minute of sitting down at the table, I was being presented with a feast of fried eggs, six in all, on a large plate. Now, in normal circumstances, two eggs would be plenty for me and the thought of eating six might be stomach-turning. But, in my present circumstances, this felt like a god-send. There was plenty of bread to go with the eggs. The man explained to me, "We've prepared this for you because we were certain you must be hungry." I managed to express my thanks before tucking into the eggs. As I sat there, gobbling down this meal, I looked at the kids, who were looking back at me, and wondered guiltily if I was eating a month's ration of their eggs. But, I told myself, they live in the country, so surely the family can get eggs when they need to. That's the kind of internal dialogue you have with yourself when you are doing something you desperately want to do but aren't entirely sure is right. This was the first proper meal I had had in 24 hours and it was fantastic. But I've never forgotten the expression of those kids, probably one mostly of surprise and curiosity, as they watched this dirty, ill-shaven stranger sitting at their table, eating this feast of eggs.

The whole time the man and the wife were asking me questions, trying to learn my story. Of course, I could understand their curiosity but the effort of speaking in French, at the end of such a tiring day, was too much. Also, it seemed best not to tell them too much, for their sake and for mine. So, sensing my wish to be reticent, they switched after awhile to telling me about themselves. I cannot remember the details but the friendliness of it all was wonderful and I was grateful.

Yet time was marching on, it would be completely dark soon

and I did not want to endanger these people who had so unexpectedly helped me. We were, after all, right at the edge of the village and my continued presence could well be a danger to them. I got up, and explained this briefly and said that I must be on my way now. The man wouldn't hear of it. He said, "I'm going to put you in a barn up the road and I'll come back at dawn tomorrow morning with some food and we can then discuss what to do."

I felt that I probably should have refused this hospitality, for the sake of this couple and their family. But while I felt restored by the wonderful meal, I could hardly face the thought of making my way down more country roads at night, as tired as I was, and not knowing what or whom I might run into. So, after a moment's hesitation, I accepted his invitation. I said goodbye to the family, again thanking the wife for the food. And by the last light of the day, at dusk, he led me to a nearby small barn, with a good mound of straw in the loft. He told me that he would be back in the early morning, with some breakfast, and that we could then discuss what to do. He then wished me good night and left. By the dim light, I could just see what poor repair the place was in. There were gaps between the boards of the wall and it felt, as a result, almost as if one was in the open air. Worse, there were rats scurrying around. This was the worst barn I had yet been in, if not the smelliest. But I was exhausted and didn't really care. The rats didn't bite me and I thought, as I drifted off to sleep, bone tired but with the comfort of a decent meal inside me and, having bathed a few hours before, cleaner than I had been in weeks. And I dozed on and off. Dawn came early and I woke just as it was beginning to be light. I checked my RAF watch; it was just past 5.00am. The place looked unfamiliar and it took a few seconds to remember where I was and what had happened. I sat up and thought about it. My new host had said he would bring breakfast but it seemed to me that the longer I stayed, the greater would be the risk to him and his family. I decided to get going and within a minute of that decision, left the barn, my sack over my shoulder, and was heading out across the field, in the early morning light of a grey dawn, going south again, away from the front.

I crossed several fields and came to another back road. There was no one about and I turned southwards on it. Within a couple of hours, perhaps a distance of 6-8 kilometres from the place where I had spent the night, I found myself walking through another village. Its name was Norrey-en-Auges. It must now have been about 8.00am or so but, at first, I did not see anyone up and about. There was a line of houses to my right, some fields with cows on the left, and beyond a village green, and beyond that a church. Against the front wall of one house, a whitewashed stone building, there was an old black bicycle. It was not locked to a railing, but simply leaning up against the wall. Not a fancy bike. It had no gears or any extras, just an old-fashioned balloon tyre bike. It immediately occurred to me that this might be my best chance of escape. If I was going to get to the Pyrenees, it would be much easier to get there, or at least part of the way, by cycling rather than on foot.

I tied a loop in the top part of my sack, swung it over my head, so that it was hanging down my back, took a quick look around – I now saw a woman doing something in the garden at the other house but maybe she wouldn't notice what I was doing. With just a second rapid glance around, I mounted the bike and was off. This was great. Even on this kind of bike you are moving at least three times faster than on foot. I felt like I was flying along, compared to my previous plodding pace. I was now heading east but within a kilometre, I came to another crossroads. There were several ways to go, which meant that if anyone had been following me, I might lose them here. I turned south and kept on cycling. I was just beginning to relax, as I sailed along, but maybe only 5 minutes after I'd made the turn, there was a hell of a shout behind me. Three young Frenchmen, teenagers actually, were chasing me on their bikes and telling me to stop, yelling "Arrêtez, arrêtez." Though I wasn't feeling nearly as tired as I had been the previous day, my legs were still stiff from all the walking I had done and I simply couldn't pedal as fast as they could.

Within a minute or two, they had caught up with me, and forced me to stop and dismount. One was maybe 16 or 17, the other two looked a little younger. The eldest was sputtering angry, furious really, and said, "You've stolen my bike. Show us your papers. Who are you?" There would have been no point in denying that I had taken the bike – they had me with the stolen goods in hand after all – and it seemed equally pointless either to try to get away or to explain. As for showing them my papers, that was impossible, I had none. The only thing was to stay calm and just walk away from them, hoping that they would let it rest there. Although they were kids, there were three of them and I was in no mood for a punch-up. So, I just said, "I'm sorry, here's your bicycle back. Thank you very much, sorry about this," and turned to walk off, sack shifted to my shoulder, down the road.

"Come back," one of them shouted behind me, "we're going to take you to the gendarmerie."

Being turned over to the gendarmerie was the last thing I needed at this point. I turned around and said, "No, don't do that please. Just let me go. I meant no harm."

Somehow the arguing went on with them for a few minutes. The leader kept on demanding to see my papers, wanting to know who I was, where I was going, why I had stolen the bike. I was not disposed to tell him so I kept trying to fob him off with non-answers. After a bit, he looked hard at me, I'm sure noticing that my accent was odd, and said, "You must either be a German who has deserted or you're a British pilot."

From the way he said it, I felt certain that he would view me in a much kinder light if it was the second possibility rather than the first so there was nothing to be lost at this point by telling the truth. "I'm a British pilot," I replied.

But he was sceptical, at first, and I couldn't blame him. If I'd been a German deserter, it would be smarter in these circumstances to claim to be a British pilot than an AWOL German soldier. "How do we know that?" he asked.

Quick as a flash, I told them that I would show them my RAF watch, with its wings' insignia on the back. I took off the watch and handed it to him, adding that I had my uniform in the sack, if they wanted to see it. They did. I undid the sack and showed them the uniform. That did it. They believed me and, instantly, the atmosphere changed. Within seconds, it had gone from hostility and suspicion to friendliness and a wish to help.

One of the others immediately said, "Okay, we believe you. Come back to our village. We can help you." I could see that they'd had a change of heart but, given my experiences the previous day, I was doubtful that they could give me much actual help. A little food, perhaps, and then it would be a matter of hitting the road again, in this case, retracing the distance I had just come. Besides, their village wasn't all that far from the one I'd spent the night at, where it seemed half the populace had watched me walk down the street. I reckoned that the odds of staying in Norrey-en-Auges undiscovered for any length of time were slim. It would be best to just keep on going. I said, "No, no, no, I'm not coming back with you. Thanks for the offer but it's best if I just keep on going."

Now the leader of the group, the one who had challenged me, chimed in, trying to convince me. "Come on, come on back, there are no Germans in our village. We can look after you, we've got somebody who can look after you."

But I persisted. There really seemed no point in retracing my steps, when I would only have to get going later that day or the next. "No, no," I said, "thank you but I'm heading for the Pyrenees and that's that. But thank you for the offer of help." They remonstrated with me for a bit more but could see that I was determined, so wished me well on my journey. And, saying our adieux, I turned around and started walking south again. From the quietness behind me, they must have just looked at me for another 10 seconds or so, and then I heard the sound of their bike tyres, which diminished and then vanished behind me as I put one foot in front of another, going south. Once again, I was walking through the Normandy countryside, past fields, between the endless hedgerows, up and down gentle dales, under the ever-grey skies. My legs no longer ached and I thanked God I'd resisted the temptation to give myself up. There was nothing more I wanted now than to reach the Pyrenees and make my escape.

Yet, an hour later, or not much more than that, I heard shouts from behind me. I looked around to see what it was all about. It was the same three young Frenchmen. I was completely amazed to see them again. I thought that I had been given away and my hope of escape rescinded. But no, they had come back to help me.

They had brought me some food in a hamper. They quickly explained that they knew that I must be hungry and felt that, at least, they should give me some food. Well, of course I was hungry and I felt grateful to them to have brought this meal. There was some meat, cheese, a chunk of bread, and some water and red wine to drink. We sat down on the grass by the road and I devoured the food. I hadn't been thinking about food but now, eating, realised that I had been famished. But, beyond that, it was good to feel that, once again, I was not completely on my own, I was getting some help.

Again, as I was eating, they returned to the subject of what I should do. The eldest, whose name was André, André Delattre, made the argument again that I should come back with them and that they would look after me. He reiterated that there were no Germans in the village, that it would be safe for me and that they could arrange some accommodation. And now it began to seem like a better proposition.

Was it the effect of the wine or the evident friendliness of André and his companions that persuaded me? Probably a mixture of both. A little more than an hour before I was determined to keep on going. But now, having eaten and drunk with them and seen that they were really keen to help me, I decided to accept their offer and go back with them to Norrey-en-Auges. André motioned me to get on his bike and I balanced on the cross-bar as he pedalled back the four or five kilometres to the village. It was probably only a 20-30 minute or so ride but the effect on my poor backside was noticeable and it was such a relief to get off that bike, when we arrived back in the village. But we hadn't gone straight back. To reduce the chances of being seen, we had taken some back lanes and paths and arrived by a somewhat roundabout route, at a big stone farmhouse in the village where I had taken the bike. As I got off the bike, André said to wait for a minute, that they had an idea for somewhere safe for me to stay but that he was just going to talk with the man he had in mind. It had been a rough ride down the dirt lanes and by-ways and my backside and I were delighted to be off the bike.

He disappeared into the back of the house and a few moments later, motioned me to come in. I was greeted by a short Frenchman of about 35 years, with brown hair. His name was Henri Lair and he greeted me with a handshake and a friendly "Come on in, you can stay with us." Henri was the farmer-owner of the property and he lived there with his wife, Marie, and his as yet unmarried 25-year-old sister, Alice, who worked on the farm.

They offered me some cider and wanted to know something of my story. Though secrecy had become quite a habit with me over the preceding three weeks of being on the run, I told them the basic story. They repeated what André had said, that they almost never saw German soldiers here, and they assured me

that they could shelter me in safety. It could be done with no one
else in the village knowing, they said, because the three boys
who had chased, and then befriended me, could be trusted to
keep quiet and no one else besides them knew. They had a little
outbuilding facing the front door, which had a bed and where I
could stay. The bed, in fact, was as I soon saw, a big,
comfortable French bed, with wooden sides and a decent
mattress. It was really just a storage room with a big bed; I
would have to wash outside. But it would be a safe hideaway,
safer than the main farmhouse, because it was just an auxiliary
building, to which no one came specifically and was hidden from
the nearby road, within the L-shape made by the farmhouse with
the big barn. The whole set-up was small but perfect. I thought
how wonderful it would be to be able to sleep in a real bed, once
again. Then we went back to the kitchen.

By this point – it was sometime in the early afternoon – I was
feeling very tired, not so much from the day itself as from the
whole experience of the previous 30 hours since I had left Lion
d'Or. It hadn't really been that long, when measured in hours,
but it felt much longer, in terms of what I'd been through and
seen. My body was beginning to relax from the tension of the
whole journey and it was as if I could, at last, let my guard down
and experience the weariness. The key thing was that I felt I
could trust these people. Henri had to go about some work, as
did the two women, and for several hours, I just relaxed in a
chair in the kitchen. I think I must have dozed on and off. The
time passed in a haze and I remember little about the next few
hours except for the warmth of the stove and being grateful that
I was no longer trudging the roads of the Normandy
countryside.

Dinner was a simple affair, being just a supper in the late
afternoon. I don't remember what the food was but I do
remember their being surprised at my choice of drink: milk.
They had offered cider and calvados but it was milk I craved

and, though they clearly thought it was a bit humorous for a grown man to want milk, they obliged. And like all the milk I had had, it was good fresh creamy milk straight from the farmer's cows.

Henri showed me back to the little guest house and said good-night, as he went off to milk his three cows. That was part of his evening ritual, milking the three cows they owned.

One of the women had left me a bowl of warm water for washing, a toothbrush and some cold water for cleaning my teeth. This all felt like luxury. Though it was still early evening, I undressed and went to bed almost immediately, and slept like a log. It was the first real bed I'd had in three weeks and it was heavenly, beneath the quilt, on a good mattress and soft feather pillows. A huge improvement on filthy, lumpy straw. There were no rats and there was a decent roof over my head. It was wonderful.

7

A refuge in Norrey-en-Auges and I become "Roger Gasnier"

I'm not sure how long I slept, maybe 10 hours or so but I woke with a start. It was about 6.00am and daylight was just beginning to show through the curtains. What had woken me up, however, was not the light but some noise. There was the sound of loud banging nearby, the sound of someone knocking hard on a door. Once again, because my sleep had been deep, there were a few seconds of disorientation, trying to remember where I was and how I got there. And then it all came back. Still, there was this banging sound, not on my door but nearby. I'd better investigate, I thought.

I quickly got out of bed and went to the curtained window of this little chalet and peeked out cautiously through the crack in the curtains. To my horror, I saw two German soldiers, rifles resting on their shoulders, standing at the back door of the farmhouse, waiting to be let in or talk to someone. In deep fear, I only watched them for another few seconds but long enough to see the door opening, then I pulled back from the window. Christ, I thought, had these French people, who had been so kind to me the day before, actually been lying about the safety of the village? That is, lying about there being no Germans about? But there was no time to lose, wondering about this. I simply had to get out of sight quickly and just pray that I wasn't going to be turned in. Where could I hide myself, though? It was a small, open room, the wardrobe probably wasn't deep enough to hold me and, even if it were, it would be the first place that anyone would look if there was a search. There was only one possible place: under the bed.

But this bed, its wooden frame made of oak, felt as if it weighed a ton. Still, there was nothing for it, I had to get under it somehow – and fast. It's amazing what strength you can muster when the motivation is there. I say that because, somehow, on my knees, I managed to lift this heavy farmhouse bed just enough to be able to crawl underneath it. Fortunately, there was adequate space underneath and a cover coming down to the floor, which effectively hid me. I lay there, heart pounding at first, both from the exertion and from the fear. Even where I now was, I could hear a conversation going on outside, some of it in German phrases. I'm not sure how much time went by. It felt like ages but was probably only five or ten minutes. And then the conversation stopped. The two soldiers must have finished their business, whatever it was, and gone away.

The silence and the waiting were broken by a knock on the door. Not a loud knock of the kind the Germans had been making but a softer one and then there was the sound of the door opening and someone coming in. A woman's voice, Alice's, said in wonder, "Frank, où êtes-vous?" "Where are you?"

"I'm under here," I said.

A pause and then she said, "Under the bed?"

"Yes."

"Mon Dieu. Ce n'est pas possible!"

I assured her, from under the bed, that it was. But there was no way that I could now lift the bed to get out from under it and Alice knew that she wouldn't have the strength for it either, so she went and got help. Well, it took three people to lift it, Henri, his wife Marie, and Alice, so that I could crawl out. It just shows how much strength complete fear can give you for a few moments, as I had when scrambling to get underneath that bed. I would never have been able to do that with just ordinary motivation.

As soon as I had crawled out and stood up, I explained, "Look, I was frightened the Germans were after me." Henri reassured me immediately. "No, no, they only wanted some eggs and butter and milk. And they paid for them, too." But there had been a threat, as well. If Henri had not agreed to sell them the food, the soldiers let him know that they would search until they found what they wanted and then just take it. So their offer to buy the milk and eggs and butter was one that Henri could hardly refuse. He also told me that they had told him that their unit had just moved into the village the preceding night and would be billetted there for awhile. In effect, I had arrived in Norrey-en-Auges one step ahead of the Germans.

My sense of the previous day, that of having, at last, found a temporary safe haven immediately began to vanish. I was now in the heart of a village actively occupied by German troops, not just a place for them to pass through. Henri reassured me again, saying that if I kept to the little outhouse, I would be safe. The Germans must be falling back slowly under the Allied assault, moving south, but there was no reason why, if I stayed hidden, I shouldn't be safe. In fact, when I thought about it, it seemed a better bet than either trying to go north or continuing south, if that was the direction more of the enemy were heading in.

Then, something happened which gave me an unexpected degree of protective cover. Later that day, a whole crowd of refugees, fleeing the bombardment of Caen, had arrived on foot. A group of these people, carrying their few possessions in valises and sacks, maybe 15-20 in all, had come to the farm, knocked on the door and asked if they could be allowed to stay in the large barn for a few days. Henri immediately agreed. A few days later, he suggested that I leave my little room and mingle with the refugees, but without talking, to make it look as if I too was one. He guessed, correctly, that they were in too much shock about their own situation to care at all about this other stranger in their midst.

This seemed a good idea. So, for several days, I did just this. It allowed me to melt into the background, as just one more person displaced by the war, and not have to spend all day hiding in the cottage, out of sight. As far as I could tell, these refugees were a small number of family groups, who did not know each other except as fellow travellers who had lost their homes in Caen. As an isolated individual, I would be, Henri argued, just one more anonymous person fleeing the Germans. He was right. The refugees showed little curiosity about me and I got by with no more than the occasional, "Oui, merci", "Non", "Eh bien?", etc. Henri mingled more and talked with them. But the whole time I was conscious of, and increasingly nervous about, the fact that I had no papers. If the German soldiers now staying in the village should decide to do an identity check on the refugees, I would be caught immediately.

When there was a moment to talk with Henri alone, I brought this up. I knew that André himself had false identity papers. Like many young Frenchmen, he had been conscripted by the Germans to work in Germany but he had evaded their net twice. He was from Paris but had come to Normandy to stay and hide out in this village under a new identity, staying with his sister and brother-in-law. It was their house from which I had nicked the bike that first day. I asked André about the possibility of obtaining some false identity papers and he indicated that he thought it could be arranged and that I should leave it with him.

Three days later, he presented me with my new identity card: "Roger Gasnier, Agriculteur" – Roger Gasnier, farm labourer. There it was, at last, my "papers", a new identity and, at the same time, an excuse for my new situation: I was, clearly, a farm

labourer who had been driven from his place of work by the war.
Mind you, it was a pretty poor job as a forgery. Anyone looking
at it closely or with a modicum of suspicion would probably see
that it wasn't genuine but it was a lot better than nothing. And it
would probably pass muster on any quick routine inspection by
German troops. Having it gave me a sense of security that I had
not had since I'd started on my journey from Lion d'Or.

From then on, I was "Roger" to Henri, André and Alice and
the few others who were in on the secret. They addressed me as
"Roger" no matter who was around and I responded as
"Roger". In fact, I started forgetting to think of myself as
"Frank". But that was all right: I didn't need to do so here.

Within a few days, the refugee group from Caen soon drifted
on, further south I think. With my new identity, and the cover
story that I was a friend of the family, this did not arouse
suspicion. Also, I was now eating regularly, I could wash when
I needed too, I had a very comfortable bed, and with my identity
card, I no longer feared being stopped by any Germans in the
village, when I went for the occasional walk. And as the
Germans settled in, so did I. They would often come to the
kitchen door, with a request for eggs or chickens. But I no longer
jumped out of my skin when I saw them at the door.

There was only one problem. I was beginning to be bored.
Just a few days before, I had been an escaped RAF pilot, rather
desperate and more than a little afraid, carrying his uniform in
a sack, on the run, increasingly exhausted and discouraged. I
had even had my moments wondering if it wouldn't be simpler
and safer just to turn myself over to the Germans and wait out
the war as a POW. Now I was a fairly contented house guest of
these great people who were sheltering me, providing me with
good food, a good bed and a sense of safety. As a result, time
was beginning to hang heavy on my hands. It just shows how
quickly a change of circumstances can alter one's frame of mind
and attitude.

Why not join in the work on the farm, I thought? After all, I was now officially an "agriculteur". So, one evening, a few days after becoming Roger Gasnier, I said to Henri, "I want to come out into the fields and help you to work." At the time, they were hoeing up their potatoes so this seemed to be the natural thing to join in on. Henri looked a little surprised at the request – it had never been part of our understanding that I would earn my keep while his guest – but he shrugged slightly and said something like, "Well, of course, if you would like to…"

The next morning, I began my career as a true "agriculteur", hoeing up potatoes, with a group of women, as it happened. It looked easy enough. You plunged the tines of the hoe in the earth, and raked up the soil over the growing potatoes. But I was slow. It seemed to me that each of these women managed to do two rows while I was struggling to complete half a row. By noon, I was knackered, and had the beginnings of blisters on both hands. When we quit at lunch-time, Henri came to see how I was doing. With one quick look, he sized up the situation and said to me – with kindness and no hint that he found it funny, which he must have – that digging up potatoes was clearly not my thing and that it would be fine if I just stayed at the house out of sight and passed the time there. He assured me that there was really no need for me to try to earn my keep. I forget the exact words he used on this occasion but the message was clear enough and I had to agree with him. It was true. I had grown up as a town lad, not a farm boy, and it wasn't likely that I was going to be much good as a farm labourer. So, that was my first and last attempt to do any serious work on the farm. But, often in the evening, when Henri and Alice went out to milk the cows, I accompanied them and their mule. The milk was poured from the milk pails into large aluminium containers, and I would help load the containers on to the back of the mule, who would carry them back to the house. And sometimes I would help in small ways at the open oven on the farm, where Henri and his wife and Alice baked their bread for themselves and their helpers.

During the days, I increasingly wandered around the village to break the monotony of staying in my little room. With my rough French country clothes and my identity card, I felt safe as long as I didn't say too much. On the first walk, which I took with André, we met a number of German soldiers, "Huns" as I thought of them, and they were surprisingly polite, greeting us with "Bonjour" and the occasional offer of a cigarette. In fact, I soon found myself coming into contact with them and having short, friendly conversations about this and that – but not about the war itself. I suppose one might say that I was fraternising with the enemy but since they didn't know who I was and I was careful not to express any opinion that might give my identity away, it seemed more a game on my part, one that I enjoyed.

By and large, they were most friendly to the French, including me, and their relations with Henri and the others on the farm were quite correct, considering that they were occupying the country. They would often bring some sugar or coffee for which Henri would give them, in return, eggs or butter. On one occasion, two Germans sat a whole evening and told us their life histories. One came from Essen and his wife and children had been bombed out of their house on one of many Allied bombing raids of that city, the children having become separated temporarily from their mother. He proudly showed us pictures of his wife and children and since his French was poor, I felt safe talking to him in my poor French. He was clearly fed up with the war and wished it would end soon, though he didn't say so in so many words. He was clearly not any kind of dedicated Nazi. His mate had a similar story, his wife and children having had to flee Allied bombing of his town in the Ruhr and he too was tired of the war. I suspected that many of the German soldiers felt the same way. Altogether, it was quite a friendly and enjoyable evening, not least because I could enjoy the fact of knowing that they were talking to an Englishman, an RAF pilot no less, and they didn't have a clue. I did, however, mostly just listen when the Germans were present, talking little.

Of course, there were die-hard cases amongst the Germans, too. One day, some leaflets in German, aimed at the German troops, wafted down from British aircraft flying high over the village. André picked one up and asked a German who spoke good French to translate it into French. This he did most willingly and told us that it said that the Russians were approaching Berlin, that the Allies had landed huge quantities of war material and men in Normandy and that to fight on was useless. When he finished, he sort of snorted and said, "Propaganda!" He looked at us and said, without a visible doubt in his face or his words, that Germany could not be beaten and that they would fight to the end. He seemed utterly convinced that Germany would win the war. We did not argue against him as we did not want to arouse any suspicion or hostility. But, as we discovered, this was still the general belief amongst the German soldiers.

A lighter moment came one day when I was visiting André's sister at her house, while she was cooking lunch, with her little boy, Pierre, running around the kitchen, playing, making noise. Two Germans knocked at the door with a few eggs, which they politely asked her to cook for them. Though they were courteous, this was not a situation where any answer except "yes" would do. She therefore started frying the eggs, while the two Germans who had pulled up chairs at the kitchen table, waited. In broken French, and probably more simply to pass the time than out of any real curiosity, one of the soldiers asked me if this woman, who was both young and very pretty, was my wife. It seemed simplest just to say "yes" and because André's sister, Suzanne, was, indeed, very attractive, the two soldiers indicated that they thought I was a lucky man and indicated their approval. Naturally, the other one asked if Pierre was my son, to which I replied, "yah yah". Having told the first lie, it would have been a mistake to start telling the truth. Fortunately, Suzanne had her back to these young men and a good thing too. A quick glance at her and I could see that she was quivering slightly, obviously trying not to betray that she was almost splitting her sides with silent laughter. But she controlled herself and by the time the eggs were ready, she was able to serve them with a completely serious, and polite, demeanour. These two soldiers became quite friendly and would visit the house with small allotments of sugar, coffee, and cigarettes. One day, they also presented a whole roll of some material that had been looted from Caen. Though it was stolen French goods, it was very welcome, given the shortage of material for clothes making and mending.

Time passed very pleasantly and my fears of the Germans decreased as each day went by without my being found out. In a sense, I had settled into a rather comfortable life, with my own room, enough to eat, and a social circle that consisted of Henri Lair, his wife and his sister, and André and André's sister's family. I even went to church with them on Sunday, in black Sunday outfits, mine being rather ill-fitting. There were also the polite exchanges with the German soldiers on these occasions and others in the town. I was taken for just another villager from Norrey-en-Auges by them and the whole thing soon began to seem almost normal.

One day, we saw two Germans trying to catch Jacko, the donkey we used for carrying the milk. I think that it was just for sport, just for something to do. These two soldiers were not doing very well in controlling Jacko, so, knowing that the mule knew and trusted me, we walked over to them, to lend a hand. Jacko let me hold his head gently, while the two Germans mounted. The whole time I was trying to keep a straight face because I knew that as soon as I let go, they would not stay on board long. And I was right. As soon as I let go of Jacko's head, and stood back a couple of steps, Jacko bucked and threw both of them over his head. There was an unintended audience of both Frenchmen and other German soldiers for this scene and there were roars of laughter from both groups when Jacko threw off his passengers. As it happened, one of them broke his ankle as he hit the ground. He had to be helped, hopping on his one good foot, by one of his fellow soldiers, not exactly a glorious casualty of war. But I have to say that he took it in good spirit, without too much obvious embarrassment for what really was a stupid and unnecessary accident, and I felt a little sorry for him.

But while my own situation had begun to seem quite safe, even positively quiet and domestic, the whole time the war was still going on around us and we were aware of it constantly. And not just from the presence of German troops in the village. Throughout most of July, we were at most only 30 miles from the front and you could often hear the artillery further north. Also, of course, there were frequent overflights by British and American aircraft and German ones. Overall it was clear that the Allies had primary control over the skies, even if they didn't on the ground. There were, however, a number of dogfights that we saw. But only once did I see one of our aircraft shot down. The fights usually ended with the Huns as the losers, either shot down or fleeing. When I saw one of these kills, I had to restrain myself and never show my feelings about it, certainly not shout anything, as I had outside my barn in Lion d'Or, since there were often German soldiers around witnessing the same events. But I silently rejoiced every time an enemy plane was shot down.

In the Lair household, we kept up with the news by means of an old crystal set hidden in the chimney, which we took out from its hiding place and listened to at least once every day, usually at night, around the kitchen table. The sound was fairly terrible – you literally had to bring two crystals together to get the transmission – but it was good enough to get the gist of what was happening in the war. It was on this radio set that I first heard about "doodle-bugs" being used to bomb London. The French term was "avion sans pilote". Hearing about these reminded me immediately of course about our earlier attacks on the V1 installations.

Using this set, however, was not without risk because of the German soldiers who were camped out in the village. They all felt free to enter the house without much more than a quick knock, or not even that, to ask for an egg to be cooked or the like. If any of them had caught us listening to the crystal set, the least that would have happened would have been confiscation of the radio. But there might have been punishment of some kind as well. Still, we were never caught. So, it was the secret broadcasts that were our main source of news from the front. And it continued to be disappointing. Progress was being made on the Cotentin peninsula and the fighting around Cherbourg, mostly involving American troops, was pretty fierce before the Allies broke through enemy lines. The Germans were clearly fighting back strongly, especially around Caen. It was apparent, four and more weeks after the start of the invasion, that Normandy was not being taken by the Allies in a walk, not by a long shot. Patton's army had come south from the Cotentin peninsula and was now coming around the back of Caen, as it were. But the city was still held by the enemy and the progress of the American and British forces seemed agonisingly slow.

Yet, it was also clear that the Germans were taking some heavy punishment and that this was beginning to take its toll on their morale. One day, two Germans, driving two large wagons, stopped in front of the farmhouse, got out and demanded cider and eggs. André questioned them and learned that one lorry was filled with ammunition, the other with petrol. They were taking both of these loads to the front at Caen. They admitted that they didn't like doing this job in the daylight because they felt they were sitting ducks for the "Tommies" of the RAF. (To many of the Germans, all British servicemen were "Tommies", not just those serving in the Army.) In fact, they said they would rather have the Tommies machine-gun their trucks from the air well before they got to the front rather than at the front, where the fighting was so intense. In a way, I was surprised to hear this from them, that they would be so candid about their fears to French civilians (plus one Brit in Frenchman's clothing!) in occupied France. In telling us this, did they really think we would be sympathetic to their plight? Or were they just getting it off their chests, thinking that it didn't matter really what we thought. (Probably the latter.) Of course, we tried to look poker-faced at this, and certainly didn't say anything unsympathetic. But in incidents like these, you could get a glimpse of German morale beginning to crack.

To my great satisfaction, they got their wish. Four miles down the road, this two wagon convoy was strafed by Spitfires and the vehicles were turned into wizard flamers. The two drivers, however, escaped since they abandoned their lorries at the first sign of the Spitfires. This incident was seen by several Frenchmen, who expressed their pleasure later that evening. In fact, the German fear of strafing of their vehicles was quite general. Many of the vehicles had a soldier stationed on the running board, whose job was to look out for approaching British or American aircraft. If any were spotted before the aircraft saw them, the lookout would immediately tell the driver and he would quickly try to conceal his vehicle.

As the fighting drew nearer, the danger to the village was two-fold. First, that it could become a battle-site itself, with all the dangers to life and property that would be involved. The second, and even more imminent, danger was that the Germans would evacuate the village, as they had done repeatedly on their retreat from the coast. Why did the Germans turn villages that they themselves were leaving into ghost-towns? It was just total war that they were fighting, as simple as that. The more refugee French civilians there were, the greater the headache for the advancing Allied forces and, potentially, the slower their advance. Anything that could help German forces, even marginally, they would do.

In any event, when the order to evacuate was given, the Germans expected total and instantaneous obedience. Civilians who refused to cooperate risked paying with their lives. I know this because I watched one man, who ignored their commands, pay the penalty.

It was early one evening in early August – I had been with the Lair family for more than five weeks at this point – and two of the lads and I were returning with the mule from milking the cows. We were going down the road, returning to the farm, when we came up with a group of refugees, maybe a dozen or so, moving south. We fell in with them; there was no reason not to. All of a sudden, maybe just two or three minutes later, a German lorry came along. We moved out of the way but the lorry came to a stop just in front of the group of pedestrians. An officer got out of the front seat and ordered everyone who had been trudging down the road, the refugees and us, to line up by the side of the road. For a moment, my heart started beating faster with fear. Had someone tipped them off about me? Were they looking for me or escaped British pilots? Or were they going to shoot the whole group of us, perhaps in reprisals for some act of the French resistance? That there were reprisals, of course, we knew from word-of-mouth and they happened not infrequently. One of the lads from the Lair farm could sense my tension and fear that this was about me, however, and he told me to relax, no one was looking for me. How he could know that, I didn't ask myself but his words had a calming effect.

But in a moment, all became clear. An old Frenchman, with a grey fringe and a grey moustache, he must have been about 70 or so, was pulled out of the lorry by German soldiers. He was then frog-marched to the edge of the wood that bordered the field just across the road from where we were lined up. He was blindfolded and roped to a tree. The German officer explained to the crowd, in good French, what was happening. The old man, it seemed, had disobeyed the order to leave his village, when the evacuation order had been given. For this he was to be shot. Our role would be simply to witness the execution. In effect, we were there to help spread the word and tell everyone whom we might meet what the penalty for disregarding an evacuation order was.

Altogether, eight soldiers were now lined up, their rifles set, aiming at the old man tied to the tree. He was just an old man who hadn't wanted to leave his house, probably the house he had lived in most of his life and he was now about to be killed for that. He had taken it all very calmly and resignedly – he wasn't fighting or struggling to get free or hysterically begging for his life or anything like that. Yet he could have been in no doubt, even blind-folded, about what was about to happen to him. Suddenly, the order to fire was given, the shots rang out, and he slumped against the tree, his head hanging forward. The German officer then designated four of the men in the crowd to remove the body and bury it. One woman and several children were crying, while many people were trying to keep back tears. It had been murder, cold-blooded murder, and carried out just to make a point and to spread fear.

At that moment, I really hated the Germans, in a way that I do not believe I had previously, at any point in the war until then. It's one thing to hear about atrocities. You ask yourself how human beings could do such things, you shake your head in disbelief and anger and disgust but then you go on about your business and forget it. But it's quite another thing to be an actual witness to one, especially when you have been deliberately forced to watch it. At that moment, I boiled with hatred for the Germans, not just the German soldiers who had killed the old man or the officer who had given the command but all Germans – men, women and children. I wanted to see them all killed, every last German. That mood didn't last long but it was what I felt at that moment.

But it was certainly not just I who had been shocked by this execution. The incident was talked about for days in the village. In a sense, the Germans had accomplished precisely what they had wanted to accomplish. Everyone in the village was afraid now, afraid that the order to leave their homes might soon come, afraid to disobey that order, should it be given.

In a way, this event was part of what set the stage for what followed next. André and his sister and brother-in-law, the very tall Roger Hervieux, held a council and decided that it might be best to leave before being ordered to do so. There was a house near Sees, a big town about 50 kilometres almost due south, which was owned by a relative, the aunt of André and Suzanne. They had been told they could find shelter there, if need be, and they decided that this was what they should do. I started discussing with André and Henri the fact that I should probably also get going too, and continue my way south. After all, it was beginning to look like an odds-on possibility that the safe haven in Norrey-en-Auges, which I had stumbled into quite by accident, might soon disappear.

But just a day or two later, there was a specific event that occurred and it was this that directly led to my departure. That day, I had dropped in on André, Suzanne and Roger, at their house and was chatting with them in their sitting room. It was about noon. Roger worked on the farm owned by the mayor of the village, partly as a horse trainer, partly doing various odd jobs around the mayor's farm, which was one of the larger ones in the vicinity of the village. He had just returned from work for lunch, maybe 5 or 10 minutes earlier, when there was a knock on the front door. Roger got up and went to the door, which opened on to the lounge, to see who it was. The visitor was his employer, the mayor. The discussion started in an easy enough fashion but then built quickly into quite a fierce row though I couldn't make out exactly what it was about. But one sentence of the mayor's came through loud and clear. "If you talk to me like that, I shall tell the Germans that you are sheltering a British pilot," as he nodded toward me. The argument spluttered to a close within a few seconds or maybe a minute after that and the mayor left. Roger turned around, looking a bit shaken.

What had it all been about? It seems that Roger had been hinting that he might leave to take another job and the mayor was determined to keep him. Labour in the region was quite scarce because of the war and good workers were even more so. He wanted to keep Roger and this was the rather stupid way he chose to do so, by trying to frighten Roger into staying on.

The immediate consensus amongst my friends was that it was no longer safe for me in Norrey-en-Auges. In my weeks of wandering around the village, practically everyone except the Germans had learned that this stranger who had settled into Norrey-en-Auges was an escaped British pilot. It was no surprise that the mayor knew, too. His threat may have been empty but nobody really trusted him. He could easily have shopped me to the Germans, either out of spite, to hurt Roger or to curry favour with the Germans. He was believed to be involved both with smuggling food supplies out of Normandy and of having some sort of dealings with the Germans. As a result, he was trusted by few people in the village.

I returned to the farm, with André, and we discussed the situation as we walked from Roger's house to the Lair farm, and then with Henri, as soon as we arrived. Henri heard our account, without interrupting, then made it clear that he had no doubt that the situation was serious. The mayor was unlikely to carry out his threat immediately but the longer I stayed, the greater the danger. He felt that there was little time to be lost and decided, on the spot, to take me by horse-drawn cart early the next morning south to Sees. There I could stay with André's aunt, who owned a house on the outside of that town. From what we gathered from the news on our crystal set, Sees was

already closer to the American lines than we were in Norrey-en-
Auges. In effect, British and American forces were working their
way around Caen by going south and east and there was thus,
at least, a reasonable chance that I would be able to cross from
Sees to our lines fairly quickly. Henri's plan was to leave at
3.00am in the morning. The darkness would provide some cover
for two to three hours of the first part of the journey. I had
hardly any packing to do but spent the rest of the day getting
myself mentally ready for the departure. The atmosphere at
dinner at the Lair's place that night was tense and there was less
than the usual amount of conversation. I am sure that they were
sorry I was leaving them. In my six weeks, I had become
practically a member of the family and, for my part, there was
also some regret at having to leave this safe and friendly place.
But there was truly no choice. And it would not be good-bye to
everyone with whom I had made friends in Norrey-en-Auges
since it had also been agreed that Roger and his family, along
with André, would travel by bike later in the day, by a slightly
different route, to the same destination.

I turned in early but was already awake when Henri's knock
on the cottage door came about 2.30am. I shaved and washed
quickly in the usual way, using a basin and cold water. Then
I dressed hurriedly and grabbed my burlap sack, took one
last quick look at the room which had been my refuge for   so
long, and went to meet Henri at the back of the barn. It was
August 8th. I had been evading capture in Normandy for nearly
nine weeks.

8
Journey back to Allied lines

Henri was waiting with his two-wheeled cart, already hitched to the horse. On the top of the cart was a mattress for me to lie on, and a pile of old furniture, which left some room for me to stretch out on the mattress. The story would be, if we were stopped, that he was delivering these items to a farmhouse in Sees and that I was helping him with the loading and unloading. We had a thermos of coffee, some bread and some cheese for the journey; that would have to be enough to see us through the day.

I climbed onto the cart, sat down on the mattress, legs outstretched and my back against the side-board, while Henri began the trip by leading the horse. After a while, he mounted to the seat, took up the reins and rode. Throughout the trip, he alternated between leading the horse and driving, the former being somewhat easier on the horse, who was well past his prime. The first couple of hours passed peacefully and uneventfully, with neither of us speaking, just thinking our separate thoughts about the journey south and, in Henri's case, I am sure, about the fate of Norrey-en-Auges. About 5.00am or 5.30am, the night-time darkness began to give way towards lighter sky in the east and by 6.00am or so, dawn had arrived, though it was another grey morning. We continued without a break, me on the mattress on top of the cart, Henri sitting up front, wielding the reins and urging the horse on with gentle clucks whenever the animal seemed to be slowing down. There was no need to stop and a journey of 40 or more kilometres, like this, necessarily proceeds slowly, not much faster than normal walking speed of 5-6 kilometres per hour. Occasionally, we were passed or overtaken by a German military vehicle or motorcycle and small groups of German soldiers. But no one stopped us or asked for our papers and, after a short time, I stopped worrying about being stopped and questioned. The occasional flight of an aircraft overhead in the grey, cloudy skies could be heard but, apart from the German soldiery we passed on the road, the war had begun to seem far away again. About 11.00am, we found ourselves approaching a young woman, standing by the side of the road, who waved us down. She had a big haversack on her back and was most attractive, with longish brown hair and nice brown eyes. She was also wearing shorts, which was both unusual and provocative. "Can you give me a lift to the next town?" she asked Henri, in a friendly and winning fashion. There was really no way he could refuse, since he had halted, but he turned to me and asked if it was all right with me if she shared the space in the cart. I said, "Oui, bien sûr," and Henri nodded, at the same time, giving me a look which I knew meant, "Be careful what you say."

This young woman mounted and climbed into the cart with a great show of very pretty legs and settled down, her haversack plunked down beside her. There was only a foot or so of space between us and she, quite naturally, wanted to talk with the person sharing this rather cramped space. She seemed lively, bright and curious. And I, naturally, did not want to talk to her, knowing that my accent would soon betray me as, at the very least, a non-local if not outright as a foreigner. Still, she was persistent and I had to say something so I told her that I was a refugee and that this man, the driver, was kindly giving me a lift south. One could see immediately that she was sceptical. More conversation would surely be dangerous so I tried to indicate that I needed to sleep and lowered my cloth cap over my eyes, leaning back against the side-board of the cart. But, it was no good, she persisted. She wanted to know who I was and whether I was truly a refugee or not. I said, "Of course I am" and tried to ignore her. A platoon of German soldiers passed our cart, going in the opposite direction at this point.

Finally, perhaps after ten minutes, a good part of which was spent in thoughtful silences on her part, she looked at me hard and said that she found me interesting, that she was certain I was not a refugee. And then she came out with it, she said that she wanted to know if I was an AWOL German soldier or an escaped British pilot. There it was again, the choice of the only two likely possibilities, which André had put to me five weeks earlier, when he and his friends stopped me on the stolen bike. And, just as it had been for André, it was a reasonable deduction on the part of this young lady. This was long before the age of mass tourism and, in any event, Normandy at this time was on no tourist's itinerary. So, if you were a foreigner moving about Normandy, you were most likely, if you weren't one of the very occasional American soldiers who had become well separated from their units, either a German deserter dodging his own military authorities and the Allies, or a British serviceman dodging the Germans.

I weighed up quickly what to say in reply – whether to just insist that she had it all wrong – that of course I was a refugee, couldn't she see that? – or to admit that I was a British airman trying to escape. It seemed certain that continuing to protest I was a Frenchman was pointless, so I told her. It was apparent that she believed me. Perhaps, again, my accent indicated English rather than German origins or perhaps it simply seemed to her much more likely that a French farmer would be helping a British serviceman than an AWOL German soldier.

"If you are English, I can look after you," she said, with warmth and a certain gleam in her eye.

I am sure that I must have looked surprised. I certainly felt it, to be made this offer out of the blue. "What do you mean, you can look after me?" I managed to ask.

She replied, "I've got a flat in Paris and I come up to Normandy to buy butter, then go back to Paris to sell it on the black market. I've got everything you could want in the flat and in Paris there's no problem. You wouldn't be caught, you would be safe. Why don't you come back to Paris with me? I can give you food and find you clothing until the Allied troops arrive there. I'm getting off at the next town."

Well, this was an interesting situation, I thought: I was sharing the back of a horse-drawn cart with a butter smuggler and a most attractive one at that, who had evidently taken a fancy to me. She clearly had more in mind than just giving me food and shelter in her Paris flat. This was a proposition. I confess that I was flattered and, for perhaps two or three seconds, I entertained the idea, with a vision of being kept and pampered by this very pretty Parisienne in her flat, sitting out the next weeks or months of the war, however long it might take until the Allied forces reached Paris. After all, there could be far worse fates. But the temptation passed quickly. Margot and Paulette, after all, were waiting for me back home and it was really inconceivable to think of not rejoining British forces if there was any chance of doing so. Hiding in Paris while my mates in the 184th and all the other units continued the fight against the Huns? No, it was impossible to consider doing that, attractive as this young lady and her proposal were. Also, it has to be said, I was a little distrustful of her. Why was she so willing to make me this offer? I was no Errol Flynn, so I couldn't flatter myself that she was smitten by my looks. Was it a trap of some kind? I didn't think so but, in wartime, you are more likely to have a long life if you are suspicious of the new situations you find yourself in – and the offers you get – than if you are completely trusting.

"No, no, thanks but I'm going to continue on my way," I said. She argued with me, saying that the thought of getting through the German lines back to the Americans or the British was crazy, impossible. I turned to Henri, in case he had missed this by-play, and said, "She's invited me to go back to Paris with her but I'm going to stay with you." He grunted assent, indicating that he had heard and he approved my decision, and probably would have been surprised if I had decided anything else. My new Parisienne acquaintance just gave me a look as if to say, "Well, I tried to be nice but have it your own way."

We went on in silence, a somewhat uncomfortable silence, for another hour or so, passing the occasional German military vehicle and group of German infantrymen, until we came to a village and stopped in the middle, at a crossroads, with a café on the corner. By this point, Henri and I had been travelling a long time, eight to nine hours and were getting close to the village outside Sees where André's aunt lived. The young woman indicated that this was the village where she had intended to get out, and since we were not taking the route to Paris, asked Henri to stop, which he did. But once again she looked at me and repeated her offer. This time I asked her why I should be so sure that I could trust her, mightn't she turn me over to the Germans? How did I know she wouldn't? Quite rightly, she pointed out that if that had been her intention, she could have signalled to any of the German soldiers we had passed on the road and had me captured. That answer made perfect sense, increased my trust in her but still, I insisted that, while I appreciated the offer, I really had decided to go on and try to get back to the British forces.

She shrugged, accepting this as my final answer, stood up, swinging the haversack, laden with her contraband butter, on to her shoulders, and dismounted from the back of the cart as elegantly as she had got into it, when we first picked her up. She then turned to me and asked me to join her for a coffee at the corner café. I could see no harm in this and sitting down for a few minutes, having a coffee, sounded like a pleasant idea. I asked Henri if he thought this would be all right and would he mind waiting. It was fine with him and I followed her into the café.

When you enter a shop or a restaurant, it may take a second or two to take in the scene, particularly if it is somewhat dark, but almost instantly I realised that this place was filled with German soldiers, laughing and drinking beer. A few gave my companion an admiring look. Oh Christ, I thought, I've just walked into the lion's den. I immediately whispered to my new friend that she should take a certain table, and face inwards to the crowd, while I would have my back to them and say as little as possible. I also told her that if she should give me away, I would shoot her. She almost certainly knew that this was a bluff. In fact, I had left my pistol in the sack in the cart.

We ordered our coffees and she chatted happily away at me, as if we were old friends, while I gave short non-committal grunts for the most part. She told me that her name was Jeannette and gave me a little of her history. After a minute or two of this, I could see that she was playing her part well and that she wasn't going to betray me, and the tension in my body eased up. We were there probably only 10 minutes or so, long enough to finish our coffees and therefore long enough to show sangfroid in a café full of German soldiers.

Outside again, we crossed the street to the cart, where Henri was waiting, and when we got there, she pulled out a small piece of paper and a pencil from one of her pockets and wrote down her name and address in Paris. She urged me to keep it in case I changed my mind. This time I simply came out with the question that had been nagging at me and asked her why she should be so "kind" to me, with her generous offer. She explained that she loved the adventure of the idea of helping an escaped British airman. So that, at least, explained part of the friendly gleam in her eye when she first made her offer. It wasn't all my sex appeal, such as it was. She was, as much, lusting after the adventure.

I got back in the cart and Henri and I were on our way. When I looked back a few seconds later, she was still standing on the corner opposite the café we had been in and smiling and waving at us. I waved and smiled back and then she disappeared from sight, as the road took a bend and we left the village. I hoped that she would be all right. The experience had been a short, totally unexpected, and completely innocent adventure with a pretty young woman.

But then doubts and fears returned. Maybe she would, after all, tell the Germans about me, I thought. There would be nothing stopping her from doing so if she wanted to and she hadn't seemed the least bit bothered by all those laughing, beer-drinking German soldiers. For all I knew, her little smuggling operation might be done with the tacit or even active cooperation of the Germans. On the other hand, she had ample opportunity to betray me earlier and hadn't, so she was probably on the level. Nevertheless, for the first five to six kilometres after we had left the village, I kept a watchful eye for any German military vehicles that might be coming racing down the road. I was prepared to jump out of the cart and make a dash for it, if necessary. And then, as nothing happened, I relaxed again and decided that she had been completely sincere after all. Jeanette was, after all, a true Frenchwoman and her offer had been genuine. But, if it was, then it occurred to me, if I were caught, she might be in danger if the enemy found the slip of paper with her name and address. Since I had no intention of taking up her proposal, I should destroy the piece of paper and I did, by the simple expedient of chewing it and spitting it out.

Although we were most of the way towards our destination, there were two more incidents on the journey. The first involved being waved to a halt by a German soldier, who demanded a match. Neither Henri nor I had any matches, so we couldn't cooperate. He was furious, perhaps not believing that we didn't have any or maybe not understanding that that was what we were saying. Perhaps he thought we were just being bloody-minded. He called us all the names under the sun, in German, and threatened us with his revolver. Henri kept calm though I was certainly nervous, but soon the soldier quietened down and let us get on our way, with some kind of snarl and a last curse.

The second incident was actually more worrying. A few kilometres further down the road, all of a sudden, up ahead, we saw two German soldiers stopping some French cyclists and evidently demanding to see their papers. I figured that if there was going to be a search of papers, they might just ask the driver for his and leave the passenger alone. My fake identity card had not yet been put to the test and I was hoping that it never would be. We had a moment's discussion and then Henri clucked the horse to get going and we proceeded toward the two sentries. To my great relief, they treated us just as refugees and simply wished us good-day and good luck as we went by. We returned this with a wave and a "merci" and were soon past them.

An hour later, we finally arrived at André's aunt's house, which was situated in a small field in the village of Planches, just outside Sees. André, his aunt, and his brother, Abel, were already waiting for us. From what they said, André, who had come on his bike (the same one that I had tried to get to the Pyrenees on) had had as little trouble getting through as we had. I was welcomed by his aunt, who was a pleasant, friendly woman in her late forties, I guessed. André's father lived nearby and we met him the next day. It was now about 2.00pm. Henri and I quickly unloaded the furniture, which lightened the cart. He was determined to leave soon for the return journey, to make it back to Norrey-en-Auges before the curfew. If he travelled smartly, and the cart was now lighter by one load of furniture and one passenger, he could probably make it before dark. The goodbye was fairly hurried and I tried to express my thanks to Henri. I owed him a lot and I believe he knew how much I appreciated this. I felt sorry for both him and the horse having to make the return journey, all in one day.

But I was soon focused on my new situation and prospects. The news was that American troops under General Patton were advancing toward Sees from the west and north. We were on the eastern edge of Sees, essentially opposite the line of approach of the advancing American army. The house was fairly small but we all settled in. For the seven nights in all that I was there, I slept on the sofa in the living room. The first three days, in fact, we did little because it was not, at first, clear just what the best approach to the American forces should be.

André, having grown up there, knew the area well and we went on some long walks in the countryside. He introduced me to several of his old acquaintances as a refugee whom he and his family were helping. Again, I said as little as possible while trying to indicate friendliness.

The day after that, we went into the village for a look around. There were German soldiers actively patrolling along the main street and many of the villagers were on the doorsteps of their houses, watching this show and, undoubtedly, wondering whether the village was going to be reduced to ruins in a battle between the oncoming Americans and the Germans. The tension in the air seemed so thick that you could cut it with a knife. Yet, not all of the enemy soldiers were Germans. To my surprise, and amusement, one of them was a little Japanese, in a German military uniform, who when he passed us by, wished us good-day in German. We, of course, all knew that the Germans and Japanese were allies but this was the first sign I had had that any of the Japs were actually involved in the European war. Perhaps he was a liaison officer of some kind. But the place was so thick with enemy soldiers that I was able to persuade André, who seemed to have no fear of them whatsoever, that perhaps it would be unwise for us to stick our necks out too much longer in this way.

We then returned to his aunt's house and continued making our plans. We had by this point heard that the Americans were only 15 or so miles away and this gave me great heart. I urged André to help me reach the Americans at this point and we began to lay plans as to how to do so. Three bicycles were obtained – the same simple, balloon tyred-type, with no gears that I had stolen that first day at Norrey-en-Auges. And early the next morning, André, Abel and I set out. I was sorry to leave André's family and there was a fond farewell at dawn. But, at the same time, I was excited by the possibility that I soon might be back with our forces.

The plan was to make for the chateau in which both André's aunt and Abel had worked, which was only an estimated three miles or so from where the American lines were now believed to be. From there, it should be easy, we figured, to reach the Americans. We had, however, gone no more than 8 kilometres or so when we came to a barricade across the road, manned by German soldiers with machine guns. There were also some Red Cross units. We were signalled to a halt by a soldier and told that we could not go any further, that there was a battle raging just a few miles down the road and all civilian traffic was being halted. Again, for me, there was a moment of fear that they might want to check our papers after giving us this news but they didn't. Once more, it felt like a lucky escape.

We had no real choice but to turn back yet, instead, we simply started thinking of alternative routes. We soon found out that all the roads in the area had been blocked to travel. There was nothing for it but to return to the house of André's aunt, where we heard about a visit of the German soldiers trying to commandeer as much help as possible. We also discussed what we should do. The simplest alternative was to abandon the idea of making the trip by bike and cut across the fields, staying out of view of the roads, and the sight of any Germans, as much as possible. Abel knew the area well and was certain we could reach the American lines across the fields.

We did not try the next day but the day after that. That morning, the three of us set out on foot and were soon cutting across fields and woods. And here I have to confess something, namely a bit of cowardice on my part. Sixty years after the event, it is hard to put this down in black-and-white but it would be dishonest not to mention it. Throughout this long walk, of perhaps 8-10 kilometres, I let André and Abel lead the way at all times. They probably would have insisted anyway since they knew this countryside and I didn't. But the reason for my hanging back was simple: fear of mines. I rationalised my willingness to let them take the risks by saying that it would be a terrible shame, after all these months, to die just a few miles away from rejoining our forces, and that was part of it to be sure. But, I have to admit it, there was also just plain simple fear of dying, stepping on a mine. If André or Abel had that worry, neither showed nor mentioned it.

After about three hours, we came out to a road that was only a short distance, maybe a kilometre or so from the chateau where Abel and his aunt had worked. There was no sign of German soldiers or roadblocks or any impediments to our journey. We simply walked toward the chateau and were soon there. At no point had we come close to the battle that the Germans had claimed the day before was raging nearby. We had either skirted well clear of it, by chance, or the fighting had moved on or, perhaps, the day before, Germans were simply eliminating civilian traffic from the roads to ease the movements of their own military units.

We were greeted by two of Abel's mates, who worked there. After some brief explanation of my presence, we made our way to the kitchen and began a celebration there, using the stocks in the wine cellar, which was an excellent one. The Americans were only three miles away, we were told, and that certainly seemed worth celebrating. Since the owners of the chateau were away and had given no indication of when they might return, it seemed only right that we should "liberate" some of the excellent wine that they had stocked. Apart from the occasional glass of red wine I had had during the previous two months, this was my first serious exposure to alcohol during my time in Normandy. By the time we decided that we should go, I was in a wizard mood, though hardly sozzled. One thing we discussed was the best way I should present myself. Since there seemed to be no Germans nearby and little chance of meeting any, between the chateau and the American lines, it was decided that I should change into my uniform. It was about 2.00pm when the three of us set out again, walking fast across the fields, eager to get there, and in the knowledge that André and Abel would have to make the whole return journey on foot as well, before darkness fell. It only took an hour and, suddenly, the three of us were walking across a field toward Sees. As we approached, a small group of American soldiers came forward, several with rifles at the ready, and others were coming along to see what was happening. One of them asked us in English, "What are you doing here?" And then he looked at me specifically and said, "Are you taken prisoner?" I realised immediately that they thought I was a German officer who had been captured by these two young French civilians. More soldiers had gathered and they were mostly young lads, maybe only 18 or 19, many with their rifles half-raised. I suspect that most of them were relatively fresh off transports that had landed near Cherbourg and had never seen any RAF uniforms, unlike the American military who had been part of the invasion forces for months before D-Day. All of a sudden, the situation seemed plenty risky. They might not want to bother with the trouble of taking someone prisoner. I didn't know that, of course, but did not want to take any chances. So I told them immediately that I was a British officer, with the RAF but that my aircraft had been shot down and I had escaped. The only thing I wanted now, I told them, was to rejoin my squadron. There was a lessening of tension. Someone patted me on the back, someone else gave me a cigarette.

I had, at last, made it back to Allied lines. But there was hardly time to take this in and I still did not know how long or how difficult it would be to get back to 184 Squadron.

An officer who had joined the group heard what I had to say and told me that the American forces were now in charge of Sees and that he would organise a jeep to take me to the American army headquarters in the town.

I turned to my two French companions, André and Abel, who had successfully seen me through to American lines. I was incredibly grateful to them and tried to express it. But they needed to get away quickly, so our farewell chat was brief, as the one with Henri had been four days previously, though we promised to stay in touch.

It was now August 15th. I had been alternately on the run or in hiding in occupied Normandy for 68 days and I was now back with "our" side. But I still had to get back to British forces and, in particular, my squadron and I wanted to do this as quickly as possible. Being treated as a suspicious character by the Americans was irritating, to say the least.

It seemed that no more than a couple of minutes went by after André and Abel had left that the jeep pulled up. I got in and sat in the back and we were off toward the American headquarters in Sees. At one crossroads, a makeshift traffic light had been set up and we stopped for the red light. A group of American troops were also standing there. One of them noticed me and immediately raised his rifle, saying "You don't want to take the bastard prisoner," he shouted to the driver, "shoot him." It was exactly what I had feared for a moment when I had crossed over into the American lines. As rapidly as I could get the words out, I said, "Don't shoot me, I'm a British pilot." "Oh, hell," he said and lowered his gun. For a couple of seconds, once again, it had looked like a close call. The whole incident wasn't too surprising actually. RAF battle dress looked very similar to that of the Luftwaffe pilots.

We arrived at the headquarters a few minutes later. The whole drive from the encampment in the field to headquarters had been fast, maybe 15-20 minutes. I was, after a short delay, escorted in to the office of a colonel and his adjutant explained the situation to him.

Was I welcomed as a brother-in-arms, someone who had had a narrow escape and was now safely returned? Not at all. The first words of this colonel, who was of medium build and dark hair, and very much full of himself, were, "Our tanks are going faster than the infantry can keep up with them and I've got enough on my hands right now. I don't need any more complications. We're on our way to Paris and I haven't got time to deal with you. You'll have to go in the pen with the others."

"In the pen?" I said. I was gob-smacked. This was not what I had imagined during all the weeks I'd been hoping and thinking about returning to Allied lines.

He said, "Yes, in the pen. Those are our orders for anyone claiming to be a pilot who was shot down. They go into   the pen and stay there until there's been a chance to interrogate them. How do I know you're British, after all? Someone else will have to find out. You'll be escorted there." He was about to turn away. As far as he was concerned, the matter had been sorted.

"There's no way I'm going in there," I told him. "And if you shoot me in the back when I walk out of here, it'll be reported because my friends know that I've been handed over to you." I was bluffing, of course. The only people who knew that I'd arrived and was now with the American forces were André and Abel and they were not only well on their way back to the house but had assumed that I was safe.

But the colonel bought it. He took one slightly disgusted look at me and said, "All right, off you go then."

I lost no time. Less than a minute later, I was back on the road walking away from headquarters, on the road to Cherbourg. I stuck my thumb out and a minute or so later, had hitched a ride in a lorry with a black driver. He had a heavy American accent and asked me where I was headed. I told him Cherbourg but almost as soon as we'd had this exchange, we saw a small van parked by the side, which had the RAF filming logo painted on its side. I asked the driver to stop and let me off, saying that these fellows would probably be able to help me locate my unit.

I walked over to the van and said, "What are you doing here?" They looked at me, took in my uniform – these fellows, fortunately, had no trouble recognising an RAF uniform when they saw one – and said to me, equally puzzled, "What are you doing here?" I replied, "I'm trying to get back to my unit which I think will now be stationed somewhere on the coast, the other side of Caen." I was guessing about this but it seemed the likeliest possibility as to where the 184th would be based, now that the Normandy coast had been secured. I also gave them a thumbnail sketch of what had happened to me. The driver was glad to help but there was something they had to do first. He said, "Right, okay, but look, we're going to St Malo for the capitulation of the fort there, to take the photos. You'd better come with us." St Malo is on the coast, at the northern edge of the Brittany peninsula, about where the peninsula begins to jut out from the mainland, hence about 80 miles west of where we presently were. It was now about 3.00pm in the afternoon so the side-trip to St Malo would delay my getting back to my squadron wherever it was yet there seemed little option but to accept. It would be better to go with these fellows than rely on random lifts from the Americans. So I readily agreed and got in.

The journey to St Malo lasted between two and three hours and the three of us were jammed pretty tight in the front seat of the van. But I didn't mind. Though these men were just part of a photography unit, I felt I was back with British forces, at last. And it was a pleasure to be having a ride in a motorised vehicle again and to be talking English. As we drove along, I noticed that the war had hardly touched this part of Normandy. From the undisturbed look of the fields, the hedgerows and the woods, one would never guess that a big war was raging not far off. Though there had been some tense moments for me with the Americans earlier in the day, the great relief as we motored along was knowing that no one was going to ask for my identity papers in German or German-accented French. I had not only survived my 68 days in occupied France but had not ended up as a POW. I was on my way back to my own people, both my squadron and, soon, I hoped, my family.

We arrived at St Malo about 6.00pm, late in the day but it was still light. The driver of the van, who seemed to know the lay-out of St Malo, drove it straight to the old medieval fort on the coast. This huge edifice was connected by a causeway to the beachfront of the town. The citadel had been the seat of German military control for the town and its commander was the "mad" Colonel von Aulock, who had vowed for several weeks that all of his forces would fight and die to the last man. Yet, the futility of such an ending must have finally struck him. He was now in the citadel and surrendering to the Americans. We parked, got out and one of the men confirmed this with a soldier waiting nearby. Apparently, the surrender itself was just about to take place. It was a massive, centuries-old stone fortress, fitted with large German pillboxes pointing over the sea. A ramp led out of it to the short causeway that led from it and connected it to the town at high tide. A jeep was waiting at the foot of the ramp that led out of the fort and two American soldiers were waiting by its side. There was also another photographer, in battle gear, whom I did not realise at first was a woman. I later found out that this was the well known American photographer Lee Miller and she seemed to be one of the few American journalists there. She had been a great beauty in her youth, a model for *Vogue*, but had then gone behind the lens to become a photographer. After the war started, she dropped the kind of art and fashion photography she had been doing and joined the American forces as a war photographer.

A few minutes passed and suddenly we saw a German officer leave the fortress, coming down the ramp. He had dark brown hair, and was wearing his full officer's uniform, with ribbons, an officer's peaked cap, and a shabby camouflage coat that flapped about his knees as he walked. A monocle over one eye made him the very picture of a Prussian officer. He was tall and thin and was obviously trying to look dignified. This was, it turned out, the famous Colonel von Aulock. Yet, as the American woman photographer tried to get a picture of his face, he put his hand up in front to shield himself, calling her "Frau" something or other, and trying to dodge being photographed. Coming down the ramp, he had been accompanied by two German soldiers, carrying his two suitcases, and a police dog. When he reached the group of us waiting at the bottom of the ramp, his men put down the bags and stood back a pace, beside the jeep. He turned to the two Americans and said, in good English: "Put my luggage in the jeep." They both looked at him as if he must be mad and the taller one said, sarcastically, "Do you want us to clean your f...... boots, too?" The colonel looked pretty startled by this, for a second or so. You can be sure he wasn't used to being addressed in this way. Without replying, however, he turned to his own soldiers and gave the same order. But the same American who had spoken to him signalled "No" to the German soldiers and said to the colonel, "You put the luggage in yourself." He looked furious but he saw there was nothing for it. He did as he was told and a minute later was being driven away in the jeep. One of my two RAF friends took some photos of this, as did Lee Miller, and then the three of us went into the fort for an exploration, after a large number of German soldiers came out and gave themselves up, to become POWs.

My RAF companions apparently had complete freedom to

roam in the newly-surrendered fort, though they had to show their ID a couple of times. We thus had a look at everything from the labyrinth of tunnels in the base, where the Germans had sheltered, to the big guns at the top of the fortress. These guns looked thoroughly warped, probably from the excessive firing they had been through during the final defence of the fort. Someone, however, told us that they had been deliberately damaged, in order to make them unusable when captured by the Americans. The Germans in the fort must have known in those final hours that there was no way they would win the fight but they could prevent the Americans from getting hold of usable artillery. I have no idea whether this was true but this may have been the intention, namely to wreck them so that they couldn't be used by the Americans. The RAF boys took some pictures of the guns and the room where the surrender had been signed. But in the course of looking around inside the fort, we found one store-room in the underground tunnels, which was packed with large containers of rum and other supplies. We felt that it was only fair to "liberate" a couple of these containers, which we did and loaded them into the van.

It was, by now, even later in the evening and there was no chance of getting away this day. We were put up at a building that had been converted to a temporary barracks. After a simple dinner and a couple of tots of our liberated rum, I turned in with some borrowed blankets. It had been a long day. My RAF companions had promised to get me back to the aerodrome where the 184th was billeted but for reasons that I no longer remember, we did not go the next day but the day after. And that day, in the morning, there was some heavy action on another small island just off St Malo. While the forces at the fort and in the town had surrendered, the island which was garrisoned by German troops had refused to. The Americans bombed it repeatedly from 500 feet with napalm as a fire-bomb weapon. The island was an inferno from one end to the other. This was one of the first uses of napalm in war though its identity as a new weapon was being kept under wraps by the Americans for the time being. I couldn't see how anybody on that island could have survived that fire bombing and, unlike the soldiers who had hidden in the rabbit warren at the base of the fort, probably none did.

We got under way after that sobering performance of military might, heading north and east toward Caen. The German forces occupying the city had still not completely capitulated but they had been pushed back to the eastern side. The western side of Caen was now completely under the control of the British forces. Again, the journey was a couple of hours but, unlike the trip to St Malo, now the signs of devastation were everywhere.

We found an RAF unit situated west of Caen and ascertained the whereabouts of 184 Squadron only to discover that the squadron was situated at an airfield near the coast. My film unit friends, however, weren't going to leave me in the lurch at this point and agreed to drive me there. Once again, we got into the van and after a hazardous journey over war-damaged roads of about 30 miles, we arrived at our objective. The airbase had been built on four or five large fields and a temporary runway had been laid across the middle of these fields. A great deal of activity was going on but after a considerable time, and stopping to ask lots of men who didn't seem to know anything about the squadron, we finally found the 184's dispersal area.

I got out of the van, thanking my two companions both for the lift and the company they had provided, and began to take my bearings. There were a fair number of people around, and it seemed a hive of activity, with several aircraft being serviced, but before I could take much in, I saw someone coming toward me, saying, "Dutch, we knew you'd get back but we didn't know what had happened to you." It was Doug Gross, one of our Canadian boys, someone with whom I had always been friendly. He got into a truck to be driven out to his aeroplane and as he boarded, he said, "Get some flying time in, Dutch", as if I'd been a schoolboy playing truant. I had to smile and replied, by way of returning the compliment, "And you get some time in behind the lines and see what that's like." He heard me, smiled, said, "See you when I get back", waved and was driven off. He was off to a sortie over the Falaise gap.

But that was the last time I saw Doug Gross. The air battle over the Falaise gap, which was the main artery for the retreating German forces, was fierce. Following the defeat of the German forces around the Normandy beaches, the Falaise gap was the main conduit for the Tiger tanks and the German troops trying to reach northern France, crossing the Seine, for a regrouping there. Thus, the war was still raging in this area in mid-August, more than two months after the D-Day landings, and this was the deadliest period for the RAF Typhoon pilots since the start of the invasion. That afternoon, probably less than an hour after I saw him, Doug was shot down and killed over the Falaise gap, one of the 289 Typhoon pilots killed in the battle for Normandy. Of this total, 55 were killed and 90 Typhoons were downed in the August fighting, most in the battles around Falaise. At the aerodrome, the aircraft were being readied as quickly as possible for these sorties. For those lucky enough to return, the whole trip, including the action at the Falaise gap, was in the order of 45 minutes.

For me, however, the war was about to go on hold, though I did not understand that immediately. I quickly found out where the CO's office was and that our CO was no longer Jack Rose but one S/L J.W. Wilson. Wilson had been first a flight lieutenant, then a flight commander with 245 Squadron from August, 1943. Bunny Rose went on to fly Hurricanes in the Far East, doing support missions for the Army in Burma at first, and was in the Far East until the end of the war.

But before I could reach the CO's office, I ran into a reporter whom I had met before, one Stuart McPherson, who was a well-known war correspondent. He had been present at the demonstration on the Isle of Sheppey when we had destroyed the tanks with rockets and I knew him from that time.

"How are you, Dutch?" he greeted me. I said, "I'm fine." He wasn't going to let it go with a couple of pleasantries, however. He must have known that I'd been missing and wanted to know my story. So I told him that I'd just got back through the lines and went over the basic facts of my adventure quickly, not really wanting to spend much time with him but to report to the group captain. From what I'd told him, however, he immediately scented a newsworthy story.

He said, "I'm on my way out of here soon" – it was now about 3.00pm – "and I can have you on the air by 4.30pm. What do you say?" Well, I'd already had another idea while we were talking and, anyway, the thought of going on the news with my exploit had no temptation for me. "No," I said, "my old CO used to say get your name in the headlines and you're a dead duck the next day." This was a superstition, of course, and I didn't think that it always came true but I wasn't going to tempt fate by bragging about my escape. McPherson could see that I meant it and he went on his way, wishing me luck. Yet McPherson's report went out at 4.30pm that day, referring to the return of a British pilot who had been shot down on D+1, but not naming me. My family, as I found out later, heard the report.

A few minutes later, I found the commanding officer and reported for duty. He welcomed me back and told me he was glad I was back safely. But I was quick to get my request in. Could I take a plane and buzz Norrey-en-Auges, dipping my wings, so that my French friends would know that I had got back to British lines safely?

I felt that this was a small request but permission was denied instantly. "No way you'd be allowed to do that," he said, "you won't be allowed to fly at the moment. You've got to go back to England." All pilots who had been shot down had to be debriefed, explaining their whereabouts and actions during the time they were away. And, perhaps more constructively, supplying any useful information about conditions behind enemy lines.

By 6.00pm, I was leaving France on a Dakota, strictly as a passenger, not a pilot, flying back to Blighty for my debriefing. I remember looking down at the waters of the Channel, which I had crossed so often on combat missions and thinking that it had been more than two months since I had last seen England. But there was a tumult of other thoughts too. I had always believed that I would make it back and I had. My luck had held and I had made it. I wondered how Margot and Paulette were and wondered again whether Margot had been worried sick about me the whole time. I also thought of other family members and how good it would be to see them again, especially my mother. And I asked myself how long it would take before I could let everyone in the family know that I was all right and back. There was also some confused thinking about what the debriefing in London would be like. Did they think I had given away any secrets to the enemy? I had had none to give, of course. Or were they curious about any valuable information I might have about the German position behind the lines? But I really didn't have any such information. And there were thoughts about my friends back in Norrey-en-Auges and when I would get a chance to let them know that I had made it back safely, as I looked out at the stretch of water beneath me, during the brief flight. I had, after all, actually survived more than two months on the run in enemy occupied territory and not been captured. The whole experience had been pretty incredible, really. Now, I was on an RAF aeroplane again and going home; that was wonderful, of course. But first there would be a debriefing. What would it be like? Had André and Henri returned safely to Norrey-en-Auges? How soon would I see Margot?

We landed at Northolt air base, west of London, just around

dusk. I reported in and was given a clean uniform, underwear, and a toilet kit. There was a standard RAF dinner in a mess hall – my recollection of that evening is pretty hazy but I don't remember meeting anyone I knew – and then a night's sound sleep in a clean bunk. That brought to a close one very eventful day, which had begun that morning with the sight of the fire bombing of the last German redoubt in St Malo harbour. The following day, I stayed at the base but was told that I would be taken to London.

Then, the next day, August 19th, I was escorted by train to London for my debriefing. This should, I suppose, still be a vivid memory but it is not. It was in a building that was part of SHAEF (Supreme Headquarters Allied Expeditionary Force) head-quarters. The interview room was fairly small but well lit. The questions were put by a British officer and his questions and my answers were all recorded by a stenographer. For the most part, the final written record was a narration of the events plus whatever I could tell them about the activities of German forces that I had seen. Finally, there was a statement to sign that I would divulge none of the details of my experience until the war was over. For each kind of escaper or evader, there was not only this set statement that you had to sign but advice on how to deflect questions from family and friends.

I have a copy of the form and for "RAF evaders" (that was my category), there were some instructions on how you should respond to any questions – whether from your wife or your parents or your friends. It read as follows: "I was shot down by flak and baled out. I managed to evade capture and get back to this country. As many others are trying to do the same, you will understand I cannot tell you anything till after the war. In any case, I have orders not to say more than I have already told you." Did I maintain absolute secrecy to my family until after the war? Well, let's just say, and leave it at that, that I tried to keep to the general spirit of the pledge.

At the end of the interview, and after the paperwork had been signed, there was a "Well, I think that will be all," and brief congratulations, again, on my having survived and made it back.

Yet, while the details of the debriefing have largely vanished from memory, there were two events that immediately followed that I remember clearly. The first was that I was allowed one call home. It was a choice between ringing Margot or my parents. I decided to dial my parents. My mother should perhaps know first and, of course, she would tell Margot immediately. There were a couple of rings and then the sound of the 'phone being picked up. The person on the end of the line was my father. I said something, which he didn't hear and he said, brusquely (that was his manner), "Who's this?" I said, "It's Frank. I'm back, I'm in London."

I'm not sure what I was expecting, maybe a whoop of joy (though that would not have been his style), or at least, a "Well done, welcome back son," or "We were so worried about you." But there was nothing like this. It seemed like just silence. I must have put him into real shock. And then I realised, as I listened, that it wasn't silence. He was crying. My father was actually crying, crying for joy that I had survived. He had never shown the least emotion about me before. I was touched, as you can imagine, but maybe more astonished even than moved. I remember the sound of his quiet crying on the 'phone that day, more than sixty years ago, as vividly as if it happened yesterday.

The second event that sticks in my mind was seeing the doctor for my medical exam. This was, of course, routine for any serviceman who had been missing and come back. They wanted to know if you had been injured or, if not, if there was anything the matter with you that they should know about or that you were concerned about. Clearly, I was not injured so the physical exam part was pretty perfunctory, it was mostly a chat. And that gave me a chance to tell the doctor about something that, in fact, I had been worrying about.

There were two normal experiences of everyday life that I simply had not had during my time as an escaped airman in Normandy. The first was dreaming. As far as I could tell, I had not had a single dream during the entire time. And this seemed odd. But what really worried me was that I had not had an erection the whole time either. Now, it is a fact of life that for most men in their 20s, 30s and 40s (and often beyond), you wake up in the morning with an erection. I always had done so. It may not be the kind of thing one talks about in polite society but it is a fact, this is just part of normal male physiology. But not once had I had a morning erection in the more than two months that I had spent in hiding and on the run. I was worried. Would I be able to return to normal marital relations? I told the doctor about the situation and asked for his view. He told me that he really did not think I should worry about this. After all, I had been under quite a lot of tension and fear the whole time, he pointed out, and this could alter all sorts of things, such as dreaming, sleep quality and other things. If, however, there should be a problem, he said, then of course I should seek medical advice about it. But he did not think it would be necessary. I left his office somewhat reassured.

It was late afternoon by this point. The decision was made that I should stay overnight in London and could go up to Cambridge the next day.

9
My war ends...
so on with the business

The next morning, I boarded the train from London back to Cambridge. I was told that the RAF would let me know in a few weeks what my next assignment would be. For the next few weeks, I should just get some rest at home with my family and get over my Normandy experience.

It was wonderful to be going home, of course, seeing again the familiar fields and villages from the window of the train, even under grey, overcast skies, as it travelled northwards to Cambridge from London. But, oddly, today, I remember little of my actual arrival back in Cambridge. Of course, it was a joy to be reunited with Margot and the rest of the family but none of the details of that day, or the following weeks, are as vivid in my memory as are the events of my time in Normandy. I suppose that difference reflects the power of fear. When you know that you are at great risk of capture or being killed if you make one wrong move, you are paying strict attention to everything that happens. As a result, those times become imprinted on your mind in a way that if time is just passing peacefully, as it did once I reached home, it does not. So much of what I saw and experienced during those 70 days in Normandy remains as sharp and clear as if it happened yesterday.

As one can imagine, Margot, though heavily pregnant, and I had a very fond reunion the night of my homecoming and my fears of not being able to function properly were immediately shown to be groundless. I also found out, I think it must have been around the dinner table that first night, that Margot had not once, during all the time I was missing, not for one second, thought I'd been killed. The whole time, she was certain I was alive and was sure I would get back somehow. I heard later from Doris, my sister, what happened when the news came through in Stuart McPherson's report on the BBC that an RAF pilot who had been shot down in Normandy the day after D-Day had just returned to British lines. My name wasn't reported, only the fact that a British airman who had been shot down on D+1 had returned safely. But, as Doris told me later, Margot, upon hearing this news item, had leapt up and said, "That's Dutch! I know it!" Did her certainty that I was alive come from the power of love? Or was it just faith in Providence? Or was it even some form of ESP? I really don't know. But when I found out that she had always believed I was alive, I was very glad. So often during my days on the run and in hiding I'd wondered and worried what she must be going through, knowing only that I'd been shot down but not knowing my fate. I had hoped, of course, that the letter I had written early in my adventure and which I had entrusted to M. Laloy had reached her. But it had not, the whole time I was missing. It arrived about one month after I got back.

Of course, I hadn't just come home to my wife. There was my baby daughter, Paulette. When I had last seen her, she was only 10 months old, a blonde little baby and only starting to crawl. Now she was a toddler, just beginning to get about with baby steps and she was adorable. She had no idea who I was – I hadn't seen her that often, in fact, since she had been born – but that didn't bother me. There would be time later, I felt, to get to know my daughter, that is if I survived the rest of the war. But, even in my most anxious moments in Normandy, I had no doubt I would.

During the past year, Margot had been living with Doris on Scotland Road, the house in Cambridge that we had bought, with my father's help, in '43. I returned there. From being an escaped airman on the run in occupied France, I had, within the space of a few days, come home and stepped into a little island of domestic tranquility. Of course, the war was still going on – the V2s were still landing on London, there were military flights overhead even where we lived, turn on the BBC news and the reports on the war flooded into your living room – you could never really get away from it. But I came as close as possible to doing so for about six weeks. Again, it is all kind of a blur, after sixty years. What remains is the memory that it felt good to be home, and safe, with Margot and Paulette and the rest of my family.

But then, in early September, we had a real blow. Margot gave birth to the baby on September 9th, a baby boy. But he was sickly and four days later, he died. We had a huge amount of sadness, as you can imagine. And this came as such a contrast to the relief and joy we had all felt at my homecoming just two weeks earlier.

Nevertheless, life is often like this and we accepted it, we had to, and looked forward to the future. But, after about six weeks at home, I began to be restless. There had been no word from headquarters about my next assignment. I was fit, after all. I hadn't been injured and I felt that I should be back on duty, flying ops. It was all too much like the time before, near the beginning of the war, when I had been told to go home, wait for my assignment, and then just seemed to drop out of the RAF's collective consciousness. So, I wrote to them, as I had the previous time, tactfully reminding them of my existence, and asking: what did they want me to do next? Within a few days, again without any admission from the RAF that they had forgotten about me, there was a letter in the post. I was to report to an aircraft testing unit at Westhampnett. Two days later, I kissed Margot and Paulette good-bye and was on my way. And, so, for the last week in October and throughout November, I was back on duty testing aircraft – Spitfires, Typhoons, Tempests – before they were allocated to squadrons. After having been on ops and after my adventure in Normandy, this seemed rather tame.

Then, in the second week in December, I was at last given a proper assignment to a new squadron. I would be flying ops again, this time with 33 Squadron under Squadron Leader Bill Bowyer. Yet, when I arrived at the air base in Portanoch, there was an unwelcome surprise. I was shown into Bowyer's office and after the preliminaries, he told me that the squadron was just learning how to fly Tempests. They had been a Spits unit and were now making the conversion, learning the ins-and-outs of the new aircraft. When I told him that I had already had 50 hours of flying time in Tempests, he looked at me in a kind of sour way, not especially pleased and told me to go back home for a month or six weeks. They would let me know when to report back. I had to wait until the others had done enough flying time on the Tempests in order to become operational.

This, I should say, is the kind of thing that was all too common in the war and which never gets into the films about the war – the bureaucratic cock-ups and waste of time that they involved. The term "snafu" – for "situation normal all fouled up" – was invented by the Yanks but during the war we had plenty of experience with home-grown British snafus, I can tell you.

Well, there was nothing for it. There was no point in my hanging around while the others trained. It was back to Cambridge to wait. Of course, it was good to be with my family again and it was great to celebrate Christmas at home. But there was still a war on, I was still in the RAF and I did not feel that it was quite right that I should be cooling my heels at home, while others were doing the fighting and the dying.

Finally, in early January, word came through: it was time to report back to 33 Squadron. The squadron was now combat ready and eager to start ops, with the Tempests. My first assignment was to fly one from Tangmere and join 33 Squadron, which was now fully operational, at Gilse-Rijen in Holland. The special feature of the Tempest, I should mention, was that it was very fast below 12,000 feet and it was intended to be used against low flying German aircraft. It had four 20 millimetre cannons and could out-manoeuvre the new German jet aircraft below that height.

I flew my Tempest to Holland as ordered and was soon flying missions regularly, with bombing and rocket runs to Belgium and Holland, in particular. By this point, the Luftwaffe had largely been cleared from the skies and many of the missions seemed like just another day at work although of course there was always danger from anti-aircraft batteries. In one mission, our goal was to destroy as many Luftwaffe aircraft as possible at the Hamburg aerodrome. We made three passes and did a pretty good job of demolishing the aircraft. But the cost was high. We lost six out of a dozen planes.

Another time I was chased by four Focke-Wulfs. I quickly dropped to 0 feet and sped back to the base. But, as it happened, my course took me right over the bridge at Arnhem, which had been successfully held by the Germans against the Allies in September of '44. All hell broke loose from the German anti-aircraft batteries. Flak was bursting all around the aircraft. I was probably in harm's way only 5 or so seconds, because I was flying low and fast, but it felt like a close run thing and I was lucky to get through it in one piece.

And there continued to be other close calls, including ones from equipment failures. On one mission to Berlin, leading a group of four Tempests, it must have been in April, '45, right near the end of the war, there was clearly something wrong with the engine of mine. It just didn't sound right. I radioed to Red 2, to take over, and headed back to the base. As I taxied in and got out of the cockpit, the flight sergeant came up and asked what was the matter. I told him and he then fetched the wing commander. Meanwhile, I was filling in Flight Form 700, "unserviceable, not to be flown". Well, the wing commander, whom I had never liked, didn't believe me and was all set to take it up himself. I warned him that it was dangerous and persuaded him to have it checked on the ground first. The verdict: one of the pistons had melted and fused into the first plug. When we got this report, I told him that had he taken it up, he undoubtedly would have been killed. He didn't say anything but from the colour of his face, I could see he was thinking about it and knew that he believed me.

In April, a lot of the fighting was still fierce, even as the Germans pulled back. Apart from the offensive that the Germans had launched in the Ardennes in December, they had been retreating for months back toward Germany. But they were still putting up a fight. By late April and early May, however, it was clear that they were just about beaten. And, then, surprisingly quickly, it seemed, the war was over. Berlin fell to a pincer movement from the Russians in the east and the British and Americans from the west. And on May 8, 1945, it was official: Hitler had killed himself more than a week before and the Germans had unconditionally surrendered. After nearly six years, the war in Europe was over and so was my war. Of course the Americans were still fighting the Japanese in the Far East but as far as we in the RAF were concerned, the war was history.

The personal event that I remember most vividly from this period, however, came not long after the Germans surrendered, in late May or early June. By this time, I was stationed at the air base in Celle in Germany. This incident was my visit to Norrey-en-Auges, to see my friends and to settle a score with the man who nearly betrayed me and my friends to the Germans, namely the mayor. I went to see the CO and asked him if I could borrow an aeroplane for two days. I explained what I wanted to do. He gave me permission without any fuss, just reminding me that I had to be back in two days. I took one of the Tempests and flew to the aerodrome in Caen. It was still in quite a mess but I managed to land without any real problems. I immediately reported to the headquarters there and asked them if I could borrow a jeep to pay a visit to Norrey-en-Auges where I had been in hiding for many weeks, protected by the villagers. Again, there was no objection, they were glad to help. I was granted a jeep and an MP driver. We drove the jeep to the village, which only took about an hour to reach. We pulled up near Henri's house in the late afternoon and immediately several people recognised me. It was like a big homecoming. It was absolutely great to see Henri, his sister Alice, André, Roger, and the others and to show them that I had survived the war since leaving them and was fine. And it was a great relief to me to see that all of them were all right too.

I was also pleased to see the village looking just as it had when I'd left. Though much of Normandy was battle-scarred and some of the towns and cities, especially Caen, lay in ruins, Norrey-en-Auges had been physically untouched. In fact, one of the first things I found out was that it had probably been unnecessary for me to flee the village at all. The Germans had not only never tried to clear it, as they had other villages in the two months following D-Day, they had just melted away from this part, shortly after I had left. "The Germans just disappeared and there was no problem at all," someone said to me. Of course, when I thought of the mayor's threat to reveal me, I was not so sure that it really would have been all that safe for me to have stayed.

I asked about the mayor and told people that I wanted to confront him about his treachery, not just to me but to Henri and to Roger and his family. Well, I was told, this should be easy. On Fridays, and this happened to be a Friday, he always came through the village, on his way to Paris. As someone explained, "He comes past here every Friday with a lorry carrying timber to deliver to Paris but what he is really doing is smuggling butter to the capital and selling it on the black market." At this bit of information, a memory of my butter-smuggling popsy, my companion on the cart ride to Planches, immediately came to mind. Clearly, some things had not changed, even though the enemy was gone.

The MP and I stationed ourselves outside Roger's house, just by the road and waited. Henri, André, Abel, and Roger also stationed themselves nearby to watch what would happen. And we waited and waited. I began to think that either the mayor had changed his route or that the information was somehow wrong when, about 11.00pm, we saw the headlights of a lorry approaching.

We stepped out into the road, the MP signalling with his revolver in his hand and motioning the driver to stop. As soon as the lorry halted, I went to the passenger side and immediately recognised the mayor. "Come on, out you get," I said in French. He looked frightened but had enough presence of mind to say, "Who are you?" I said, "Never mind who I am. But you must recognise me." He acted as if he didn't know what I was talking about but he obeyed and sullenly and slowly, got out. I motioned him to stand in front of the headlights and stood just a couple of feet from him. Roger had come over to my side and was standing next to me. "You must recognise me," I said. "You stood outside that door," I pointed to it, "and you threatened Roger that you would tell the Germans that there was a British pilot sitting in his living room. That was me." He wouldn't admit it, though we went over the same thing a couple of times. I gave up trying to get him to confess and said, "All right, have it your way, but we're going to search your lorry. Get down on your knees." He didn't obey at first. "Now, get down," I repeated. This time he did. And then he started to cry. I was still covering him with my pistol, a little surprised to see him break down this way but not at all sorry to see him blubbering, in fear for his life. But at this point, the MP got scared and said in English, "For Christ's sake, sir, don't shoot him, we'll all be in trouble." I just smiled over at him and said, "I'm not going to shoot him, I just want to make the bastard cry." And he did, he cried, pleading for his life, saying he hadn't done anything wrong, that I was mistaken.

Finally, I let him get to his feet. We got the driver out too and then searched the cab of the lorry and the shipment of lumber in the back of the lorry but found no sign of smuggled goods of any kind. In the end, there was nothing for it but to let them get back in the cab and go on their way. A couple of years later, I visited the village again and Henri gave me the explanation of how we missed the butter. Apparently, there was a special compartment on the underside of the lorry in which the butter was hidden. But we hadn't thought of that and hadn't looked there. This fact had come out later. It was a shame that we didn't know it then. It would have been a great pleasure to turn the mayor in for smuggling.

The next day, we drove back to the Caen aerodrome and I flew my Tempest back across northern France to the base in Germany and reported back for duty.

I was in for another 6-7 months but, of course, it was now a totally different experience. Mostly it was enjoyable, with more time to relax and have fun. But there was one event that was, at the time, simply beyond anything I had ever imagined. Shortly after the surrender, a group of us went to Bergen-Belsen. I cannot remember precisely why our group went but we did. The horror of the place, and the other extermination camps, has been described often enough but what is hard for many younger people to understand today, when we know all about the Nazi death camps, was the disbelief we all experienced at first. How could human beings do this to other human beings? Nothing like this, nothing on this scale had been seen before. I had been enraged at the Germans for the execution of an old man in Normandy but what we saw in Bergen-Belsen was beyond belief. Apart from the fact of this kind of mass murder, there was the smell. You could smell the stench of rotting flesh from the camp 5-10 miles away. It was all unbelievable.

But fortunately, there were lighter moments. At one point following the war, there was a training session at the Isle of Silt, off the west coast of southern Denmark. The German civilians were generous and friendly. Perhaps they were beginning to sense relief at no longer being under the Nazi regime. One day, a military parade was scheduled. Air Vice-Marshal Broadhurst was in charge. But that day it was pissing down with rain. The CO, Johnny Johnson suggested to Broadhurst that it would be a huge mistake to make the men march under these conditions. Instead of a parade, Johnson suggested, why not just open the bar? Well, Broadhurst did not need too much arm-twisting. A good time was had by all. I remember having a chat with one of the German waitresses who spoke fairly good English. She said that the Germans had undoubtedly deserved to lose the war. I agreed, of course, without saying so but asked why she felt so? She pointed to Broadhurst, who was not physically the most impressive-looking of men, and said that if we had been led by men like him, and the Germans had still lost, then the German army must not have been very good. I thought that this was a bit unfair to Broadhurst but it was, if nothing else, a novel take on the war.

And then, finally, in late November, I got word that I was going to be discharged soon. In early December, maybe a week after I had been notified, I reported to the relevant office in London and was officially demobbed. There was no ceremony to it. You were handed a piece of paper, concerning your discharge, and you had to sign it. And then you were given a suit, a trilby hat, a new pair of shoes – there was nothing very fancy about any of these items, I can tell you – and then you were out of the door, a civilian once again. For me, it had been almost exactly six years since I had started active service with the RAF. I felt lucky. We had won the war and I had not only survived but was in good health. It was only a question of what I would do next. That was all but I was optimistic, I'm always optimistic. Precisely what sort of work I would do, however, was not clear. And there was no time to be lost. Once again, I found myself taking the train back to Cambridge from London and arrived back in my home town the afternoon of the same day I was demobbed.

My father offered me a job with the family company but, as before the war, this lacked appeal. I just did not want to be working with him. The possibility that I thought of first, of course, was taking up where I had left off, namely working with the Cambridge County Council. I walked up Castle Hill, it was a bitter cold December day, and entered Shire Hall and asked if I could see the county clerk. Of course I could, the receptionist replied. A few minutes later, I was in his office. The clerk, an older gentleman, remembered me immediately, got up when I entered his office and said, "Nice to see you back, Holland," as we shook hands. It was almost as if the six years had just been a week or two and nothing of importance had happened in between my leaving and returning. There were no questions about what sort of war I'd had or anything of the sort, just a welcome back. Perhaps at the Shire Hall, however, very little had happened or changed from 1939 to 1945. But for me, those six years had been a formative experience. I had grown up. The six years had felt like a lifetime's worth of experience.

But after the opening pleasantries, I immediately got down to business with the county clerk, asking if my old job was still available. Of course, he said, the job is yours, we'd kept it open for you. That was nice to hear, of course, I said, even if unexpected. But I needed to know, what would the salary be? He looked a little startled, I thought, at the question. Why, just what it was when you left, he said. In other words, £150 per annum. At that, I must have looked rather surprised myself. This was well below what I had been earning as a flight lieutenant in the RAF for the past two years. I now had a wife and a child and a family allowance from the RAF. We were hardly rolling in money but things were comfortable. Yet the county council assumed that I would be satisfied to make just what I had been earning as a single man six years earlier. I didn't need any time to consider it and told him straight-away that, if that's what was on offer, I would resign from the service. I then told him I had an option to join my father's business and that is what I intended to do. He expressed his regrets at my decision but clearly was not going to make me a better offer to keep me. I bid him good day and went around and said good-bye to some of the people I had known from before, many of whom were still there.

And, there I was, about to do something I had sworn I would never do, join my father's firm. There were not, in fact, a lot of other possibilities. We may have won the war but the British economy was on its knees. Rationing was still in operation, and would be for nearly 10 years more. Britain in early '46 was pretty grim and, in the quality of life, it still felt like war-time. But I wasn't going to give a lot of thought to that. I had a family to support and I was determined to make a go of things. And I was determined to start by setting my own conditions for joining C. Holland's.

The business had been founded in 1894 by my grandmother and, in 1917, the same year I had been born, my father had joined it. Sometime in the '30s, my brother Fred then came in and Grandma Holland stepped aside at that point, to let her son and grandson run the company. Initially, when the business started up, it had been located on Sedgewick Street in Romsey town, near the southern-most part of Cambridge. Sometime later, but before I was born, C. Holland's had moved to 213 Mill

Road, where it had been ever since and where, in fact, I had spent my early childhood.

I went to see my father in the small room that he used as an office in the house. As with the county clerk, I got right to the point. I told him that I had thought things over and would like to join the business. But, I added, I really did not think I could work with him but that I could work with my brother Fred. In effect, I was asking him to turn the business over to Fred and me. Perhaps he had been expecting the question, I don't know. But he agreed almost immediately, making my second surprise of the day. He thought about it for a few seconds, not much more it seemed, then said that he was prepared to split it 50:50 so long as we promised to give him a certain amount to live on for the rest of his life.

This proposed deal would have been too generous to me, I thought. And I told him so, that it would not be fair to Fred, who had already worked for many years in the firm. I proposed that Father give me a third and Fred, two thirds. "If that's the way you want it, fine," he said. We shook on it. In the space of a few days, I had gone from being an unemployed, ex-RAF pilot to having a foothold in civilian life. Not everyone was this lucky. In fact, a lot of the pilots had trouble finding work. Eighteen months later, Len Thorpe was still looking. A lot of firms and organisations did not want men who had shown the pluck and courage to be fighter pilots. They wanted more docile, subservient types.

Once again, my luck had held. It was clear to me, however, and to Fred, too, that we could, and should, try to do more with the business. Our first decision was that it should be expanded from a yeast supply firm to something bigger, distributing bakery goods and then, eventually, if all went well, some kind of wholesale food supply firm. But, for that, we needed more space. We made an offer to the neighbour next door, a Mr Newman, to buy his house. He liked our offer, apparently, and accepted it without too much haggling. After Mr Newman moved out, Fred moved into that house to be closer to things and to have additional office space. For the time being, my family and I stayed in our house on Scotland Road.

What the purchase did, in particular, for the business however was to give us more storage. For the kind of expansion we had in mind, we certainly needed more space for the stocks than the two existing garages out at the back provided. Therefore, the next step was to tear them down and build a warehouse behind the two houses. The third step was to build an extension of the road to reach the front of the warehouse. Obtaining the finance for this was surprisingly easy.

Initially, we were going to expand on the bakery side of things rather than jump into doing every kind of food. But for this, we needed supplies, in particular, fats and sugars for making cakes. These, however, were in relatively short supply, due to the rationing regulations in force. Our solution was to import a special product available from Belgium called "Sweetfat", which was not covered by the rationing scheme. As its name implied, this was a mixture of sugar and fat and we would buy it at a ton or two each time. I remember moving job lots of it around in wheelbarrows. In addition, during these early years, '46 to '48, I drove the vans for deliveries and did a lot of the footwork getting more custom for us. Fred, in contrast, tended to stay deskbound and handle much of the paperwork though I did the weekly accounts on Saturday. Though I was, by my own choosing, in the agreement I had struck with Father, the junior partner in the enterprise, I have to say that I was doing more than my fair share to get it up and running. Fred may not exactly have been a sleeping partner but he was certainly a less energetic one. And never a particularly happy person. But that was no change from before; he had always been something of a sourpuss.

Yet the key thing is that we prospered, we were expanding the business and it was succeeding. It was also tremendous fun, I was really enjoying it, all aspects of it, even though it often meant workdays that went from 7.00am to 7.00pm, with just a short break for lunch and a 20 minute lie-down in the middle of the day. The work involved not only planning the expansion, making sure we were getting all the supplies we needed, but driving the van, dealing with customers and, as I mentioned, going and finding new ones. But it was exciting to take what had been a stable but small business and expand it into something much bigger, more dynamic and more interesting.

Of course, that first year, of '46, involved more than just work. There was also a lot of catching up to do with people I had known. One of them was Hubert Middleton. He had been assigned to the British Education Service in Berlin at the start of the Michaelmas term in 1945 and had worked there for a year, returning to Cambridge in September of '46. Soon after returning, he invited me to be his guest to high table at Trinity one evening in the autumn. Of course, I was delighted to accept. For all my experience of Trinity as a chorister, this was the first time I had been invited to join the fellows as a guest at high table at one of their dinners. Dinner would be in the main dining hall with the long stained glass windows. This building, which looks like an old converted chapel, overlooks the Great Court, just across at a slight diagonal from where one enters through the main gate to Trinity at the porters' lodge.

The term "high table" implies a certain grandness that the table itself does not really have. It is just a long wooden dining table at one end of the hall, which is filled with similar long wooden tables and benches for the undergraduates. What distinguishes the high table from the others is not just its position but the fact of being on a platform raised perhaps 2-3 inches. This is just enough to trip you up if you are not careful when you step up to it but not enough to give the kind of exalted view of the hall that the word "high" might suggest.

The food itself, as I recall, was not exceptional but certainly better than what the average Cambridge family was having for dinner at the time. What made the experience special was the atmosphere of the hall itself, with its high ceilings, the stained glass windows and the walls hung with the portraits of the great men who had been masters and fellows. And, of course, there was also the fact of the company of the fellows themselves, in their black gowns. The evening commenced with the saying of grace in Latin by one of the fellows, everyone standing behind his chair, following which there was some sort of discreet signal to sit. The occasion was presided over by the Master of Trinity, the great British historian, G.M. Trevelyan. He was the Regius Professor of History at Cambridge and was a distinguished looking man with his white and grey hair and moustache.

After dinner, all of us made our way out of the dining hall to the master's lodge next door, where a gleaming polished dining table had been set for the guests. We took our places. It was indicated to me that I should sit on the right of Professor Trevelyan, as a protégé of Hubert Middleton, and was thus the honoured guest at this gathering. Dr Middleton, in turn, was on my right side and soon engaged in an earnest conversation with another historian about some historical matter. I had only known Hubert Middleton as my choirmaster but he had the reputation of being phenomenally well read, knowledgeable about all sorts of things. The madeira was passed around, to the right, and the port, to the left. A waiter came and offered us each a cigar at some point in the evening. A good cigar, too. I don't know if cigars were covered by the rationing rules in force throughout the country but around this table, the privations of the war and its aftermath seemed a long way off. While Hubert Middleton was having his conversation, around the table the other guests seemed involved in equally earnest conversations about various academic matters. It would have been impossible not to be impressed with the learning and intelligence of this group of people, made all the more special by the luxury of the setting. And, yet, while I was enjoying the experience, the situation, and the kind of talk, seemed so disconnected from my world and the life I had had in the war.

I turned to Professor Trevelyan and said that I could easily see the great brain-power seated around this table but what I didn't understand was why it wasn't being used to more practical effect, being harnessed for building up industry in the country. Britain may have won the war but it was still going through incredibly hard times. Trevelyan looked at me, with what looked like a trace of condescension. And he said, "Holland, can you think of a better place to spend your life, with your own rooms in this magnificent college, looking out on the Great Court here, and with all the time in the world to think about your subject and what you want to do with it?" Perhaps I did not look as appreciative or sympathetic as he expected me to be because he added, "Can't you understand why people want to do this?" I said, "Yes, I can but I still would have thought it was more interesting to go into business." The slight kindness in his eye, however shaded it might have been by condescension, went out, as he said, "It's a rat race."

Well, that may have been the view of the business world from the master's lodge at Trinity College but it wasn't mine. To me, building our business was certainly not a rat race but a challenge and an exciting and enjoyable one, at that. Furthermore, the business was clearly growing and thriving, as Fred and I had hoped when we had laid our plans for expansion. And in March of '49, my second child and daughter, Louise, was born. From early days, her nickname was "Lollie", perhaps because this is how Paulette, having trouble with saying "Louise" pronounced it.

One surprise of being in business as a partner with Fred was that we got on quite well. We had never been close as children or young men; there was the six-year age difference between us, as well as basic differences in personality. Yet, as business partners, we were compatible and worked together well. Yet, by 1950 or '51, I could tell that Fred was beginning to be tired or slightly bored with it all. He had, it has to be said, been working at it a lot longer than I had, having started before the war. And he kept on dropping hints about how maybe it was time to sell the business. The buyer he had in mind was the United Yeast Company, which was a subsidiary of the Distillers Company Ltd.

Finally, I decided to put him to the test about this, to see if he was serious or, at least, to shut him up about it. Late one week, I wrote out a letter to the head of the United Yeast Company, stating that we had reached the point in our development of the business where we thought that they might possibly be interested in buying it. Was this the case and should we discuss this matter? I typed in Fred's name under where he would put his signature. Since he was the major share-holder, it was only proper that the letter should come from him. On that Friday, I handed it to him and told him that if he was serious about selling up, he should just post the letter over the weekend and I would leave the matter with him for his decision.

Early on the following Monday morning, I asked him if he had posted the letter over the weekend. He said that he had. I immediately told him that he should expect a 'phone call from the company before noon of the next day. I had no doubt that they would be interested. The next morning, I had a delivery to make in one of the vans, to St Ives, a small town about 10 miles north of Cambridge. When I got to St Ives, however, I realised that I had to check with Fred about something and gave him a ring. His news was that he had just heard from the company in London. They were interested, indeed, and could we show up at their offices at 10.00am the following morning?

We arrived at the London offices of the United Yeast Company at 10.00am, as they had requested, and were soon meeting with their board of directors. During the discussion, I said absolutely nothing, Fred did all the talking. By noon, the directors had agreed a price for our company amongst themselves and told us their offer. Fred seemed to think that it was a fair price. Again, I kept complete silence. They took us out to lunch and, as it happened, I sat next to the chairman, a man named Robin Black. As the lunch was starting, he turned to me and said, looking rather pleased with himself, "Well, we've done a good deal, Frank." I looked back at him and said, "You haven't done a deal yet. You've agreed a price with my brother and now I know the value of the shares of our company. But according to the agreement I made with him when we set things up, if one of us wants to leave the business, the other has the right to buy his shares. And that's what I would like to do." He looked taken aback and said, "You can't do that." I said, "Oh, yes, I can." At this point, he changed tack and tried reassurance. He told me that I had nothing to worry about, that if the business were sold to them, they would employ me to run the Cambridge branch of the company, which would include our company. I told him that I would have to think about it.

And think about it I did, in particular how I might actually pull this off. Having put so much effort into building the business up, I wasn't ready to let it go. On the other hand, I had no realistic idea as to how I could actually buy Fred out. The price offer that United Yeast had made was not a small one and if I was to buy Fred out, I would have to raise two thirds of it. I had nowhere near that amount of money to invest. Fred himself must have been wondering too. "What do you want to do?" he asked me. I said, "I'm going to buy you out." And he replied, "You can't afford to." And I said, in turn, "Give me another week." Well, he didn't apply any further pressure to me. He must have been assuming that the whole thing would be sorted out, one way or another, soon enough. After all, there was the definite, and good, offer from United Yeast.

The solution to my problem came through my friend Doug January. Doug was a physically big man, and he liked his luxuries. With him, a bottle of champagne was never far away when there was something to be celebrated and a good cigar was almost always at hand. He looked a bit like Churchill, and in his speech, general bearing and manner, also resembled the old man. I always suspected that these similarities were not purely accidental. He was also a number of years older than me and had already made a very successful career in the Cambridge business world, in the property business specifically.

Once again, as in my getting into the RAF, golf played a part in events. Doug was a golfing partner of a man named John Ward in the accounts department at Shire Hall and, through him, had learned that I was a golfer. One day there was a 'phone call from a Mr Douglas January, whom I hardly knew at the time, asking me if Margot and I would like to play a round of golf that Saturday at the golf club. I accepted the invitation, of course and we met them at the agreed time that Saturday morning.

It soon became apparent that it would not be a runaway win by either side. We were playing a good competitive game and on the 8th hole, I had hit a long drive but there was still some distance to the green. Margot asked me whether she should play short or go for the green. I said, "Go for the green, show them all you've got." And Doug turned to me a couple of seconds later and said, "Dutch, I've never heard a man say that to his wife." That was the start of our friendship. This must have been in '47 or '48.

Well, several years later, on the Saturday following the meeting in London with the United Yeast directors, I was playing a round of golf in the morning with Doug alone. Maybe that day my golf game was a bit off or maybe I just looked preoccupied. But he evidently sensed that something was not right.

"What's wrong?" he finally asked.

"Nothing, Doug, nothing."

"Yes, there is something wrong with you. You're not the same chap you were last week."

"Well, I've got a bit on my mind," I admitted.

He didn't press to find out what that was and we didn't discuss it any further during the game but, as pre-arranged, he came to my house for lunch. As always for our Saturday lunch, Margot served a delicious beefsteak and kidney pudding. And, after we had tucked in, Doug came back to the earlier conversation, wanting to know what was behind my bad mood. I really did not want to go into it in any detail – this was my problem, after all, and I felt that I had to find my own way out of it – but he must have had some idea what it was about. Because he said, "Dutch, if this is a matter of money, I will support you. And if you want my support, ring me up Monday morning and we will go and see your bank manager immediately."

After he had left, I turned to Margot and said, "Do you think he really meant that, about financial support if I need it?" "Yes, I do," she replied, without a second's hesitation.

Monday morning, I rang Doug up first thing and I asked him if he really meant what he had said. "Dutch," he replied, "I will ring your bank manager. You're at the Lloyd's on Mill Road, right? Make an appointment for tomorrow afternoon."

The next day, at 1.00pm, we showed up for our appointment with the bank manager, a Mr Bill Smart, who was also a golfer, and a good one at that.

Doug was blunt. "Whatever Mr Holland wants, he can have. I will take responsibility. Please make up a document to that effect."

"Mr January, you can't do that," Bill Smart said. He looked a little shocked.

"Yes, I can. I can do whatever I want."

Smart still hesitated. "Well, you've got to have a lot of confidence in someone, to give them this kind of support."

Doug said, "I will be responsible for anything Mr Holland needs in the future," and he repeated the request for the document.

The document was duly prepared and Doug had it for his signature the next day. And I now had the backing I needed to buy Fred out.

That Thursday or Friday, I saw Fred in the office and said, "Here's the cheque for your two thirds shares in our business," and I laid it on the desk before him.

He looked hard at it, as if he could not quite believe his eyes, then he looked at me and said, "Where did you get this from?"

"Never you mind where I got it from. There's the cheque. If you want to take it, then take it. If not, we will just carry on."

"I want to get out," Fred replied.

"Fine, it's agreed. You now have your money."

But that wasn't exactly the end of the matter. Fred's son, Pat, had been working in the business for the past few years and I didn't think it was fair that Pat should have to go, just because Fred was. So I told Fred that I was willing to give Pat a third share in the company. Fred thought that this was fine and Pat was pleased to accept. But he didn't stay long. Pat had trained in the bakery trade and that was what he really wanted to do. After two years, Fred had persuaded him to set up a bakery, under their joint management, in Teddington, Middlesex. Pat then surrendered his share of the business to me and joined his father, having been paid out for his shares. This would have been in '52 or '53. Hence, I was now the sole owner of C. Holland's, just six or seven years from having joined the firm as the junior partner.

My first step was to see if I could put it on a basis that would allow Doug to be released from his undertaking with the bank. I went around to all the companies we did business with and asked them for three months' credit. All except one agreed. That freed up enough money for me to make a payment to the bank, which, in turn, induced them to release Doug from his responsibility. We had been good friends before but this taking on the responsibility for any of my debts really cemented the friendship.

And the business continued to thrive and grow. Within a few years, I was able to pay off my bank loan. Yet, when you are in business, if you have a certain temperament, you don't rest on your laurels. You are always looking for new opportunities, new directions. And that was the case with me. We had pretty much covered the market for the kind of food items we were supplying. A new direction was needed.

And one such possible direction was petrol. This was the late '50s and England was, at last, really recovering from the war. There were more cars on the road all the time and cars need petrol. Petrol stations, as a result, were good businesses. It seemed to me that here was an opportunity, if I went about it in the right way.

It turned out that one of our employees, a man named Bob Johnson, who had been one of our van drivers, had left us to be a salesman for Texaco. Texaco was selling us petrol for our vans and one day in 1958, Bob came to me to discuss the matter. But I had a different question for him and a request. "Bob," I said, "can you get your company to tell me if I can put a petrol station in front of this building?" He agreed immediately, "Yes, I will," he said.

A month or so later, he came by to make his usual call on us and I asked him if he had put the question to his managers. His response was, "You didn't mean that, did you?" "Of course, I bloody well meant it," I told him and asked him again, firmly, to please put the question to his company.

This time he actually did it and a few days later was back but the answer wasn't at all encouraging. He told me that Texaco wasn't interested in discussing it unless I had planning permission for it and he somehow implied that they didn't think it likely I would get it.

But I was determined to try. I submitted an application to the local authorities responsible for such things and it was a good plan, even if I say so myself. I was proposing to knock down the front part of what had been Mr Newman's house and build a forecourt with four petrol pumps and a kiosk. True to Texaco's prediction, it was turned down. But I knew it was a good idea and I wasn't going to just drop it. So, I appealed against the decision of the local authorities and was granted a hearing, one that would involve the inspectors. The hearing started at 9.00am or 10.00am and there was actually a lot of opposition. Finally, at noon, the chairman of the meeting, the chief inspector, said that it was time to call a recess for lunch and that after lunch, he wanted to inspect the premises where I intended to put up the forecourt.

After lunch, that was exactly what he and I did. We went around to our business premises, I described my plans on the spot, and I could tell that he thought it was a reasonable plan. But, as we were winding up, he turned to me and said, "Who's got their knife into your back?" I asked him what he meant. "Oh, never mind," he said. But what he had seen convinced him and he was able to bring the other inspectors around. The plan was approved. Then there was the question of how to finance it but I was able to raise the money. We then went ahead, just as I had imagined it would be, with a forecourt with four petrol pumps and a kiosk. And it was a success. We made money.

The next step, it seemed to me was to expand by building a showroom and selling cars. More of Newman's old house was converted for this purpose. Texaco were now willing to be co-investors and they put some of the money into this. We got a small concession from the agents for Morris cars, King and Harper's. And when I say "small", I mean it. The initial agreement was that we would sell six Morrises a year. We had no trouble doing that and it seemed to me that we wanted more ambitious backing. So we changed agents and were soon selling Simcas. Within a short time, we were selling 20-30 a year. This was not a huge number but certainly more than six and enough to show the promise of the business.

In 1966, a new property came on the market, further south on Mill Road, Turpin's yard, at 315-317 Mill Road. Doug January suggested that I buy this for a second petrol station. The owners were asking for £25,000, not a small sum in those days but I managed to get it for £22,500, which was still a considerable investment. My specific idea was to make it a self-service station. The labour costs would be less and my hunch was that it would be popular because it should be a fast way of filling up your car.

Now, at the time, in all of England, there was just one self-service station, in Essex, just south of Cambridge. It would take some additional investment to set this up and my thought was that, once again, I should try the major petrol companies. I had been dealing with Texaco so they were the ones I would try first. I made an appointment to see the chairman of Texaco at the company headquarters in London, just off Fleet Street at the time. We discussed my proposition in his office and I can remember his exact words to this day: "We do not think that self-service can ever take off in this country. We are not prepared to give you any money for this."

Well, that was clear enough. But if that was Texaco's position, it wasn't mine. I left there resolved to finance the project myself, rather than trying the other companies first, where I might well get essentially the same brush-off. And I did just that. We converted the buildings at Turpin's yard and built the forecourt, with six self-service pumps and all the gear that was needed for recording the sales amounts. A kiosk where the customers would make their payments was also put in.

And we had a name all picked out: "Hel-up yoursel-uf". But I knew that we needed some publicity if we wanted to get this thing off the ground properly. One asset for a promotion of the kind I had in mind would be the right sort of car for the publicity pictures. At that time, the Triumph Tiger, a six-cylinder sports car had just been introduced. I went to the Triumph dealer and secured one for four days. In addition, we should have somebody well known to the public involved in the opening. Someone suggested the well-known actress of the time, Liz Fraser. She was happy to agree, provided we paid her £500 – and in cash. We agreed. If we were going to do this thing, we were going to do it right and not on the cheap.

The opening was a big success, with good pictures in the local paper of Liz Fraser driving up in the Triumph Tiger, smiling, looking gracious, receiving flowers from us, the whole bit. The real success, however, came in the following week. It was our sales figures: we sold 15,000 gallons of petrol that first week. There was every sign that we were going to prove the prediction of the chairman of Texaco completely wrong.

The next step was as before: to build a showroom to sell cars. This would take more investment and having just extended myself to buy the property at Turpin's yard, it seemed a good idea to try to get a backer to help with the costs. Again, a major petrol company would be the obvious choice but this time I tried Mobil instead of Texaco. And this time, the outcome was as I'd hoped. They offered £35,000 for the development, to be repaid with interest in quarterly instalments, over a 15-year period. This seemed completely feasible so a deal was struck. We went ahead and built the showroom with a car-wash facility on the forecourt. At the time, we were selling Rootes cars. Initially, we were getting our supply of cars through another agency, Robinson's, but this was not always easy. What I wanted was a direct dealership from Rootes and they soon obliged. The understanding was that I would strike the specific arrangements with their main sales manager, a man named Jack. The phrase

"Jack the lad" rightly describes him. He was a good-looking young fellow and clearly very popular with the ladies. One day, I said to him, "Jack, why the hell don't you get married?" And he replied instantly, "Frank, why buy a book when you can use the library?" I had to laugh. It would have been hard not to like Jack and he and I got along fine. But after awhile, he left to do something else. And about this time, Rootes – I think it was under pressure from Robinson's – cut out my direct dealership. By this point, we had been selling about 80-90 cars a year. It was good business but not spectacular. I decided that it was time to look around and see if we could strike a deal with another motor car manufacturer that would give us more freedom to sell more cars.

By the early '70s, the Datsun company, was beginning to make a strong entry into sales of motor cars in the UK but there was, as yet, no Cambridge dealer for Datsun. It seemed that it would be worth a try. In 1974, I went down to their headquarters in Brighton and talked to their sales director. He was a hard chap and made clear what they wanted: if I guaranteed to sell 100 cars a year, they would give me the Datsun dealership for Cambridge. I told him that that seemed quite a lot – though, in fact, it was not that many more than we had been selling for Rootes. He was unmoved by my objection, wouldn't budge. Those were the conditions, he insisted, take it or leave it. So, I took it. And, what's more, we made our goal easily that first year. In fact, our sales boomed. Within a few years, we were selling about 380 a year, or more than one a day on average.

By the time the contract renewal came up, the headquarters had moved to Worthing and the new owner of the Datsun franchise for the UK was a businessman from the Continent named Amar Botner, a short man with close-cut iron-grey hair. As a businessman, Botner was an even harder case than the sales director in Brighton. But he was an interesting man of European background, with a French mother and a German Jewish father. Botner had fought with the French Army at the beginning of the war and had been captured. Sometime after that he had managed to escape and then fought with the Free French, right until the end of the war. But I only learned this much later and when I tried to draw him out a bit, to tell me about his experiences, he simply said something about having to act in accordance with one's convictions – if you are to be able to live with yourself. He was a hard man but I respected him, even before I knew about his history.

The new conditions for sales that he had set were that we should agree to sell 500 cars a year, redecorate the showroom once a year, and some other items. All of this seemed like a fairly tall order and I hesitated. The business, however, had thrived under our Datsun dealership and I had no wish to give it up at this point.

Nevertheless, a problem soon appeared. There was a certain model that none of the dealers was having much luck unloading. Botner had, of course, noticed this and decided to force the pace. He summoned 50 of us, probably the whole complement of UK Datsun dealers, to a big meeting at the headquarters at Worthing and assembled us around a large half-circle wooden table.

"Gentlemen," he announced, "we have got to get rid of these cars." He then went around the room, calling each dealer by name and assigning each a number of cars of the troublesome model to be sold that year. Each one agreed, saying "Yes, Mr Botner." Until he came to me, in the middle of the group. He assigned me 10. Having seen what was going on, I had already made up my mind and said, "No, Mr Botner, I won't take any, we can't sell them." Well, he didn't pause. It was as if he hadn't heard. He just continued around the group, assigning the numbers to be taken. No one else objected.

But he had heard me, all right. A few weeks later, at the Earl's Court Motor Show in London, I ran into him or rather he came up to me and with a sad and serious look, a more-in-sorrow-than-anger sort of look, said, "Fronk" – that's how he pronounced my name – "Fronk, you have let me down." I denied it, "I haven't let you down, Mr Botner. You know that. We have been selling many cars, we just cannot sell that model, that's all there is to it." He then offered me 10% more for each car sold of this particular model if I took a quota of 10 for the year. I refused. He lowered the number to 7, while keeping the extra financial incentive. I still refused. We ended with an agreement for 5 to be sold each year, and with an increased margin for my dealership. Neither of us was thrilled by the outcome but it was an acceptable compromise on both sides. And somehow Holland Motors managed to sell five of these a year in Cambridge until the model was withdrawn, when I breathed a sigh of relief.

Some time in this period, Datsun was swallowed up by the Nissan company, so we were now selling Nissans. Soon after this take-over, a group of five British dealers were invited, along with our boss, Botner, to Tokyo to meet with the chairman and board of directors of Nissan. I had been picked to be part of this group. This would be my first trip to Japan and I was pleased to have been invited.

The day after we landed at Tokyo airport, we went to meet the chairman, who spoke to us through an interpreter. After the preliminary greetings and welcome, the chairman said to us, "Gentlemen, you can ask us any questions you would like. And we would also like to have any suggestions from you for improving sales of our cars in England." There were several questions from the group and then I asked about the company's plans once we had reached the present sales' targets for Britain.

Botner immediately tried to intervene, saying, "You can't ask that!" The interpreter now relayed both my question and Botner's comment to the chairman in Japanese. The chairman turned to Botner and said in Japanese but which was rapidly put into English by the translator, "Mr Botner, I said we would answer all the questions that are put to us." Botner, a proud man with a temper, looked quite put out but said nothing more. You don't argue with the ultimate boss of your company, after all. The chairman then answered my questions, saying that once sales targets had been reached, the Nissan company planned to set up one or more factories in Europe, quite possibly in England.

Two days after this meeting, a group of us were being given a tour of one of the Nissan factories, when Botner's public relations man, a chap named Peter, came up to me and took me aside. He told me that I had been chosen to give the response to the Nissan Motor Company, on behalf of the British dealers, at the big Gala dinner a few nights hence. I looked at him and asked, "Who said so?"

"Why, Mr Botner, of course."

"Well, you tell Mr Botner that if he wants me to do this, he should ask me to do it in person."

Peter looked slightly taken aback and said that he couldn't ask Mr Botner that. And I said, "Why not?" I then insisted that he do so. Peter looked unhappy but agreed to relay my request to Mr Botner.

The next day, there was another trip to a different Nissan factory and Peter came up to me to inform me that I would be on Mr Botner's bus that morning. As soon as I boarded, Botner signalled to me and said that I should sit next to him. He then asked me why I had made this condition. I told him that I thought that this was an important matter, and if it was, then it was only right that he should ask me directly rather than relaying it through his PR man. Well, there was a bit more back-and-forth about this but finally Botner did put the request to me. Public speaking was not one of his strengths and though he probably should have been the person to give the reply at the banquet, he was clearly relieved to be getting out of it. Once he had asked me himself, I told him that I would be pleased to accept. He then, however, immediately started to tell me what I should say. At that, I told him that I wasn't going to be directed and that if he wanted certain things said in a certain way, then he should be giving the speech. He backed down and it was settled, I would give the talk in my own way.

The Gala night took place three days later and it was quite a large and posh affair. I was sitting at the main table with the chairman and the president of the company, Botner, and the translator, a Mr Goto. I was seated between the chairman and Mr Goto. A beautiful young Geisha girl was serving us the drinks – she knew that my drink was whisky, somehow – and I couldn't resist asking Mr Goto, in a quiet voice, whether she was one of the chairman's perks. Instead of answering me, he translated the question to the chairman, who laughed his head off. And the chairman replied, through the interpreter, "No, Mr Holland, she is not one of my perks but she will look after you while you are here." Botner had heard all this and he was furious, saying to me, "You can't ask things like that." But I had and, clearly, no harm had been done.

As the meal was nearing the end, there were some brief words of greeting to the assembled guests by one of the top officials of the company and then it was my turn to give the reply. I walked across the dance floor, got up on the stage, picked up the microphone and proceeded to give my short talk – in Japanese. That was my special surprise for the group. You see, I had written it out in English then had enlisted the help of our lady guide to render it into phonetic Japanese. And I had practised for the preceding three days and had it, if not perfect, at least quite good.

Well, it was a small sensation. As I finished, people stood up and applauded. But I wasn't finished. I then gave the talk in English and then made my way back to the table, to more applause. As I was sitting down, I heard the chairman say something to Mr Goto, who then promptly translated it for me. The chairman had said, "That is the first time we have ever had the response to the Nissan Motor Company made in our language." And he had then added, "Mr Holland, you and your wife will be guests of the Nissan company whenever you visit Japan."

When this was translated, Botner, of course, overheard it and was livid. I think he found it almost intolerable being upstaged by someone whom he regarded as an employee. But he said nothing, just silently fumed.

And then there was dancing. The chairman signalled to the Geisha girl, who immediately came over, and indicated to her that she and I should dance. So I got to dance with this beautiful young woman.

Furthermore, during the parties over the following two evenings, she was on hand to bring me drinks and whatever items of food I wanted. She was delightful.

The whole trip had been great, just great. Nor did it do any long-term damage to my working relationship with Botner, who, after all, regarded my dealership as a success. Yet, Botner himself eventually came to grief with the government, who claimed that he had fiddled the books and that he owed them £25 million in back taxes. I do not know the truth, or otherwise, of this, but the fact is that Botner left the country and took up residence in Switzerland and never returned to Britain. His managing director, however, did a year's time in connection with this claimed tax fiddle. Yet it was a fairly gentle sentence. Apparently, he was allowed out between 9.00am and 5.00pm to do business but had to be back by 5.00pm every working day. Our criminal justice system often works in mysterious ways, particularly when it comes to white-collar crime, and this might have been one of those times.

Some years later, in the early '80s, we switched from Nissan to Fiat but that is a long story and I won't go into it here. Yet, our Fiat dealership was, if anything, even more successful than what we had done for Nissan. In the mid-1980s I semi-retired, handing over the day-to-day management to a small but loyal team who had been with me for many years. The truth is I wanted more time to relax, in particular to play golf, and by this time I was spending more and more time in France, as I will explain in the next chapter. But I found it hard to give up the business, which had been my pride and joy. I had, after all, taken a successful but small and highly specialised family business, catering to the bakery trade, and first built it up to a successful wholesale food business. Then it had branched out in the late '50s and early '60s, in a wholly new direction, the motor car business and I had made a big success of that. In the early '60s, the two halves of the enterprise had operationally separated, with the motor car business under my name and C. Holland & Sons Ltd. continuing under the original name, and being run by its own manager, a man named John Cox. In 1980, my nephew Robert Bakewell, Doris's son, joined the company and later took over the management when John Cox retired. Given the independent management of C. Holland's, I had been able to focus all my attention on the motor car side of the business from the early 1960s onwards.

Yet, as anyone who went through the '80s and early '90s in Britain will know, this period wasn't a good one for business. Sales had declined and we went through harder times than we had ever experienced before. Perhaps the fact that I was in France half the year didn't help. Whatever the reasons, it was clear to me by the mid-'90s that it was time to wrap things up and in 1996, we sold Frank Holland Motors. The company was bought by one of our competitor agencies, Robinson's, in fact. And 1996 was an anniversary of sorts: it had been just over 50 years since I had first joined the family company, becoming a junior partner to my brother, right after the war.

But the story of my life from 1946 to 1996 was not just one

of local business success or business ups-and-downs in Cambridge. It was filled with events on the personal side, which led me to reconnect to France and my memories of the war and Normandy. In the next and final chapter, I will describe how my life came to be tied up with France and the French for a second time.

10

My continued French connection

My war-time experience in Norrey-en-Auges virtually guaranteed that there would be some ongoing ties to the people in France who had helped me. They had risked their lives to do so and there was no way I would forget them. I made a visit in 1947 to the village, my first since the night-time confrontation with the mayor in '45, and saw many of my friends, though not André, who had returned to Paris after the war was over. And in the early '50s, I took a car ferry over, in my MG saloon car and attended André's wedding in Brittany.

Margot encouraged these contacts and visits. She felt tremendously grateful to Henri and André and the others for having sheltered me during those weeks in Normandy, but she did not come herself. After all, we had two young daughters to look after. In addition, she participated in the business and helped keep an eye on things while I was away. So, altogether, it was simplest to go by myself.

And then in 1957, an incredible blow fell. Margot was pregnant again and though she had had several miscarriages, we had high hopes that this time, everything would go well. One day in June, however, she started feeling very ill. We did not know what was going on and rushed her to the hospital, the old Addenbrookes (as it came to be called after the new

Addenbrookes was put up). This was no trivial or quickly-mended complication, however. Margot had had a pulmonary thrombosis and died two days after being admitted to hospital.

I was completely thunderstruck. I couldn't believe it, at first. I had suddenly, without any real warning, lost my beloved wife while my two daughters had lost their mother. I did not allow myself to be carried away by grief, that's not the way I am, nor did I show much. But it was an incredible blow. If you have ever experienced anything like this, you won't need the description and if you haven't, there aren't words I can find to describe it adequately. Of course, what kept me going was the thought of my responsibilities. I had my two girls to look after and my employees, as well. By now, of course, the company was a medium-sized going-concern in its holdings and operations and we had a corresponding work force.

If anything, having the work to attend to undoubtedly helped me through this period. But the following two years were a pretty dark time for me and, I am sure, hard on my girls though we didn't talk much about it at the time. The two grandmothers, Nanna Holland and Nanna Notley, and Margot's sister, Peggy, whom the girls called Pippy, rallied round and were a tremendous help. These three ladies really kept the household going.

And then, in 1960, I decided it was time for a holiday, a foreign holiday, something special, for me and my daughters. I didn't take many holidays – the business seemed to take constant attention – but that summer seemed the right time to do something of this sort. I don't remember how the particular idea came about but maybe it was from Doug January because we went with him and his family. The plan was to have a holiday in the Mediterranean, on the island of Majorca. Today, this island and its neighbours are overrun with tourists but in 1960 going to Majorca for a summer holiday was still an unusual thing to do, at least for Brits.

We flew to Majorca and landed at Palma, then travelled from the airport to stay in the beach town of Magaluf. Our reservation was for the Hotel Atlantic which, at the time, was the only hotel on this otherwise deserted stretch of beach.

It must have been our first or second day there. We were all down on the beach, the Januarys and I lying on reclining beach chairs, the children were off playing in the sand. It was a pretty glorious summer day. And then one of us noticed that our children had been joined by two others, a teenage girl and a somewhat younger boy. I might not have paid much attention but Doug pointed out the apparent mother of these two children, a strikingly attractive auburn-haired lady.

Later that day, while I was waiting for the lift in the hotel lobby, this same lady came up, also to take the lift. I said something about noticing that our children had been playing together on the beach. She made some sort of friendly reply and I could tell immediately that she was French. Well, sometime before the lift had reached our respective floors, I had invited her and her children to join our group for dinner and she had accepted. Later that evening, she and I went for an evening stroll on the beach. I remember she took off her shoes to walk barefoot in the wet sand. That's a friendly sort of thing to do, it shows the woman likes and trusts the man she is walking with.

Her name was Suzanne, though to me, once I got to know her better, she was always Suzie. She was a divorcee, raising her two children by herself. She was well-organised, intelligent and had class, in her looks and the way she dressed. She also had business skills. She was the managing director of one of France's biggest shipping companies, "Navigation Mixte". An impressive woman and I liked her right from the start.

A few months later, I went to Paris to pay her a visit. She suggested that we have dinner at the restaurant, "Chez les Anges", owned by one of her friends, a man named Armand. At that time, "Chez les Anges", though I did not know it when she first mentioned it, was probably one of the top restaurants in Paris. Certainly, the meal we had there was first-rate, as were all our subsequent dinners there. And she introduced me to Armand that first night. Armand, a stocky but distinguished looking man of medium height with black hair and a black moustache, was, I think, surprised to meet an Englishman who spoke French. And, of course, he found out about my Normandy experience some time fairly early in our acquaintance. Whatever the reason, he and I hit it off from the start.

In fact, over the following months, when I would visit Paris to see Suzie, he would let me stay at his flat. I think that during those times he went to stay with his fiancée, Alice, whom he married either that year or the next. Sometimes he and I would, after the restaurant closed, go and have a drink at one of the nearby night clubs. This period was the start of my friendship with Armand. Nevertheless, when Suzie told him that I had proposed and she had accepted, he had said – she told me later – that she must be crazy to marry an Englishman. Whatever his general views about French-English "mixed" marriages, I don't know, but I am fairly sure that he changed his mind eventually about this particular case.

There was, of course, no question about what country or place we would be living in; it had to be Cambridge. That's where my business and my life were. Suzie, therefore, gave up her high-powered job with Navigation Mixte and devoted herself to merging the two families and running her new household in England. By this point, I had moved my family out of Cambridge itself to the little village of Great Shelford, just south of the town. Our house is situated along a tree-lined road, Woodlands Road, and the house is called Merrowdown. It is a lovely and peaceful spot. Behind the house is a large grassy lawn surrounded by trees on both sides. The grounds are bordered at the far end by a stream and the river. There is not only the usual wildlife of birds and rabbits and squirrels but the occasional muntjac will make an appearance on the lawn.

Suzie, who was a highly organised and efficient lady, faced no challenges in running the household. Merging the two families was a different matter, however. At least, fortunately, there was little problem with the three girls. Suzie's daughter Liz, who was about 16 at the time, basically got along fine with both Lollie and Paulette, who had been nicknamed Polly at school. Liz was and is a sweet, easy-going person, eager to please others. But her son, Hubert, was a different matter entirely. Maybe the problems started because he'd been growing up without a father and now he was in a new country, with a new language, and suddenly having to deal, as well, with a step-father and step-sisters. I don't know but one could imagine that that might have been his side of the story. Mine, however, was that I believe children should follow the rules laid down by the parents, even if one of those is a step-parent. That's the only way a household can function. There have to be rules and the children have to do what the parents ask them to do. It is as simple as that. Well, whatever the exact reasons were, Hubert and I were on a collision course almost from day one. He was only 11 when Suzie and her kids arrived in our house but by the time he became a teenager, he was completely out of control, going out of the house at all hours, getting up to God knows what. To say that he and I did not have an easy relationship would be to put it mildly. In fact, it would be about 30 years before we did. When he was 18 or 19, he headed back to France. He worked for a while as a golf teacher and did other things too but later became a manager of various casinos, and (in Normandy), made a big success of that. Finally, in 1997, at the wedding of Liz's son, Clive, Hubert and I had a long chat and finally put the past behind us. We now see Hubert and his new wife about once every year or two and it's good to do so.

My two girls were growing up, of course, and beginning to find their own directions. Polly, after finishing school, had helped in the business but during this time she was being courted by a young man, Colin, who was the son of another Cambridge businessman. Polly and Colin got married in 1965 and three years later, their first child, Caroline, was born. (Their second, Nick, came along two years later.) Lollie, six years younger than her older sister, completed her course of studies at the Perse Girls' School – the best all-girls school in the city – and decided to become a primary school teacher. When she was 18, in 1967, she went off to London to train for this but later, after three years of teaching, decided that she wanted to do something more ambitious and became, first, an educational psychologist and later, a child psychotherapist.

Although life is always throwing up problems to deal with, it was basically good for me in the '60s and early '70s. The business was thriving, my girls were doing well, it was good to be married to Suzie. I kept up with my golf and in 1971 became captain of the men's section of the Gog Magog Golf Club, taking up the position that Alan Gray, my first choirmaster, had held in the early 1900s. I continued to enjoy the company of a good circle of friends and acquaintances, not least Doug January in Cambridge, and Armand in Paris, whom we would see whenever we went over to France.

And then, in 1973, disaster struck again and, as before, completely out of the blue. Suzie, like all of us in the family, was an enthusiastic golfer and one day in the autumn while she was playing, she had a massive stroke. We had had no warnings or inklings that she had blood pressure problems or anything like that. It just happened and she died suddenly. Again, I could hardly believe that this had happened. For the second time, I found myself a widower. At least, now, I did not have to worry about my girls, they were leading independent lives. And, also, the motor car business we had was doing very well as was C. Holland's. In general, things were certainly more secure for me than they had been in 1957 when Margot died. But the initial shock of Suzie's death, and then the loneliness – the sense of a big gap in my life where Suzie had been – were pretty overwhelming at first. It's the kind of situation where you can't help but ask yourself, at least once, "Why me?" But there is no answer to that question. At least not for me as I have never been a strongly religious person. And, in the end, there is no point in dwelling on one's misfortunes. You face ahead to the future and get on with living.

The following year, I paid a visit to Armand in Paris. It would have been my second time seeing him since Suzie's death. It was good to see him again but, as it happened, he had someone in mind for me to meet, a woman friend of his and Alice's, a widow named Olga. Olga had been married to a much older man, who had died a year or so earlier. Well, I have described Olga's striking looks and the good impression she made on me when we met. Within a short time, I was again making trips to Paris, to court a lovely Parisienne.

But every new situation has its own aspects, of course, even when there are some close parallels to things in the past. Olga has never learned English with the same proficiency that Suzie did. She is altogether more tied to France. To her friends there, to French cuisine, to French culture in general. Hence, our life together has reflected that, with our time split between England and France. In the beginning of our relationship, we spent more time in Cambridge than in France. This was before I had semi-retired from the business and it was essential that I be present to keep things going. But, as time went on, and my direct involvement in the day-to-day affairs of the business decreased, it became possible to spend more time in France. And we did. We bought our flat in Mandelieu in the early '80s and, increasingly, that has been our base when we go to France. We still come back to Cambridge for a good part of the year, avoiding the heat and the crowds of mediterranean France in the summer. And since Armand and Alice are there a good part of the year, it is an excellent arrangement in all respects. My French has improved, though I still make plenty of mistakes in the grammar, but if I spend hours a day talking in French, it can be quite tiring. It will never be second nature to me, the way speaking English is.

Yet, if Olga's attachment to France is a major reason for my increasing ties to it, that is not the whole reason. The friendships I formed in Norrey-en-Auges continued and those in turn led on to other contacts and trips, including wine-judging contests and the like. Wine is another interest I share with Armand. For years, he owned vineyards in the village of Rully, in Burgundy, and produced an excellent white and a wonderful red.

But the fact of my having been a Typhoon pilot itself led to a new set of connections to France. Because, surprising as this may sound, a society to honour the British Typhoon pilots had been formed in Normandy, in the late 1970s. Its key figure is a man named Jacques Berhan who, as a young boy of 11, saw a Typhoon pilot, whose plane had been shot down, parachute to earth. That made quite an impression on the young Berhan and years later, he began salvaging crashed Typhoons and trying to find out the stories of their particular pilots. One of these pilots was J. Rowland, who had been in my flight group on that fateful attack on the Mezidon marshalling yards, where he had been shot down and killed. Jacques was involved in the salvage of Rowland's Typhoon, which helped serve as the model of the life-size Typhoon that is on display at the WWII museum in Caen. He, of course, was not alone in all these efforts. As I see every time I go back to Normandy, there is still a lot of gratitude to the Brits and the Americans for liberating France from the German yoke, even though so much of Normandy was destroyed in the fighting. As a result, a number of people have joined in the salvage and restoration efforts, which, of course, are really a form of homage to the men of the RAF who fought and died in Normandy.

And, of course, I've been back to Normandy many times for celebrations and commemorations, not least for those in connection with the big anniversaries of D-Day, the 50th and the 60th. The 60th, of course, was in 2004 and will undoubtedly have been the last big one and almost certainly will have been the last one for me. A group of six of my family went over, taking our car on the channel tunnel train. Our group consisted of Olga and myself, Polly and Lollie, and my two sons-in-law, Colin and Adam. It had been decided beforehand by the Typhoon Pilots' Association that there should be a separate celebration for the Tiffy pilots ahead of the main June 6th celebrations, to avoid the inevitable crowds and complications that the main event would involve in Normandy. Hence, this was scheduled for the second week in May.

We left a couple of days early, to allow time for some sight-seeing and some good meals. We visited the field where my aeroplane had come down. You can still see the large, now grass-filled, depression in the ground where it hit. Late that afternoon, there was a special commemorative celebration in the village of Croissanville, where my aircraft had come down. The gathering was held in a medium-sized room on the second storey of the municipal building of the village. Perhaps there were 50 people or more in the room, nearly all locals, who had shown up to mark the event. I'm not an emotional person or, at least, I don't like to make a big display of my feelings – that's just not my way – but I have to say I was touched. The mayor made a speech, then Yves Delauney, the son of the farmer whose family farm house my Typhoon narrowly missed, said a few words. Yves himself had been born seven years after the war but he made it clear how grateful his whole family was that the war had spared their family house – in particular that my aeroplane had not crashed into it! And, he, like the mayor, noted the gratitude of the people of Normandy in general for their liberation by the Allied forces from the Germans. Following his remarks, I made a short speech expressing my appreciation for this commemoration and recounting one of my adventures. Then I was presented with both a medal and with a large piece of one of the wings of my aeroplane! It had been kept all these years at the farmhouse. It became clear that the local people expected me to take it back to England but I had to decline politely and, instead, donated it to their small local history museum. There was also a brief visit to Omaha beach because one of my sons-in-law wanted to see it. There was a lot of mist that day and the beach was quiet in the way that beaches are when there is mist and fog. A couple of sea gulls paraded along the shore line and a young man was doing a kind of slow-motion run down the beach, taking exaggerated big steps, some form of exercise. There was hardly anyone else around. Perhaps on a clear day, there are signs of wreckage offshore to remind you of the battle but looking at the beach that day, it was hard to believe that it had been the site of so much fighting and dying. The rough stone monument to the fallen at the edge of the beach, not far from the café, provides the main testimony.

A day later, the general commemoration and honouring of the Typhoon pilots was held in the village of Noyer-Bocage. There was an impressive church service in the large modern church of the town, and two big evening meals in the hall of the local community centre. The big official event, however, was the laying of wreaths at the monument to the Typhoon pilots. This monument was also largely the fruit of the efforts of Jacques Brehin and it is quite a handsome engraved dark slate monument. It lists all the Typhoon pilots who died fighting to free Normandy. I knew a number of them, of course, and it's hard to see the names without feeling a pang of sadness for their lives cut short. One of those names is that of Doug Gross, the friendly Canadian who urged me to "get some time in" flying just before he was killed in the battle for the Falaise gap. For this ceremony, there were 18 of us – Brits, Canadians, Australians –

who came and were honoured. We each received a special medal from Madame La Maire of Noyer-Bocage. Since there had been a large contingent of Canadians flying Typhoons, there was special homage to them, paid by both the Canadian ambassador to France and the top Canadian military attaché.

This event was special and meant a lot, I am sure, to all of us who took part. But, for me, the highpoint of the trip had come the day before the main events at Noyer-Bocage. This involved a visit to Norrey-en-Auges again and seeing Alice, Henri's sister. She is now 85 or 86, a little white-haired old lady with a very sweet, warm expression. She lives in a kind of assisted residential community for the elderly. She has her own little, self-contained flat but if help is needed, it is right there. It was great to see her and introduce her to the members of my family. Of our group, she had only met Polly before.

And then we went to visit the village church and its graveyard. By this point in our visit, it was about 2 o'clock in the afternoon and the day had turned brilliantly sunny and warm. We paid our respects at the graves of Henri and his wife, Marie. Marie had died in '98 and Henri, four years later, only two years before our visit, in 2002. I missed my old friend. It would have been great to see him again and talk about old times. About 30 feet away from where Henri and Marie were laid to rest is the grave of my nemesis, the mayor, and that of his wife. He had died in the early '90s. When I think about him, I still regret that I had not been able to get him on the butter smuggling rap.

We then entered the church, which was undergoing some kind of internal reconstruction. This was, of course, the church where I had attended Sunday services, in an ill-fitting borrowed black suit, with Henri and his family back in 1944. Though the building is now a bit dilapidated and undergoing renovation, the yellow walls and the light from the windows give it a nice feeling. There is a simple wooden altar, plaster statues of saints on the wall, and that afternoon the sun was shining in through the three long thin, simply-decorated, windows at the front of the church, just behind the altar. I cannot explain why I did what I then did but it felt right. I walked up to the nave, looked at it and felt like singing. I do not normally burst into song, uninvited to do so, in churches. This was the only time it's happened. It just felt right. The song that came to my lips was, "O, for the wings of a dove" by Felix Mendelssohn. Was there a memory of sitting by the pond near the old granary in the field and wishing I were a bird who could just fly away? I think that's what prompted me but the words just came to mind and I sang them, as I had in my youth when I was a chorister. It had probably been 70 or more years since I had last sung this anthem.

O, for the wings of a dove!
Far away, far away would I rove!
O for the wings, for the wings of a dove!
Far away, far away, far away, far away would I rove!
In the wilderness, build me a nest,
And remain there, forever at rest,
In the wilderness build me,
Build me a nest,
And remain there forever at rest,
And remain there forever at rest,
For ever at rest, and remain there forever at rest,
And remain there forever at rest.

Yes, it seemed hard to believe that so much time had gone by, that my fugitive existence in Normandy had all taken place 60 years before. I had been a young man then, full of life and not a little fear, determined to survive and not be caught by the Germans. And my friends at Norrey-en-Auges had made sure that I stayed safe and had made it back to Allied lines. The whole Normandy experience had been the greatest adventure of my life – though, at the time, of course, it seemed more like the greatest problem I had ever faced than the greatest adventure. But I had not only come through it and survived the rest of the war, but afterwards had had the good fortune to have a fulfilling and basically happy life. A life marked by some terrible losses, to be sure, but a life that I really cannot complain about. I have been lucky in so many ways.

Not least, I suppose, I feel lucky to have had such an unexpectedly interesting life, one that I would never have imagined while I was doing my rounds as a boy on my bike in Cambridge, delivering parcels of yeast. Though British to the bone, the experiences I had in Normandy, in particular being sheltered in Norrey-en-Auges, and then the various vicissitudes of life later, led to a completely unpredicted life-long set of links with France.

I was very glad that I had come back for these 60th anniversary celebrations and, in particular, to have returned to Norrey-en-Auges once again. Not least, as I gave my song full voice, I was pleased to feel, for a few moments, so much like the young boy I had once been. The young boy who had been thrilled to be a chorister at Trinity College and who had sung with feeling so many times in the Trinity College chapel.

Index